SECRETS OF HOI AN

Vietnam's Historic Port

Books by the same author

Dragons on the Roof, Unravelling Vietnam

Hanoi of a Thousand Years

Hue, Vietnam's Last Imperial Capital

ABOUT THE AUTHOR

Carol Howland is an experienced travel writer, a former feature writer for a national magazine and a contributor to more than a dozen British newspapers. Following a mid-career foray into stockbroking, she edited two finance magazines. But early in her career, she wrote and revised guidebooks and more recently, returned to travel writing. Enthralled by the country, she has published four books exploring Vietnam's cultural heritage. She now lives in France.

'Carol Howland has written four travel books, that had they been written and read by the intelligentsia of America before the Vietnam War, would have made the US pause and take stock of the state of affairs in this small, now well-known country.

'The author's meticulous research into the customs, traditions and cultural history of Vietnam are a mind opening revelation to the uninitiated traveller. She explores the exotic venues of an historically turbulent culture that is vibrantly alive and growing in spite of today's conflicts among the powerful nations of the world.

'Reading her series of books on Vietnam, *Dragons on the Roof, Hanoi of a Thousand Years, Hoi An – Vietnam's Historic Port, and Hue – Vietnam's Last Imperial Capital,* is a deeply rewarding experience. Without even mentioning the Vietnam War, she leads the reader on a journey through the cities and countryside of this beautiful Asian country and the mysterious mindset of the proud, persistent and independent people of Vietnam. Her descriptions of the ancient civilizations in the early years and how the country developed through Taoism, Confucianism, Hinduism, Buddhism, and Catholicism leave the reader with an astounding wealth of information to synthesize in order to appreciate the varieties of experience one can expect when visiting this country.

'From the tale of the two Vietnamese Trung sisters who repulsed the An Chinese in 40 AD through the expulsion of Kublai Khan, the Japanese in WWII, the French Colonialists, and infamously, the US, to the beautiful flower gardens, architecture, cuisine of the rich and poor, to the type of jewellery worn in the imperial court of Hue, she writes in great detail of the marvels of manners and grace still apparent in the Vietnamese people.

'First published in Hanoi by Vietnam's publisher of foreign language books, her books celebrate Vietnamese culture, a remarkable series of books that elucidate the many faces of Vietnam. Her wit, insights and thoroughness permeate the writing and bring joy, excitement and expectation to the would be traveller and historian. Read them, go to Vietnam, and follow her suggestions to have a really rewarding experience in Vietnam!'

Ken Embers, Vietnam representative for Globalism; Director of English Programs and Projects for Vietnam Children's Libraries International; Captain, helicopter pilot, Vietnam 1968-69.

'Like a military reporter, Carol Howland embeds herself with her subject. However, her strategy is less military than empathy and Howland has not only the gift of insight but the gift of friendship: she leaves her subjects like a long lost pal, a priceless asset in this big hearted but still endlessly enigmatic country.'

Peter Howick, Columnist, *The Evening Herald,* Dublin

SECRETS OF HOI AN

Vietnam's Historic Port

CAROL HOWLAND

MYNAH BIRD BOOKS

Published by Mynah Bird Books 2018
1 Regents Court, 10 Balcombe Road
Branksome Park, Poole, Dorset BH13 6DY

First published 2011 by The Gioi Publishers
46 Tran Hung Dao Street
Hanoi, Vietnam

ISBN - 13: 978-1-999843625
ISBN - 10: 1999843622

To all those scholars from whose works I have so heavily drawn and to friends in Hoi An for their unflagging encouragement and support.

CONTENTS

PART FOUR – WITHIN MEMORY

LANDFALL

The swallow skims over the ground
Rain will swell the pond
The swallow flies high
The shower will be short
– Vietnamese proverb

In the late afternoon sun, the sea is empty. Far to the east, the blue-grey outline of Cu Lao Cham – Cham Island – floats on the jade horizon. The brilliant light glances off the surface, the only sound that of the boat, slashing through the water. At a signal from the lookout perched in the prow, the pilot turns the boat gingerly to the west, feeling his way towards an inlet eighteen miles south of Danang. He has no need of the map reading: 15°88'N, 108°34'E.

The sparkling surface of the sea bears no imprint of what has passed by before. The waves roll ceaselessly as they might have done on the first day of eternity. This same jade water has floated men in small wooden boats and later ships, sailing along this South East Asian coastline for two thousand, perhaps three thousand years.

Under the searing sun, the boat rolling with the waves, the sea rippling its muscles as though it were a colossal living being, I empathise with those first brave people in their single and double-hulled outriggers, flimsy, wooden boats hardly bigger than canoes, who sailed these treacherous, rocky and coral-laced waters in the mists of pre-history, their fears and hopes, perhaps their desperation, stashed as cargo. Where did they come from? Why did they come? *Why have I come?*

The question was put quite bluntly by a BBC-TV producer: 'In a phrase, why Vietnam, why this town?'

In a phrase? One phrase is insufficient: 'It's a charming old Asian port town with probably the finest concentration of historic merchant houses in Vietnam, possibly in Asia, now a World Heritage Site, with ruins nearby of an earlier, mysterious civilisation.' No, not possible in a single phrase.

11

Sometimes a journey seems to become imperative to satisfy a niggling curiosity about a place. I longed to probe the three cultures that the locale of Hoi An has hosted over a period of two millennia, to forage into the stirrings of the town's origins, to burrow into the history that has made Hoi An the town it is, to hear the stories of its past and present inhabitants. Little did I imagine that its turbulent past would draw me deeper and deeper into a thicket of convoluted controversies, the enigmas of much of its early history still hotly disputed by scholars.

Other, more personal reasons, more emotional, press for your going. You respond to the lure of the exotic, the yen to wander through the labyrinth of an alien culture. While you are young, you go for the sheer adventure and the exuberant excitement of the unknown; when you are old, you go to see and maybe to understand a bit more about another world before it is too late to go at all.

During my first journey through Vietnam thirteen years ago, I stopped in Hoi An. Drawn back by its intimate charms, I have returned time and again, lured by the homely beauty of its old merchant houses, their dark-stained beams elaborately carved and inlaid with mother-of-pearl. Neither the grandeur of a stately home, a chateau, nor a cathedral fashioned in stone has quite the sensuous appeal of wood, warm to the touch, wood touched by a succession of generations past.

Unwinding Hoi An's history – and what a mysterious, tumultuous and colourful past – piecing it together like a puzzle and searching for the stories of its old families have spun my curiosity through a fever of spiralling perplexities. Hoi An is a town intermeshed in the histories of China, Japan, Malaysia, Indonesia, India, Persia, the Arab world, Portugal and Spain, Holland, France and Britain. These days, scholars in more than half a dozen countries are studying the old records of their compatriots' early trade – forced to 'translate' their own archaic languages into modern language in order to understand – in a collective effort to reconstruct the multi-national history of Hoi An. In 1990, scholars from Japan, Poland, the Netherlands, Canada, Thailand, the US, Australia and Vietnam took part in a symposium, delivering academic papers on various aspects of the town's history. Fortunately, the original publisher of this book, The Gioi in Hanoi, has published their papers in English.

Traditionally, academic papers tend to be rather dry, couched in quiet, neutral tones with numerous qualifying clauses, rarely expressing a modicum of emotion. But during that two-day seminar held in Hoi An, it is clear that even these academics could scarcely suppress their excitement at discovering overlaps in one another's work, pieces of the conundrum suddenly falling into place or raising further questions.

Reading their papers, I found my own excitement mounting as Hoi An's multi-national history continues to unfold. My scribbles in the margins of the collected papers are full of wow's, really's, where's – queries regarding strange, now long-forgotten place names, which I have tried to chase down. But the wow-factor remains. And I could not help wondering during the sleuthing process, what in two thousand years time, archaeologists will find of our own technological and cultural achievements, picking over the remnants of our civilisation. Or will we have destroyed the earth so thoroughly by our over-indulgence that there will be only primitive life forms left – and plastic bags.

As I am a travel writer and not a historian, I shall try not to write a history. But inevitably, a town and a locale that has given rise to three distinct civilisations over a period of two thousand years demands some historical explanation. Why here? Who were the people who lived here and what happened to them?

'Shallow here,' says the pilot as he veers the boat around an unseen, underwater shoal. The boat scrapes the bottom – the lookout shouts to the pilot. The boat scrapes the hull a second time and mercifully, keeps moving.

The horizon above the prow softens into a feathering of casuarinas; then a golden necklace of sand rises above the sea as the boat rolls and sways. Then a patch of haze dissolves – the opening to the harbour. Fishing boats returning home now float alongside us. Others are heading out to sea; Vietnamese fishermen mostly fish at night.

A wide rectangular fishnet, stretched high above the water to dry, shimmers in the rosy, late afternoon light, the sun slipping low into the haze, setting the sky ablaze. The sunset over the jade sea, the fishing boats, the shimmering fishnet, the faraway shoreline – would make a pretty painting, an almost too-pretty painting to be real.

The old town of Hoi An lies tethered along the north bank of the Thu Bon River. Its estuary lies riven by sandy islands, its shifting shores flooded by lakes and salt marshes, formed over the centuries by the invading and retreating course of the river, lashing monsoon rains, strong tides, sea currents and trade winds. Rarely is a town so completely dominated by its geography. With each monsoon, Hoi An's topography changes, sometimes considerably; the river diverts its course, new streams appear, others dry up abandoned. Sand and silt drift and settle in the riverbed, presenting new hazards to the boatmen to find channels through the shallows.

In the early days, long, thin islands running parallel to the coastline made it possible to reach Hoi An's harbour from three approaches: directly from the sea – always shallow, from present-day Danang to the north, or from Tam Ky in the south. From Danang, ships sailed south, up the Han and Co Co rivers, then into the De Vong river until they reached Tra Que lake to moor. From the south, they sailed along the Truong Giang river to Thi Lai or Tra Nhieu lake to drop anchor.

From high in the Truong Son mountains that form the curved spine of Vietnam from north to south, four rivers gush rainwater and silt into the Thu Bon river, which shoulders its liquid burden laden with alluvium down the hills, through the valleys and across the narrow coastal plain. At Hoi An, the river water flows over the sandy river banks, and mingles with the sea and the ocean currents, whipped alternately by north-easterly and south-easterly winds.

Tides, sometimes once a day – sometimes twice a day during the same month – rush twenty-four miles inland, erosion swelled by the velocity of the river's flow and the sucking withdrawal of the tides. The upper Thu Bon river, the largest river in central Vietnam, lies in one of Vietnam's areas of heaviest rainfall. During the monsoon season from September through December, it receives eighty to ninety per cent of its annual rain; the dry season from January to August brings only ten to twenty per cent.

The Thu Bon estuary has changed beyond recognition over the centuries. Photographs taken in 1964 and 1985 show that the beach, Cua Dai, has moved hundreds of meters south. I have waded through several inches of mud in Hoi An's market in November and postcards show photographs of people paddling boats in the streets. Most houses have marks on a doorframe or a wall somewhere, showing where flood waters rose to in previous years. Annual flooding of at least a meter is considered normal. Come the rainy season every autumn or a storm warning, inhabitants dismantle and winch their furniture from the ground floor upstairs. Why they didn't build their houses on stilts or at least place the lower floors at a higher level is not a question that one asks.

Raucous shouts from the quay and the market waft over the water. Cumbersome ferries, more like barges than boats, await the clutter of bicycles and motorbikes at the riverside quay where pretty blue excursion boats line up for tomorrow's trade. The mellowed, ochre houses of Bach Dang Street squat facing the river, hunched together under the comforters of their mossy, tiled roofs. The older, historic, wooden houses stand along Tran Phu Street, Nguyen Thai Hoc and Nguyen Thi Minh Khai Streets, three streets running east-west, more or less parallel to the river.

Red silk lanterns bob along the eaves of the houses in the evening breeze. It may be the end of the *Tet,* Vietnam's big annual New Year season, but these days, Hoi An retains a festive mood during most of the year. Open shop fronts gush deep-hued waterfalls of silk scarves and ranks of embroidered evening bags, wacky beach bags and hats, sandals of every description, paintings from filmy watercolours to brash abstracts, ebony chopsticks and rosewood boxes inlaid with mother-of-pearl, thumb-sized to life-sized stone and wooden statues, cheek-by-jowl with trendy tailor shops and tempting restaurants, their open terraces draped with morning glories, enticing passers-by.

Thanks to a law against wheeled vehicles in the old town during certain hours, most days visitors can stroll amiably from old merchant house to shop to temple, as traders from afar have wandered these narrow lanes for centuries. Hoi An is a commercial town, a shopper's paradise. You can have a dress or a suit made to measure (best copied) at a fraction of the cost you'd pay at home – and they'll make it by tomorrow, sometimes even this afternoon.

This time in Hoi An I will stay in the rented house of a friend of friend, an Australian English teacher. The owner of the house is an octogenarian *Viet kieu* (an overseas Vietnamese, who in his case has returned), a former general in the army of South Vietnam, who after what the Vietnamese call the American War, migrated to America with his wife and ten children to live until he retired. Now he has returned to Hoi An to spend his last days.

Bags upstairs – I note a candle in a vase, which means power cuts. I stroll into town to The Eating Place, an open square where each 'restaurateur' operates from a cooking stall a meter-and-a-half wide, a long table extending out front, a tout snagging passing clients with chat and a menu. At Miss Nam's stall, I order stuffed eggplant and an iced lemon juice, then head toward the market to buy mangoes. (The Eating Place has now moved across the bridge to the island of An Hoi – left end, around the corner).

No longer the quiet, sleepy town of memory, outside the old historic centre, Hoi An rumbles with the affluent growl of motorbikes. A female singer croons over a distant loudspeaker: end of *Tet* hangover. I ring an Aussie writer of a certain age, met in passing last year, who tells me that he has 'married a mature Vietnamese woman living in Saigon' (officially Ho Chi Minh City, abbreviated as HCMC), 'the mother of a son of fifteen, a daughter of twelve – and expecting my baby in the autumn.' He has bought her a restaurant in HCMC and has no desire to live there, although he visits frequently. So an intermittent marriage, it would seem.

In the evening, I walk across the bridge to An Hoi and stroll along the new promenade fringed by tall palms, looking for one of my favourite restaurants of last year. The waitress remembers me, despite my having exchanged only a few words with her on several occasions. The people of Hoi An are very open and friendly. I always think of the Vietnamese as the Italians of South-East Asia – they are so warm, so openly welcoming – and they love to sing.

Having ordered a green mango salad topped with shrimp and chopped peanuts, a plate of stir-fried vegetables and a fresh beer – made yesterday – I sit, looking out over the boats moored in the river to the silk lanterns, beginning to glow along the eaves of Bach Dang Street across the river. No one lives on the boats these days. A memory surfaces of long, slim boats with palm leaf canopies, lined up along Hoi An quay, a father tending his toddler in the bow while his wife cooked the evening meal. A woman stops at my table and I buy a bag of peanuts.

16

'My first customer, good luck,' she says happily. By tradition, the first customer portends what kind of day a shopkeeper or vendor will have. Selling peanuts must be her evening activity.

Little girls of eight or nine with big, wistful eyes approach, warbling clay whistles and when you resist buying a clay whistle, they very carefully take out of their baskets delicately painted, wooden dragonflies. They stand in a cluster and approach, one by one. Only here, across the river in An Hoi do the little girls sell clay whistles and dragonflies. An evening enterprise.

Clusters of coloured lanterns light An Hoi bridge in lieu of street lamps and huge illuminated sacred animals – the phoenix, turtle, dragon and unicorn – float on the river upstream from the bridge, left over from *Tet*. Kids squat on the curb and race over the soft, grassy verges along the riverside promenade.

Families wedged like peas on motorbikes, children between father and mother, sometimes snuggled in front of papa, roar past. Teenagers gather in the middle of the street to admire a new baby and chatter on their mobile phones, mothers spoon food from bowls into the open mouths of their toddlers, matrons sit gossiping on a bench. A girl from each restaurant stands behind a lit music stand holding the menu.

'Happy Hour! Fresh beer! Please come in my restaurant.'

Next morning by half past eight, it is too hot to sit on the terrace for breakfast. I spend most of the morning watching a not quite English speaking technician from the post office and his father, probably a builder, install a cable and 'hub box' to hook my laptop into my landlady's internet connection.

Come evening, again I cross the bridge to An Hoi and find a new-to-me seafood restaurant. This time, a delicious steamed fish in a pot smothered in onions, herbs and ginger. The balmy tropical evening steals over the restless soul as soothing as a warm massage. Gazing across the black river, past the silhouettes of palms and boats to the festive, red and white lanterns strung along the eaves of Hoi An, with a slow intake of breath I realise that this is one of those quiet, unannounced moments of pure joy. The uncertainties of the months ahead translate into a tingling sense of anticipation. It is good to be back in Hoi An. Vietnam always feels like a second home.

PART I

EARLY PEOPLES

MYSTERIOUS MIGRANTS

Several huge burial jars found in the vicinity of Hoi An – some up to a meter high, cylindrical with rounded bottoms; others, squat with round bellies – clamour for attention in Hoi An's modest Sa Huynh Museum in Tran Phu Street.

Diagonal cord marks on the tubular jars look so sharp, they might have been made by scraping a fork across the surface yesterday. Whose grieving hands shaped these clay jars and so lovingly interred them in a sandy riverbank to be exhumed two thousand years later?

When and where the people came from, no one knows. That they came, most probably in wooden boats and settled in large numbers, traded, fished, lived and died along this coastline is not in question. We know them as the Sa Huynh people, only because their burial jars were first unearthed from a sand dune some miles south of Hoi An at a place called Sa Huynh.

It is generally accepted that by the middle of the third millennium BC, maritime technology of single or double-hulled outrigger canoes and plank-built boats had developed sufficiently to make long distance voyages along the coasts of South East Asia and there is ample evidence that the Sa Huynh people were skilled mariners.

The rounded shoulders and out-turned lips of the jars once held flattened, conical lids, but the lids have perished or broken and fallen into the jars. Some held jars within jars, a double inhumation. The Sa Huynh cremated their dead; no human remains have ever been found, only their treasures, or the tools their grieving relatives tenderly placed in the burial jars, thinking they might be useful in the next world.

Always in clusters, like family plots, all of their jars were discovered along riverbanks or in sand dunes near big rivers. More than forty Sa Huynh burial sites have been found along the

Thu Bon river and its tributaries running deep into the hinterland highlands, nearly to the Laotian border. From the dating of their burial jars, we know that the Thu Bon estuary served the Sa Huynh people as a commercial port during the last two centuries BC and well into the first two centuries of the Christian era. More than half a dozen sites lie in the near outskirts of Hoi An.

Sa Huynh settlements stretched from as far north as Hoa Qui near Vinh (about halfway to Hanoi from Hoi An), south to a site east of Saigon known as Giong Ca Vo, always along rivers. Archaeologists currently date the Sa Huynh culture from as early as the eighth or ninth century BC to sometime in the first or second century AD.

Three, beautifully-turned, pedestal bowls await fruit or perhaps an offering in a glass display case of the little museum. Yet because it is so personal, it is the jewellery that touches the heart: chunky, thick, circular earrings of jade, stone and glass, each thick circular earring projecting three or four triangular points; a myriad of minute, multi-coloured glass beads; large elongated carnelian beads cut in geometric facets; a cobalt blue, cut-glass bead necklace that might have been produced yesterday. Therefore, a society that had already progressed well past subsistence into specialisations, trades, a society that could afford to adorn itself and its dead.

Digs between 2002 and 2004 at Lai Nghi just north of Hoi An yielded some of the wealthiest Sa Huynh artefacts yet discovered: apart from iron tools and weapons, beads of gold, glass, agate, carnelian, rock crystal and nephrite, a form of jade – and four gold earrings, the first gold earrings to be found in a Sa Huynh site. Over ten thousand beads were painstakingly counted, more than a thousand made of semi-precious stones.

One jar alone held a rich cache of carnelian, gold and glass beads. Who did they belong to? A a powerful ruler or his queen, the headman of a clan, a high priest, a wealthy trader, maybe even an elderly matriarch? The dig at Lai Nghi more than any other, revealed distinct levels of wealth in the contents of the burial jars. For archaeologists, the most exciting finds were the gold-plated glass beads, the striped alkali-etched beads, a tiger pendant and a bird pendant.

It was assumed that the glass beads had been imported from India until fairly recently when the remains of Sa Huynh glass-making – using Indian techniques – were unearthed at Giong Co Vo, a site east of Saigon, dated at around 100 BC. Now it is accepted that the gold-plated glass beads and the alkali-etched, striped beads were made in Vietnam, possibly to order for the Indian market, most probably at Giong Ca Vo. It is still assumed that the gold earrings were imported – although centuries later, an Englishman named Chapman reported, 'Dang Trong is gold country. Here is the finest and purest gold in the world' – Dang Trong being an earlier name for Central Vietnam. One cannot help but wonder if the Sa Huynh people had discovered gold in the upper reaches of the Thu Bon river valley nearly two millennia earlier.

Disappointingly, the finds from the Lai Nghi site near Hoi An are not – or not yet – on display in Hoi An's Sa Huynh Museum. Even more disappointing, neither are the curious, double-headed animal earrings – unique to the Sa Huynh culture – found scattered around South East Asia, which bear witness to their widespread trade and possibly, to their origins.

These strange, two-headed animal earrings have been found in such far-flung archaeological sites as the Philippines (Palawan Island), Taiwan (Orchid Island), Indonesia (Java), Thailand, and in Borneo, where they were known 'ethnographically' among the Sea Dyaks. Which raises the teasing questions: might the Sea Dyaks have been the antecedents, or conversely, the descendants of the Sa Huynh? Or did they merely copy the designs after trading with the Sa Huynhs?

Fortunately, in passing through Hanoi, I had found the double-headed earrings at the National Museum of History. Made of glass and stone, the curious heads look like that of a goat, an antelope or an oryx in profile, nose down, the curved horns pointing upwards, the heads joined by a crossbar, from which a loop or a hook attached them to the ear. These animals were unknown to modern science until they were 'discovered' as recently as 1992 in Vietnam's highlands and identified as a hoofed animal that looks rather like a mountain goat, now classified as *pseudoryx nghetinenis*.

The National Museum of the Philippines holds a Sa Huynh burial jar found in a cave on Palawan Island, tentatively dated at approximately two thousand eight hundred years old. Red 'hooks' have been painted round the upper 'collar' beneath the rim. The flattened-dome lid of what has become known as the Manunggul Jar holds two intriguing figures seated in a boat among sea waves, their legs crossed, hands in their laps – no oars, no sails – which has led to conjecture that the two figures need no oars nor sails because they are drifting to the Land of the Dead. Tantalizingly, the chunky, round stone earrings with the spiky projections are known in the Philippines as *lingling-o*.

If the Sa Huynh were, indeed, sea gypsies, or at least wide-ranging traders, what manner of lives did they live? These ruminations were partially requited by a chance viewing of a French documentary about a present-day tribe on Palawan Island, the self-same island where the Sa Huynh Manunggul Jar and its intriguing lid were found.

The narrator explained that this family group of two couples and their children normally lives in the hills, but come down to the sea seasonally where they build straw shelters. In the film, the men collected wild honey and hunted with blowpipes, 'talking to the birds' to enable them to approach near enough to shoot – like a tribe in Sarawak. The women dug for roots and fished in a vine-draped jungle pool using what looked like minnow nets, giggling and splashing one another like children, their own offspring larking about in the brown water – to a Western urbanite, a primitive Eden.

The adults, handsome and lithe of frame, wore sarongs, the women blouses, the men T-shirts, betraying their contact with the modern world. Light brown-skinned and black-haired, especially the women with their hair tied in knots pulled away from their lean faces, looked very like the Vietnamese. They cooked in terracotta pots over open fires. Perhaps for the television cameras, they held a celebration. The smiling people sat in a semi-circle while one man, this time bare-chested, danced to the beat of a large drum. I couldn't help wondering if they might be the distant descendants of the Sa Huynh, left undisturbed in remote pastoral isolation. Or the tribes of Sarawak? Or relatives of the sea gypsies of Krabi in Thailand?

Sa Huynh archaeology is very much a growth industry. In January 2009, a bronze Sa Huynh statue of a sleeping tigress was unearthed on Vietnam's west coast bordering Cambodia. Twelve inches (30 cm) long and weighing twenty-six pounds (19 kg), it is believed to be more than two thousand years old.

Stop Press: While writing I hear via a newsletter that archaeologists have found 'hundreds of jar tombs' in a ten-hectare site along the banks of the Ky Low river of Phu Yen province, three provinces south of Hoi An.

Second Stop Press: (August, 2010) More than ten thousand objects of Sa Huynh pottery, plus artefacts of stone, copper, iron and crystal have been discovered in an excavation near Phan Thiet (on the coast east of Saigon). That they have been dated at 2,500 years old – pushes back the date of arrival of the San Huynh along this coast to 500 BC.

Even a superficial glance at Asian history is an eye-opener to the Western Eurocentric – how little we know of the East.

Very early on, Indian merchants began to visit the Malay peninsula. When the Indians heard that there was gold in Java, the rush to Suvarnabhumi, the fabled Land of Gold, was on. According to British archaeologist, Ian Glover, as early as the fourth century BC, a famous Indian how-to manual for achieving worldly success, the *Arthasastra,* ranked the pursuit of profit above all other goals in life – even over love or virtue. These early voyages made by the Indians would have been spectacularly dangerous, fraught with the risks of typhoon and shipwreck, scorching sun, hunger and thirst, and when they came ashore to seek food and water, poisonous snakes and insects – and massacre by hostile natives. A later Indian writer stated the risks bluntly but provocatively: 'Who goes to Java, never returns. If by chance he returns, then he brings back enough wealth to support seven generations of his family.'

Suvarnabhumi, the Land of Gold, was considered by the Indians not only as a pot of gold, but also as an opportunity for Buddhist proselytizing. Three missionaries – Gavampti, Sona and Uttara – were sent by the Indian Emperor Asoka, to convert the people of Suvarnabhumi soon after the Third Buddhist Council in the mid-third century BC! That there is an Ashoka pagoda near Haiphong stirs one to wonder if one of those Buddhist missionaries might have made it to Vietnam – and when?

Eventually, the Indians set up trading posts along the Malay peninsula. According to myth, the kingdom of Funan in the Mekong Delta was founded in the mid-second century AD by a hero coming from the south – across the sea. Histories suggest that as the Malay peninsula was sparsely populated, the Indians were forced to take slaves to exchange as trade merchandise from along the southern coast of the Indo-Chinese mainland. Whether their slave-gathering expeditions extended round the peninsula and up the coast to Sa Huynh settlements is open to speculation.

British archaeologist Ian Glover writes: 'It was a lust for gold and spices that provoked the Indianization of South East Asia from the first millennium AD and which also brought the spread of Islam . . . This Western demand for an aromatic flower bud (cloves of *Eugenia aromatia* trees) of rather little value to the native peoples of the Moluccas, transformed in the long run, the economic and political face of Asia. Of such little things are empires built.'

Cloves from the Moluccas islands had been known in China since the third century BC. Pliny in faraway Rome described cloves in the first century AD and regular commerce between India and Rome was documented in Classical writing from the second century AD. It is even thought likely that a trade mission from Emperor Marcus Aurelius stopped in Central Vietnam en route to the Han court in China in 230 AD!

Maritime trade between India and China began sometime around the middle of the second century BC! The Chinese conquered what is now northern Vietnam in 179 BC, established three administrative districts that extended into central Vietnam, their borders now unknown.

The route from China to India ran along the coast of Vietnam, around the Indo-Chinese peninsula, along the Cambodian, Thai and Burmese coastlines, taking the overland portage route across the narrow isthmus of the Malay peninsula, ending at Kancipura in southern India. A later route eventually passed through the Straits of Malacca.

Certainly by 111 BC, during the reign of Emperor Wudi of the Han dynasty, maritime contact between China and India was well established. Chinese annuals for 111 BC record the arrival at the imperial Han court of an embassy from the Kingdom of Huangzhi, thought to have been eastern India – bearing the gift of a live rhinoceros. That the poor creature made the trip on board ship all the way from India seems unlikely. The ship's itinerary through South East Asia suggests that it might well have been obtained, along with the tortoiseshell and ivory that formed part of the tribute, from the coast of Central Vietnam.

Having conquered Nan Yue, the three districts established earlier, it seems clear to British archaeologist, Ian Glover, that the renamed southernmost Han district, Rinan, included that part of Central Vietnam occupied by the Sa Huynh.

Maritime commerce from India westward to the Mediterranean was far more developed than trade travelling eastward. Astonishingly, at the Western extremity of the trade route, an Indian ivory figurine was excavated at Pompeii! Amphorae from Rhodes and early Italian Arrentine ware have turned up on the South Indian coast as well as hoards of Roman gold coins, numerous Classical intaglios and seals throughout southern India and Sri Lanka.

Some of these finds may have been the result of what archaeologists call 'drift' – trade from one merchant to another along a relay network, passing on prestige 'Big Man' objects, presented in a reciprocal, tribute-to-ruler type of trading, well-documented in prehistoric and early historic societies of South East Asia. The final recipients of these exotic objects may not have had the faintest inkling of their provenance.

A few remnants from this trade with the West have emerged in South East Asia: Roman, Greek, Persian and Indian artefacts at the port of Funan, Oc Eo, now inland from the Gulf of Siam, south of the Cambodian border, a kingdom that occupied the Mekong Delta from the second to the sixth centuries AD.

Curiously, German classical scholar, Albrecht Dible, believed that Oc Eo might have been the Indian Kattigara, the rendezvous for merchants from China and Rome, referred to by second century Alexandrian geographer, Ptolemy, his surmise based on the itinerary of a voyage made by a Graeco-Roman merchant named Alexander.

Ian Glover goes on to say: 'By the early part of the Christian era, these perhaps rather separate South East Asian exchange systems had been linked into a vast network of trade stretching from Western Europe via the Mediterranean and the Red Sea to South China – the economic integration by trade of most of the inhabited globe, excluding the Americas and Australia and its significance for the subsequent development of South East Asian societies cannot be ignored.'

Some call it the Great Sea Route as opposed to the overland Silk Road. The newly PR-minded Chinese have dubbed it the Maritime Silk Road and propose building a museum to commemorate it.

The Sa Huynh traded extensively, both overland and by sea along the coast with the people of southern China, with the Dong Son people of North Vietnam and the Dong Nai people in the south. They had close contact with the people of the Upper Lao Plateau, with those around the Malay archipelago and with island peoples of the Pacific.

Sa Huynh artefacts found in sites in Thailand and Burma testify to trade in ancient times, whether by the Indians, the Chinese, neighbouring traders, or by the Sa Huynh themselves is uncertain; their boats would have been quite capable of these coastal voyages.

Sa Huynh sites near Hoi An provide a stunning array of leftovers from their early trade with the Chinese: Han bronze mirrors from the first century BC, Han bronze vessels, Chinese coins cast during the reign of Wang Mang (9-23 AD), Chinese Wu Zhu coins (cast between 118 BC and the seventh century AD), Chinese-style crossbow bolts and fragments of Han seal impressions – supporting the conclusion that China's influence extended far enough south to include the Sa Huynh settlements in the Thu Bon river valley.

What eventually happened to the Sa Huynh people remains a mystery.

Suddenly, it dawns on me that the very brisk wind that comes up every afternoon and flings the curtains around – it's dead still in the morning through midday – is the north-easterly trade wind that blew the merchant ships from China and Japan south to Hoi An for their annual trade fairs during Hoi An's heydays in the sixteenth and seventeenth centuries.

This afternoon a huge box arrives on the back of a motorbike. My landlady announces that she is having a new washing machine installed on the upstairs landing – and that's what is in the box – a full-size washing machine on the back of a motorbike! The evening starts with a civilised gin and tonic to celebrate the arrival of a new lodger, a Swede doing a month of volunteer work at Hoi An orphanage. We are halfway through our drinks when he notices water streaming down the sitting room wall. Following the leak upstairs, we find a lake issuing from the new washing machine. The landlady rings the installer and to my surprise, he turns up in minutes, climbs a bamboo ladder into the loft and turns off the water, saying that he can't fix it tonight, no water until tomorrow. He then zooms off on his motorbike. So no cool-down showers at bedtime.

Next morning the installer arrives and sets to work to correct the poor connection. He leaves, saying that everything has been fixed – 'sure, sure, sure' – he even leaves the washing machine running empty to prove it.

I have stripped off about to take a shower when I hear the sound of water hitting tiles and looking round, find water running down the wall from the attic just outside the bathroom. I shove a dish-pan under it, pull the clothes tree out of the way and shout to the landlady, who rings the plumber. Having placed a bucket under the leak, we hear water dripping elsewhere – this time through the ceiling light fixture over my worktable – onto the laptop. I drag the table away from the dripping, mop the water off the laptop, plug it in and relief, it comes on.

The plumber has yet to arrive an hour later. Meanwhile, the gardener climbs the bamboo ladder into the loft and turns off the water again while we mop water. The landlady is well equipped with mops and buckets as the house flooded, as did most houses in Hoi An during last year's typhoon. The dripping only stops an hour later, presumably when the water tank has emptied.

Meanwhile, the gardener is back, shouting into his mobile, trying to get the plumber to come back. It is half past ten and at eleven, everyone goes off to lunch followed by a long nap. Not much gets done in Hoi An – or in Vietnam, for that matter – during hot afternoons. Only certain shops, banks and the post office stay open.

After helping to mop up, I go out for an early lunch to a nearby cafe where the notice board is crammed with recommendations from backpackers. An elderly Dane replaces the red tablecloth. Is he the owner or the partner of the Vietnamese lady owner? Western men, particularly middle-aged to ageing Western men, caught up in the flattery of pulling a much younger Vietnamese woman, frequently become the funders of modest ventures such as bars, cafes and clothes shops.

Or conversely, a young Western man marries an irresistible Vietnamese beauty and they open a bar or a restaurant together.

Despite it being lunchtime, I order the great Hoi An breakfast: a pineapple shake, Vietnamese tea (iced), a tomato and onion omelette served with a hot baguette – echo of French influence – yoghurt and muesli (declined) and a tropical fruit salad.

The restaurant owner next door sprinkles the pavement and road in front of her restaurant to cool and lay the dust in the heat of midday. Lorries laden with bricks lumber by, screeching their air horns. A tourist bus heaves past, its air brakes belching. A Vietnamese peasant woman pushes her canopied cart towards her daily position, shouting *sua chua.* The waitress from the cafe goes out to her to buy a plastic bag full of coconut milk, sprouting a straw. A pyjama-clad countrywoman under a conical straw hat swings past, watermelons and bananas in cane trays dangling from her bamboo pole. I offer to buy half a bunch of bananas. She holds up forty thousand *dong* (about $2). I laugh, give her ten thousand and know I have still overpaid.

That evening I meet a British woman, who I had met in Hanoi. Over a 'fresh beer' on an upper terrace in An Hoi, we gaze across the river as Hoi An's red lanterns start to glow at twilight. Back in Hoi An, we order green papaya and mango salads at the Cargo Club – a refuge for ex-pats, drawn by the tempting bakery counter. The night still young, we wander back across the bridge to An Hoi for mango and coconut shake nightcaps.

Next day the plumber does not return. I hop on the back of my landlady's motorbike and we roar off through the rice paddies to *La Plage* at An Bang beach. While she is doing yoga, I stretch out in a folding chair with a good, strong Vietnamese cafe, feet in the sand beneath a ragged palm leaf parasol.

The waves swell, curl and plunge, sending foam teasingly up the sand. A caressing, offshore breeze wafts the salty scent of the sea inland. Slim fishing sampans putter a hundred meters offshore. One tiny basket boat, a coracle not two metres wide, called a *thung chai,* raises a small square sail. The islands of Cu Lao Cham haunt the gauzy horizon.

As I watch, slowly the sampans line up, moving from left to right, turn, then weave back on themselves in a double line, bobbing up and down in the waves like ducks at a shooting gallery. The *thung chai* under sail has dropped out in deference to the motors. Every few minutes, a fisherman lifts the triangular net at the bow of his boat to check if there is a catch, the boats still moving in formation – cooperative fishing. Another idyllic picture: slim, dark sampans, slant eyes painted on their bows to ward off evil spirits, interweaving back and forth against the jade water and hazy mountains.

The sea looks so clear, so fresh. Yet through these waters, seafarers from faraway countries have sailed their ships for centuries, losing their lives to storms or pirates, their bodies claimed by the hungry sea. Perhaps the very sand at my feet holds minuscule fragments of their bones and cargoes: gold, silver, silk, china, rhinoceros horn, precious woods. The South China Sea (in Vietnam, known as the Eastern Sea for sensitive political reasons) is an old, much-travelled sea route. Men have used it as a liquid jade highway for two thousand years, and very likely, for a thousand years earlier.

A young man walks to where the waves foam, bends down and plants a bunch of joss sticks in the sand: to commemorate a relative lost at sea perhaps, or in remembrance of all those who have perished in its depths.

When I return the coffee cup to the thatched pavilion, a sharp-eyed Vietnamese woman, seated with a man at a table with a pile of papers, looks up and asks, 'Who are you?'

Now the Vietnamese are very friendly, but they are not usually this abrupt. Can she possibly be some sort of nosey official, I ask myself? But no, she introduces herself as Le Ly Hayslop, whose name I recognise as the author of *When Heaven and Earth Changed Places,* later made into the Oliver Stone film, *Heaven and earth.* In her book she tells the harrowing story of growing up in war-torn Vietnam and of her difficult life as an emigre Vietnamese widow with young children in California.

Once the book was published and the film made her some money, she returned to Vietnam to set up several charities where she grew up as a child in a village near Danang. The man with her is her local assistant. It is heartening that a good many *Viet kieu* (overseas Vietnamese) return to Vietnam, having been successful abroad, looking to do what they can either through their acquired expertise, through investments or charities to help their fellow countrymen.

From *La Plage,* we meander to the other end of the beach to Pfattys (sic) for lunch. I find myself chatting to a young Vietnamese – formerly an options trader in Chicago – newly employed in Hanoi as a consultant to foreign, direct investors in Vietnam. His father, born in HCMC, was a *Viet kieu;* the bilingual son, having grown up in the US, has now returned to the land of his fathers. I also meet a young French photographer, who suggests that I contact an Italian archaeologist. A very worthwhile, soothing and sybaritic day at the beach.

A SECOND WAVE

Sometime before the turn of the Christian era, newcomers sailed over the horizon, dropped anchor and settled virtually in the same river valleys along the coast of Central Vietnam as the Sa Huynh people. From their Austronesian language, it is assumed that they came from the Philippines, Borneo or the Indonesian archipelago.

Centuries later, they became known as the Chams.

That artefacts of the earlier Sa Huynh people – their burial jars and unique two-headed earrings – have been found in Borneo and the Philippines naturally provokes conjecture. Certainly, the Sa Huynh traded with the peoples of Austronesia. One could even wonder if the Sa Huynh, in fact, were earlier migrants from these same regions and tribes, having preceded this second wave of migrants by several centuries. Did these later arrivals follow the Sa Huynh traders home, or conversely, had these Austronesians themselves been trading in Sa Huynh ports?

Were they welcomed? Did they cohabit with the Sa Huynh peaceably? There is no archaeological evidence to prove any case. Some scholars speculate that the finding of Sa Huynh pots near Cham towers suggests assimilation, that an intermingling took place, perhaps even intermarriage between the Sa Huynh and the Chams. Or did the Sa Huynh fight to fend off these intruders to protect their homelands and livelihoods – their trade and fishing? Might the Sa Huynh have been attacked and defeated, even enslaved and sold? To the darkly suspicious mind, the disappearance of Sa Huynh burial pots and their intriguing jewellery early in the Christian era might suggest that their civilisation was not assimilated by the Chams, but destroyed, extinguished – brutally and violently, if not quite abruptly.

The fate of the Sa Huynh people remains an unsolved mystery for further investigation.

The history of the Chams is still being unearthed, literally, in the shape of brick temples, sculpture, inscribed stone stelae and potsherds. It is an exciting, ongoing, lively and contentious detective story, still being unravelled, archaeologists and historians in heated arguments as new artefacts are unearthed. Each fresh discovery proves or repudiates the last theory and debates between scholars have been raging about the dates of certain stelae since the first Frenchman lifted a Cham brick towards the end of the nineteenth century.

So who were these Chams? Where even, was this so-called place, Champa? The current thinking among scholars is that the Chams were, indeed, Austronesians – a present-day tribe in Borneo can understand modern spoken Cham. For the Chams still exist; they have settled further south around Phan Rang, in the Mekong Delta and in Cambodia – those who survived the annihilation of their culture.

Scholars agree that the Chams originally settled in the coastal river valleys of Central Vietnam, taking over precisely the trading networks first established by the Sa Huynh. For the Chams were also traders, people skilled at navigation.

Exactly where Champa was – moreover, what Champa was – is a hot issue. It is thought that each of the river valleys operated as a political entity, focused around clans, who sometimes intermarried among one another. Sometimes these tiny sovereign realms, kingdoms, city states, operated as a loose confederation for purposes of conquest or defence. At other times, they warred against one another – but here the historical waters muddy for there are no records to tell us. Mostly, Cham history is conjecture, riddled with theories and suppositions.

When the Chams started to write is uncertain. We know that their religious scriptures written on bark – and in the north of Bali the people still inscribe poetry on bark – were burnt and carried away by invaders at various times during the first millennium of the Christian era. Scholars are left to rely on trying to match up Sanskrit inscriptions on their stone stelae with Chinese dynastic records – painstaking detective work for researchers – the Chinese annuls sometimes compiled a century or more later, so of somewhat questionable accuracy, not to mention a Chinese bias.

Why Sanskrit inscriptions?

Obviously, an Indian influence, but from where? And when? More debate here. From India? Or from the Indian trading states established along the Malay and Indonesian coasts early on? Or from closer to home, from across the Truong Son mountains that act as a spine down the length of Vietnam – through Burma and

Thailand via Laos and Cambodia, as at least one archaeologist strongly believes? Or from Funan, which by the third century covered most of the southern Indo-Chinese peninsula, the southern part of Thailand, into Burma and part way down along the Malay peninsula?

By controlling the Isthmus of Kra – the narrowest point of the Malay peninsula over which merchants moved trade goods overland – Funan virtually controlled trade between China and India. A later route eventually used the Straits of Malacca.

Funan's port, Oc Eo, in the Mekong delta just south of the border with Cambodia, was certainly established as an Indian trading port. Adding fuel to the theory that Indianization spread northward from the south and over the mountains, Funan shared the same creation myth as Chenla, the bordering kingdom to the north – and of the Chams. Chenla, which conquered Funan in the sixth century, is considered to have been the precursor of the Khmer kingdom that later built Angkor.

The Funan myth relates how the kingdom was created by the marriage of a Brahmin prince named Kaundinya and the local queen, Liu-Ye, who he defeated in battle. The Khmer version calls the prince Preah Thaong and the queen Neang Neak, naming her as the daughter of the sea serpent *(naga)* king. In the Cham version – from a stone inscription at Myson dated 657AD – the prince is called Kaudinya and the queen, Soma, is again the daughter of the *naga* king.

An interesting aside, when musicians and dancers from Funan visited China in 263 AD, the Chinese emperor was so beguiled that he ordered the establishment of an institute for Funanese music and dance near Nanjing. One has to wonder if these Funan (Indian?) dancers shared their dance tradition with the Chams and Chenla, whose people later became known as the Khmers.

Cham history, because it is so dramatic and there is so little of it that is certain, sucks you in like a black hole. Once having started the unravelling, it is difficult to stop.

Archaeologists and historians agree that the Chams traded with the people on the far side of the mountains from very early on. It is also known that the Indians sent out missionaries – Brahmin as well as Buddhist – on board their trading ships. But apart from the arrival of Hinduism in the form of Saivism, the worship of Siva, stitched onto the Cham's indigenous religion centring around their mother goddess, Yang Po Ino Nagar, also known as Uroja and Uma, there is no evidence of a migration of Indians to the central coast of Vietnam – 'because the Chinese were already there!' – asserts one archaeologist.

Chinese records speak of ten kingdoms south of Rinan, their own southern-most trading territory. Rinan, which in Chinese means South of the Sun, is thought to have included the coastal area south of the Ngang Pass (a little more than halfway between Hanoi and Hue), although Rinan's borders remain a mystery.

Incredibly, the bureaucratic Chinese conducted a census of Rinan in the year 2 AD, recording a population of 69,485 people from 15,460 households. The Chinese first traded with the Sa Huynh people, afterwards with the Chams. In fact, according to British archaeologist Ian Glover, Chinese annuls tell us that their only trading partners in mainland South East Asia during the first millennium AD were the Chams!

An early Chinese book, *Shuijinzhu,* mentions a port town called Lam Ap Pho, (port city of the country of Lam Ap), its harbours along the lower reaches of the Thu Bon river, flowing down to Cua Dai (Great Port), near what through the centuries was to evolve into the town of Hoi An. Another Chinese book, *Thong Dien,* speaks of 'Mount Bat Lao, overlooking the port town of Lam Ap.' Mount Bat Lao is what today is known as Cu Lao Cham – Cham Island, offshore from Hoi An. Scholars more or less agree that Cham settlements at various times included:

Amaravati	(certain archaeologists postulate that it occupied the Thu Bon river valley, no one knows exactly where it was located)
Lam Ap Pho	a location slightly upriver from Hoi An
Simhapura	Lam Ap's capital or principality, present-day Tra Kieu
Srisanabhadresvar	Myson

And further south:

Indrapura	present-day Dong Dzuong
Vijaya	present-day Qui Nhon
Kauthara	present-day Nha Trang
Panduranga	present-day Phan Rang

With possibly three more, further north:

Van Xa	near Hue
Than Hoa	halfway between Hanoi and Vinh
Ha Tinh	just south of Vinh

Simhapura, present-day Tra Kieu, a few miles upriver from Hoi An, was one of the earliest centres of Cham political power, dating from before the turn of the Christian era. Lam Ap Pho, the port for the country of Lam Ap, in those early days was located slightly upriver from present-day Hoi An, the sandbars of the estuary having extended south and east through the centuries.

Simhapura waxed and withered in importance several times throughout Cham history and Myson, hidden away in a secret mountain valley further upriver, served as the spiritual sanctuary, not only for the rulers of the Thu Bon valley, but for Cham kings up and down the coast. Whenever a new ruler established power, he built a new tower or temple at Myson to honour himself and to ally himself with the Hindu god Siva – almost, it seems, as an act of self-accreditation.

Later Chinese annuals tell us that there was a rebellion in Rinan against direct Chinese taxation in 100 AD and another uprising in 136. Both uprisings were in the southern-most district of Xianglin, known as Elephant Forest – considered by at least one archaeologist to have stretched as far south as the Hai Van

Pass between Hue and Danang – possibly taking in at least part of present-day Quang Nam province, which includes Hoi An.

There were further conflicts in 144 and 192, when the district magistrate of Xianglin was assassinated by Khu Lien, the son of a district official, an event that led to the establishment of a new independent polity called Linyi by the Chinese, which means Forest City. Linyi was in the southernmost area of what had been nominally Chinese controlled trading territories. Certain archaeologists believe Linyi to have been Lam Ap, the Thu Bon river valley. Yet where Linyi was located and whether or not it was Cham, remains one of the most hotly disputed and unresolved controversies, passionately argued between archaeologists and historians. Was Linyi the same polity as Champa, or wasn't it?

That the Chinese do not describe Linyi as an Indianized kingdom feeds fuel to the scholarly argument that it was not a Cham revolt. One scholar even argues that Linyi was somewhere in Laos! Or might Indianization simply have taken place – after the rebellions? As far as is known, the first temples at Myson were built in the fourth century.

Whether this revolt was mounted by only one or two of the Cham kingdoms, or a united effort, or was not a Cham revolt at all – might it even have been the Chinese traders? – is not known. The Chinese-held territories further north remained under Chinese domination until the Viets freed themselves in 938.

Whatever, by 248 AD Linyi felt brave enough to attack the Chinese territories of Jiuzhen and Jiaozhi to the north, a pattern that was to continue throughout Cham history. A Chinese writer of the time described the people of Lam Ap as both warlike and musical with 'deep eyes, a high straight nose and curly black hair' – decidedly un-Chinese.

Chinese annals of 280 AD record China's rage at breakaway Linyi: 'He (the King of Linyi) is in contact to the south with (the king of) Funan. Their tribes are numerous; their allied troops aid each other. Taking advantage of the ruggedness of their region, they do not submit to China.'

The very earliest Cham inscription, the *Vo Canh,* was found – not at Myson – but in Nha Trang on the coast to the south of Myson. Written in Sanskrit, it is not only the earliest Cham inscription, it is the earliest inscription to have been found in

South East Asia and pre-dates the Khmers by several centuries. Attributed to a descendent of Sri Mara, the *Vo Canh* stipulates benevolently that his 'wealth should be used for the happiness and wealth of all.' Canadian archaeologist, Dougald O'Reilly, remarks wryly, 'Quite who Sri Mara was remains a mystery. The debate over the *Vo Canh* inscription has raged for a century' – another scholarly dogfight. Although the Frenchman, Abel Bergaigne, as early as 1888 linked the *Vo Canh's* origin 'palaeographically' to third century South India – that's as near as it has come so far to being dated!

In a layer also probably dating from the third century AD, the Go Cam dig near Simhapura (Tra Kieu), upriver from Hoi An, yielded heavy Chinese or North Vietnamese-style terracotta roof tiles, suggesting Chinese occupation from at least that time. Archaeologist Ian Glover, who participated in the dig, describes half cylindrical tablets, the sort used at the ends of roof tiles, decorated with stylized flowers; animal or demonic kala faces, one featuring a human face, its nose and eyebrows moulded in the form of a tree with spreading branches. These 'face tiles' are the earliest figurative art yet discovered in Central Vietnam.

At least one scholar believes that the Cham king, Fan Wen, was born in China and came to Champa as an adventurer where he served under King Fan Yi of Linyi. This same scholar credits Fan Wen with bringing knowledge of palace design, defensive walls and ditches, weapons and armour – and Chinese musical instruments – to Champa. When the old king, Fan Yi, died in 336, Fan Wen assumed power and sent an embassy to the Jin court of China with a gift of trained elephants and a letter, according to the Chinese 'in barbarian characters.' The Chinese refused his territorial claims and after several military campaigns, Fan Wen was defeated and died in 349.

This morning at the far end of Hoi An, I stumble across a custom new to me. In a cafe, the waitress appears with a menu and a glass of water – the first glass of water I have been offered in a Hoi An restaurant or cafe. As it is very hot, I order iced Vietnamese tea. The waitress looks somewhat nonplussed, opens the menu to teas and I see that no Vietnamese tea is listed. I ask if they have Vietnamese tea and she says 'yes', goes away and another waiter comes. I explain that I am happy to pay for a

Lipton tea, but would prefer Vietnamese tea, if they have it. This brings the young manager to explain that Vietnamese tea is always free. I say that I have paid for iced Vietnamese tea many times in other cafes. This seems to pain him. He explains that he worked in a hotel for five years and thinks it unfair that foreigners always pay more for everything than the Vietnamese – but we earn multiples of what the Vietnamese earn.

'Vietnamese tea is free, it only costs maybe a thousand dong. I will bring you Vietnamese tea, you do not pay, but order fruit juice or coffee – to make me happy.'

As my tummy is slightly uneasy from yesterday's too peppery salad, I really do not want a fruit juice or a coffee. I explain that I have only come to wait for a friend; I am waiting for a tradesman around the corner, who will be back in an hour.

'Fine, I will bring you Vietnamese tea. Order something when your friend comes.'

But my friend won't be coming to the cafe. Suddenly I realise that I have bumped headlong into a cultural tradition of Hoi An hospitality. In a Vietnamese home or office, the visitor is always offered Vietnamese tea without ever being asked if it is desired. It is simply a part of the welcome, like shaking hands in the West.

In leaving, I point to the coffee on the menu and hand the waiter ten thousand dongs, saying it is for coffee – but I don't want the coffee. Still not happy, the manager returns to my table to say that it is all right if I want to tip his staff. Oh dear, still not done the right thing.

Later, a Hoi An friend explains that the Vietnamese drink Vietnamese tea as a kind of chaser for coffee. Whenever you order a coffee in a Vietnamese cafe in Hoi An, as opposed to cafes catering for foreign tourists, a glass of Vietnamese tea is automatically served with it. So, you have to order coffee to get Vietnamese tea!

IN A SECRET VALLEY

At seven sharp I am outside the gate waiting for new friends, two *Viet kieu* and a French lady, to pick me up in a taxi. The *Viet kieu* are a mother and daughter from France, the mother an agronomist born in Saigon, who migrated to France at the age of nineteen, her daughter an environmentalist, who has grown up in France.

Their elderly French friend is fulfilling a promise made to her father on his deathbed – to visit Vietnam. When the Vichy Government took power in France, her outraged father crossed the Channel in disgust and joined the British Navy, then later served in Hanoi during the French Indo-Chinese War.

They finally arrive at half past seven; we had hoped to arrive early, before the crowds. It is nine miles (14 kms) upriver from Hoi An to Tra Kieu and another eighteen miles (29 kms) on to Myson, the secret valley of temples, hidden deep in the jungle.

Within a minute we are in the countryside. Thick fog smothers the vibrant green rice paddies, as soft and lush as a deep pile carpet. Colourful plastic bags, attached to bamboo poles flutter over the paddies to frighten the birds. Occasionally a tomb rises from a paddy field; rice farmers lie at rest where they lived and laboured.

In late February, the transplanted rice is about halfway to harvest in April; planting was late this year because of a typhoon and flooding. Billowing groves of bamboo, the lacy tracery of flame trees and cascading vines form a leafy avenue for the road. Here and there banana palms flap their paddle fronds.

Squat, tile-roofed, stucco houses loom like ghosts through the fog, flashing pots of luminously yellow chrysanthemums left over fromI *Tet,* the Vietnamese New Year. Each house stands sequestered behind a low wall or a wire fence, its side boundaries marked by a line of slim areca palms, sometimes a mango tree. Now and again, a mass of crimson bougainvillea blazes through the fog. Along the road, one solitary red flag with a gold star hangs limply and rather surprisingly, a red flag brandishing the gold hammer and sickle. Briefly, a dark pond, its surface like black lacquer, shimmers and disappears in the mist.

We are travelling grandly in Mr Duc's air-conditioned, six-month-old Toyota saloon. English-speaking Mr Duc is a one-man taxi company whose wife teaches French. On my first visit to Myson thirteen years ago, I sat tenaciously hanging onto a handle in a four-by-four, the road so rutted by potholes from the rainy season that we could travel no faster than ten or fifteen miles an hour. Now, smooth tarmac slides through the green countryside and villages.

Half past seven is rush hour; most businesses open at half past seven. Mr Duc gently steers us round hooting buses and lorries and with the briefest hoot, nudges motorbikes and bicycles toward the right side of the road in order to pass. He hates using the horn, he tells us, possibly in deference to Western sensibilities. This is very temperate driving compared to the hell-for-leather, seemingly brake-less, long-distance bus and lorry drivers, who blast their air horns the length of Vietnam's Highway One from Hanoi to Saigon.

Vietnamese riders of bicycles and motorbikes sit with shoulders hunched, under cloche hats and jackets. To them late February, the end of the rainy season, is winter, while my companions and I are comfortable in T-shirts.

A huge green plastic bag of rice lies in the middle of the road. A few yards away, a motorbike has stopped, its driver contemplating how to retrieve his lost load without unbalancing his remaining load, another identical bag of rice. Corn and cane fields leap up unexpectedly, surrounded by rice paddies. Wild morning glories carpet the verges.

Suddenly, a huge boat – a three-deck liner – looms out of the water to our left. Screened by vegetation, without realising it we have been following the river upstream. 'A restaurant, owned by a Vietnamese from Hoi An,' says Mr Duc. He is less forthcoming about how this maritime apparition got here, up a shallow backwater. Later I feel rather sheepish on the way back when the fog has cleared, to see that it is built of concrete. From behind us comes the blare of a siren and a white ambulance screams past, red light flashing – no ambulances, thirteen years ago.

At Tra Kieu, site of Simhapura, City of the Lion, the former Cham capital of the Thu Bon river valley, the sun starts to burn through the mist and the temperature to rise. In the bronze village of Dien Phuong, gongs and lanterns hang from every eave, outdoor display shelves cluttered with bronze dragons, pots and incense burners. Thick bunches of tobacco leaves dry on racks in front of a few houses.

'Old ladies like tobacco,' says Mr Duc.

Precisely an hour after our departure, we approach a huge ceremonial gate over the road reading: Welcome to Myson. Where thirteen years ago I trembled with each hesitant step over a narrow, bendy bamboo footbridge, steaming in the jungle, now a bridge for vehicles with rustic, log-look railings and brick arches in the shape of Cham towers, crosses the shallow stream. This is as far as Mr Duc is allowed to drive.

In the ladies, I recall with an inner chuckle being surprised to find bidets installed where one would expect toilets on my visit four years ago.

'We ordered Western toilets, they sent us bidets, so we have bidets,' the attendant had explained nonchalantly. Now, there are Western-style toilets and a sealed, plastic receptacle for the absent attendant's tips.

We stroll along a wide, stone-paved road for perhaps half a mile through the low-lying, tightly matted jungle brimming with birdsong. Years ago, this was a dusty dirt track, so hot in early April that the heat shimmered on the horizon and I thought my brain was dissolving – the hottest day in my living memory. My *Viet kieu* companions stop to creep up on every black and yellow butterfly. Even gossamer spider webs along the steep banks beneath the tangled jungle find immortality in their snapshots. I am secretly relieved that I will not be rushed through the ruins.

Abruptly, round a bend, a haunting, dark red brick tower and a two-storey temple, leaning slightly, erupt from the jungle (temple Groups B, C and D). At just after half past eight, we have the temples to ourselves. Birds twitter, the heady scent of warm, green jungle fills the air; you can almost smell it growing. Entering the low-walled temple quadrangle, the peace of this sacred sanctuary of the Chams descends upon us. I instantly grasp why the Chams chose the pure isolation of this narrow, hidden, green jungle valley in which to raise temples to their deities over a period of seven centuries. Tranquillity reigns. Along these rough paths tread a ghostly procession of kings and priests, redolent of a culture long disappeared. But here also swarmed marauding armies to defile and destroy, to slaughter and to plunder. Myson, at first tranquil, harbours a restless soul. So much has happened here, so many have come in reverence, in joyful triumph, so many in aggression, all to disappear.

Eerily, a deity with elongated earlobes stares stolidly from the wall of the grass-tufted remains of a temple tower. The entrance to the vestibule around to one side of his damaged tower exposes thin, corbelled bricks, the entrance supported by stone pillars, elegantly carved in extended lotus petals.

Each king, as he built a temple tower, a stupa, or one of the buildings of a temple complex, had an inscription engraved, sometimes on a temple pillar or on a stele, usually inflating his own importance. In dedicating temples, Cham kings added a suffix referring to Siva to their own names, thus identifying themselves with the deity to whom the temples were dedicated – a forerunner perhaps of the Khmer tradition of god kings?

The first known Cham king, Bhadravarman, built a temple tower (B1), dedicated to himself and to Siva, the newly created deity, Bhadreshvara. His inscription in Sanskrit translates: 'For the benefit of the sons and grandsons of King Bhadravarman.' Only the stone pit is left where treasure would have been cached away – and a few post-holes, indicating that the upper part was built of wood and almost certainly burnt. From only the pit or treasure vault, it is impossible to guess the temple's size or shape.

According to archaeologist Ian Glover, the earliest inscriptions found near Myson, known as *Hon Cuc,* were on stones about five miles (8 km) north-east of Myson on the Ba Ren river, a tributary of the Thu Bon river. Only visible in the dry season, they mark the boundaries of Bhadravarman's temple complex and have been dated (palaeographically), to late fourth or early fifth century. He is thought to have reigned 380-413. From the temple boundary markers and this inscription, Ian Glover surmises that Bhadravarman's influence was quite extensive. However, Glover goes on to say that oddly, attempts to identify Bhadravarman as a king of Linyi have proved mysteriously fruitless: 'His name is not mentioned in later genealogies of Champa.'

Linyi was sacked in 446 by the Song army. China, irked by Linyi's frequent attacks on her southern territories, retaliated. The Song army led by General Dan Hoa Chi sacked Khu Tuc and killed the Lam Ap General, Pham Phu Long, then marched south to Lam Ap where they stormed the walled town and citadel. Looting temples and treasury, the Song carried back to China an astonishing, estimated one hundred thousand pounds of gold! Whether the gold was looted from Khu Tuc near Hue or Lam Ap (Simhapura-Tra Kieu), or both, and whether or not they were Cham, Linyi was a rich prize.

The capital of Linyi has been described in the Chinese *Shuijingzhu* as having been surrounded by rectangular walls measuring 2.4 miles (4 km) in circumference, the packed earthen walls rising seven metres high, topped by brick walls for another three metres with four gates and wooden palisades of up to five tiers high, oriented east-west, with a river flowing north, the principal gate facing east. The *Shuijingzhu* also tells of fifty separate quarters, eight temples and pagodas, a brick or tiled palace and densely packed houses.

According to archaeologist Ian Glover, this type of rectangular citadel enclosure matches that discovered at the site of Thanh Loi near Hue on the south bank of the Huong (Perfume) river – but also that of the citadel at Tra Kieu. Scholars generally agree that following the Chinese victory of 446 and the fall of Khu Tuc, that Simhapura (Tra Kieu) and its port, Lam Ap Pho, swelled in importance.

A second inscription found south-east of Tra Kieu, possibly intended to protect a nearby spring, refers to Nagaraja, king of the *nagas* – the sacred snake rulers of the underworld. Although written in Cham, the inscription contains borrowed Sanskrit words. Believed to date from the early sixth century, it is considered to be the earliest text written in any Austronesian language. Cham history is still very much in a state of flux, each discovery adding fuel to the existing arguments and theories.

On the subject of the temple dedicated to Bhadreshvara, Glover surmises that Bradravarman's reign might even have dated from the late fifth or early sixth century, 'making him the contemporary of King Kaundinya of Funan, who sent an official complaint to China in 484 concerning the actions of a usurper king of Linyi.'

The Chams built their temples of low temperature fired bricks, used no mortar and carved the exterior surfaces – every pillar, window and false door; every door frame moulding, every alcove and statue, and the elaborate friezes around the base of

42

their temples – after they were built. It has recently been discovered that they used the resin of a local tree, *dipterocarpus alatus roxb,* the same resin they used and still use to seal wooden boats and basket boats. They virtually glued the bricks together! Moreover, the resin is so strong that it improves the tensile strength of the bricks. Laboratory tests in Milan have shown that instead of breaking apart under stress, the bricks remain sealed and they break in the middle! The Chams are just possibly the finest artisans in brickwork the world has ever known.

Two elephants under a banyan tree – a scene that could well have been a local snapshot when it was carved – grace the lintel of a small two-storey temple. Figures of Siva shelter in alcoves. Along one side, voluptuous bare-breasted *apsaras* under colonnades perform their heavenly dance, eternally.

A tiny museum has been arranged inside one temple, the turned-stone balustrades of its windows not unlike thick, sharp edged Victorian chair legs and very like those at Angkor. A fine, headless Siva stands firmly inside, barefooted and bare chested, his sarong in neat formal folds around his slim hips. Most of the best pieces of sculpture from Myson have been removed and taken to the Champa Museum in Danang, to the Guimet Museum in Paris or to the History Museums of Hanoi and Saigon, but one very fine lintel has been left here on display: A dancing Siva balances on one bent knee, his other bent knee lifted high, heel bent, toes turned upward, multiple arms flailing – or might this be how early sculptors indicated motion? Beside him, his consort, Parvati, kneels. An orchestra accompanies Siva's dance: drum, flute and percussion 'shakers'. The jangle of their silent music drifts into consciousness along with the heat and heavy humidity.

Beyond Siva on a high counter, two round, upturned semi-spheres – breasts – lie exposed. The goddess Uma – or Uroja, she had many names – was worshipped by the Cham people long before Hinduism took root and she continued to be worshipped as the Cham mother goddess simultaneously with Saivism. Fittingly, nearby stands the tip of a huge stone lingum, the creative, phallic symbol of Siva. For the Westerner, it is not easy to reconcile the eroticism of Cham (Khmer or Indian) religious art with the chastity of Christianity. It demands a complete volte-face to embrace the worship of the human life force in both its male and female physical aspects, rather than holding sacred a life of self-denial in anticipation of a heaven, never to be experienced in this life. I remember one of my Buddhist friends complaining that 'Christianity is so violent.' And it is true, if you think of all those martyred saints and the crucifixion.

Outside, a damaged stone Nandina bull sprawls near a line of several exquisitely carved, heavenly female dancers, poor lost *apsaras,* waiting to be returned to their rightful, original architectural positions. Nearby, a fine stone male figure sits with one knee bent flat, one knee upright, wearing decorative armbands and a finely carved braid across his chest. He might have been carved recently, he is in such fine condition.

Further into the site, heavenly *apsaras* bearing swords dance alongside the entrance of a second small museum where inside, another Siva performs his cosmic dance *(tandava)* under protruding terracotta temple roof finials. Jolly elephants, their trunks flying high behind them, trot along what was probably the base of a temple – the Chams used elephants in warfare.

A highly decorated, multi-tiered lingum is the central display here, tiny images of Siva, each sheltering under a lotus leaf, circling its round tip. Metal caps *(kosa)* often made of precious metal alloys – gold and silver – to cover the tip of the lingum, were considered as important a devotional tribute to the deity as the lingum itself in the eyes of the donor king.

Standing amongst the temples (of Groups B, C and D), their courtyards neat and tidy, it is hard to imagine what Myson must have looked like when the French priest, Father Bruyere, first led a French military attachment to Myson in 1885, nor the conditions endured by the first French architect-archaeologists, Henri Parmentier and Charles Carpeaux, who started to investigate and survey the ruins in March of 1903.

Parmentier, as *architect-pensionnaire* of *l'Ecole Française d'Extrême Orient* (the French School of Asian Studies), was charged with studying, excavating and preserving Cham monuments built between the seventh and sixteenth centuries along the central Vietnam coast. Quite an assignment.

Patrizia Zolese, heading the Italian team of archaeologists and architects from the Lerici Foundation of Milan Politechnico, currently working at Myson, has written extensively of those first efforts by the French.

'As Myson lay a considerable distance from the nearest village, Parmentier and Carpeaux faced stifling heat, unsanitary conditions and constant threats from the local insects and animals. Their journals speak of reptiles, spiders and scorpions – and Ong Cop, Mr Tiger. No idle threat, Mr Tiger. Their landlord had been seized, carried off and presumably devoured by a tiger while they were living in a *cagna,* a straw house on the mountainside that provided scant protection even within a four-metre high stockade.'

Before they could begin their survey of the monuments, first they had to excavate tons of earth and fallen bricks to find what lay beneath. Once rubble and vegetation were cleared, the vegetation would rush back.

A temple building (now known as C1) was requisitioned as a photo lab as it provided complete darkness inside. Charles Carpeaux diligently photographed everything and his collection of glass stereoscopic plates – most of his photographs were taken later in Cambodia and preserved at the Guimet Museum in Paris – were only restored, digitized, identified and partly published in a catalogue for an exhibition of Cham sculpture in 2005.

While at Myson, Carpeaux unearthed a terracotta jar buried at the base of a temple building (classified as C7). In it he found a treasure trove of gold and silver adornments intended for a deity: a crown, earrings, necklace, ornaments for chest, arms and legs, as well as two golden linga resting on silver ablution basins.

Their excavations ended in the torridly hot month of July. Carpeaux, exhausted, never saw Myson again – nor France. Tragically, he died only a year later in Saigon at the age of thirty-four. Parmentier's exhaustive survey of the Cham ruins, *l'Inventoire sommaire des monuments Cham de l'Annam,* is still referred to today as the most complete inventory of Cham temples ever made – his original classification of monuments is still adhered to – and it was he who recognized that the temples in Group E were amongst the earliest.

With World War II and the Japanese occupation of Vietnam, French archaeological work stopped. The temples lay neglected and overgrown by the jungle; then came bombing during the Vietnam War.

As the Viet Cong used Myson as a base, Myson was bombed not just once but repeatedly until, according to the oft told story,

Philippe Stern, Chief Curator of Cham Art at the Guimet Museum in Paris, sent a message to President Nixon, urgently requesting that the bombing of Myson stop. Too late, the bombing stopped.

What is less well known is that earlier, during the French Indo-Chinese War, Philippe Stern, already at the Guimet, had sent a similar message to the top French general in charge in Hanoi, requesting that Myson be spared.

Following reunification in 1975, having been devastated by forty years of war, Vietnam had little money nor energy for archaeology. Nevertheless in 1980, a joint Polish-Vietnamese Committee for Conservation of Cham Architectural Heritage was organized to investigate the state of the ruins (1980-86). Giant bomb craters had been gouged out of the site; only fifty buildings from a previous seventy-two remained in anything like a standing state, and the entire area had been mined.

Head of the Polish team was a professor of architecture, Dr Kazimierz Kwiatkowski; heading the Vietnamese team was a Russian-trained architect, Hoang Dao Kinh, who I happened to meet some years later when he was restoring Hanoi's opera house. He told me then how they had to clear mines before they could even approach the temple ruins – eight lives were lost and more than twenty were injured.

At the time, I remembered my own first timid visit in the shimmering heat of April 1997 – and it gets much hotter later in the summer. Having been told to stick to the paths, I had cautiously explored Groups B, C and D. Seeing the tip of a temple tower peeping above the trees, but no discernible path, for fear of mines, I had retreated. The jungle quickly submerges everything in an impenetrable tangle of greenery.

With the collapse of the Soviet Union, funding stopped, but Dr Kazimierz Kwiatkowsky doggedly went on working – living with the workers, using his own money to pay the workers to clear and reconstruct Groups B, C and D. It was his life's work and he wanted to finish it.

When the French first came to Myson in 1903, writes Patrizia Zolese, Groups B, C and D were buried under several metres of rubble. First the French, then the Polish-Vietnamese team, not only excavated but restored the temples – using the anastylosis system, which was new to them.

Patrizia Zolese describes the work done by the Polish-Vietnamese joint effort with almost reverential respect.

'Several hundred workers mobilized to open paths, fell trees, clear vegetation, removing thousands of metres of soil, filling in bomb craters, treating vegetation that penetrated the brick structures, clearing and collecting thousands of ancient bricks and terracotta decorative elements and identifying their former locations for future use . . . reinforcing towers urgently threatened with collapse, reconstructing lower elements of razed structures using retrieved brick and cement mortar to expose the restored areas to view.'

It quickly becomes obvious that the work of an archaeologist in South East Asia demands hard physical labour in an excruciatingly hot, hostile and debilitating climate.

It was only when Hoi An raised a granite memorial to Kazimierz Kwiatkowki in Tran Phu Street that I learned that it was he, more than any other, who had helped Hoi An and Myson to become listed as World Heritage Sites – and that he had died on the 24th of March 1997, only days before I arrived in Myson that first time. I had stood in his reconstructed temples, gazing ignorantly at the towers and the pieces of Cham sculpture that he had so cherished – that he gave his life to rebuild and preserve.

An arched bridge over a gurgling stream leads to the next group of temples in a grassy enclosure (Group A). Very badly bombed, this central temple tower, formerly one of the glories of Myson, lies in ruin, broken and overgrown by vegetation, its remaining walls rising defiantly.

British archaeologist Ian Glover laments its loss: 'This style of architecture was renowned for its elegance of pilasters and perpendicular mouldings, which gave an illusion of height to the walls of the temple, and for the sandstone sculpture on the superstructure of the tower of *devatas,* female figures, holding a lotus bud to their breasts.'

The tower of Group A was nearly thirty metres (97 ft) high, carved from the top to the bottom, Federico Barocco tells me sadly. Barocco, the young Italian archaeologist the French photographer had suggested I contact, arrived as a member of the Italian team in Vietnam almost exactly a century after the French archaeologists started that early survey. Just now he is investigating what may have been a wall two hundred miles (320 km) south of Hoi An in Quang Ngai and Binh Dinh provinces, 'making excavation tests, an archaeological survey and doing multidisciplinary research.'

No more than grass covered lumps remain of the corner towers of Group A, although in front of one, archaeologists have meticulously lined up two stone columns bearing profusely carved, curling vines and lotus flowers. Paths between the central temple and towers lie strewn with broken bits of brick and sometimes straw to soak up the rain during the wet season.

A three-tier stone lingum, once worshipped as the most sacred object in the inner sanctum of a temple tower, over which liquid offerings would have been poured ceremoniously by a priest, stands exposed in the open air. The square base of a lingum referred to Brahma; its octagonal second tier to Vishnu; the upper, rounded tier, symbolic of Siva.

Only one carved column clings to the facade of the tower. The Hindu deity, Indra, rides an elephant towards the entrance. Elephants parade round the exterior base of the temple where dragonflies flit about my feet in the long grass. Inside stands a stone basin *(yoni),* on which the lingum outside might have stood.

To one side, several stone blocks have been systematically lined up, probably missing from the base of a temple, portraying worshippers in pleated sarongs, praying under intricately carved canopies. By now, tour groups of visitors are beginning to invade.

We retrace our steps to the bridge, where log steps lead provocatively upward toward forbidding coloured tape (Group G). Reluctantly, we continue on the path to more temples (Groups E and F), thought by early French archaeologist Henri Parmentier to be amongst the earliest remaining temples at Myson.

At the entrance to the site, a life-sized, headless guardian *(dravavara)* stands bare-chested, his long sarong reaching to his bare feet. Wearing an elaborate necklace and armbands, he holds the remnants of a snake in one hand. A now faceless Nandina bull lies nearby. Beside him stands a stone stele, its message carved for eternity in Sanskrit or Cham, its meaning now locked away to all but specialist scholars.

Sometimes Chams made their inscriptions in Sanskrit on one side and in Cham on the reverse, providing a kind of Rosetta stone for archaeologists centuries later.

Whatever might have been at Myson before the seventh century, even as early as the fourth century, was built of wood and burnt by invaders. Yet it is fairly well accepted that the Chams had some sort of unified polity by the fourth century.

In the walled enclosure of Group E, one brick wall of the temple tower remains vertical atop a grassy hillock, starkly silhouetted against a glaringly bright sky, the metre-high enclosure walls now smothered in grass. What must have been another fair sized temple has now sprouted an irreverently robust crop of cane from the rooftop. Steel poles brace its walls and lacy fern and moss choke the base. Two stone, turned balustrades are all that remain to protect a square window, once again like those at Angkor Wat.

At the far end of the site (Group F), a galvanised steel roof shelters what is left of a huge temple tower, leaning dangerously, its walls braced, its bricks crumbling from the top. Of the former entrance, only a pristine, white marble step carved in the shape of a lotus blossom lies exposed at the base of a fearsome pile of bricks that look as if it could topple at any instant. Nearby, another stele heralds the greatness of a king long dead. Beside the temple yawns the source of its destruction, a deep, overgrown bomb crater.

On our way back to Hoi An, we stop at the Catholic cathedral in Tra Kieu, once the site of Simhapura. Of the once glorious Cham capital, nothing is left. The cathedral presents a shocking face to the world. Dragons ripple along the banisters of a bifurcated staircase sweeping up to a central porch and porticoes – beneath half an open dome, flanked by two square towers. The church must have been bombed in two, leaving only half the dome.

Inside a sung mass conducted by two priests, one Western, one Vietnamese, is just ending. The congregation of about fifty is mixed, Western and Vietnamese. To one side, a small informal museum hides under a porch dripping with violet morning glories. Inside, two stone Cham elephants gallop towards one another. Incongruously, a framed Lords Supper spreads along the opposite wall and a wistful white china Virgin Mary greets the visitor beside shelves of what appear to be contemporary terracotta ceramics – Cham? A Vietnamese man tells us in careful English that a miracle took place here in 1885 when twenty-four people hid in the Cathedral and were protected by the Virgin Mary at a time when the Vietnamese (Nguyen) emperors were persecuting Catholics.

At the bronze village, Dien Phuong, we stop at a shop hung with lanterns and gongs, its shelves crowded with Buddhas, dragons, elephants, incense burners, temple dogs and altar candlesticks. The *Viet kieu* daughter listens to every gong in the shop, then to every gong that comes tumbling out of a huge bag of gongs brought from the back room. At last she decides upon a large, deep-throated gong and a smaller, higher-pitched gong exactly an octave apart.

Then the bargaining begins. I am bemused to see that the shopkeeper uses the same ploy with *Viet kieu* clients as that to befuddle foreigners, offering a blank page and asking how much the prospective buyer is willing to pay. But this is a wise daughter; her mother bought a gong last year, so she knows their approximate values. The shopkeeper demands a price three hundred thousand dongs ($16 US) higher for the two than she has offered. Finally, threatened with retreat, the shopkeeper relents. Then the mother buys a rice pot and a flower bowl in less time than it takes to pack the two gongs in the car boot and we head back to Hoi An in the midday heat to cool showers.

'You have to go to Myson this afternoon. Someone on the Italian team has had to fly to Hanoi, so Mara is free this afternoon, but only this afternoon. Otherwise, she is working.'

The urgent phone call is from Thanh, the thoughtful *Viet kieu* wife of the Italian archaeologist, Federico Barocco. Mara Landoni is the Italian architect attached to the Lerici Foundation of Milan Politechnic team currently working at Myson.

Thanh kindly arranges for a motorbike to take me to Myson, leaving in an hour's time in the blistering midday sun. Slicing the wind on a motorbike is not a bad way to keep reasonably cool and there is hardly any traffic as everyone else is taking a nap. Myson, roughly thirty miles from Hoi An, takes an hour at best, either by taxi or by motorbike, an hour and a piece of string if there is traffic.

Arriving at Myson, we stop near the entrance, now deserted in the afternoon heat and I try to ring Mara on my mobile – no signal. Suddenly we are plunged back into the pre-technological

50

age. The tigers may have gone, but Myson is still a hot, difficult place to work, logistically.

We inquire at a restaurant and are told emphatically that Mara has flown to Hanoi. We then ask at the restaurant opposite. A man there points us towards the entrance and shows us on a map of Myson where Mara's site is – except that I know she is not working today. He, however, is certain that she is there. So the motorbike is waved through by the ticket checker at the entrance and we head down the stone road toward the ruins. Where the stone road ends and becomes dirt track, the motorbike stops. I ask the driver to wait, there being two stone benches in the shade, for I don't know if I will be able to locate Mara. I have visions of having come all this way and not being able to find her. But does he understand?

I head off along the dirt track, past the performance hall, now empty. Likewise, the shop and refreshment standing opposite. It's as though the party's over and everyone has gone home, not just for today but for the entire season. I am the sole person about. Mid-afternoon is clearly the ideal time to have Myson to yourself, if you can bear the heat – the Japanese carry umbrellas even in the morning.

On approaching the first Cham ruins, I see three figures, who at a distance could be Italian, one of whom might be Mara. I wave and she waves back.

'I'm not an archaeologist, I'm an architect,' she says by way of greeting. 'Patrizia Zolese is the archaeologist in our team. She had to go to Hanoi. We are standing in Group C. Normally, Hindu temple entrances are in the east. In Henri Parmentier's system of classification, Number 1 is always the main sanctuary tower, the *kalan.'* Mara explains that the valley isn't very wide and that the river originally ran on the opposite side of the temples. The river we see now is the 'new' river – it wasn't where it is now when the temples were built.

'In a Hindu complex, the *mandapa* is the place where people go inside and purify themselves before they enter the *gopura* (gate), leading to the *kalan* (main sanctuary tower). The *kosagrha* (treasure house-library) is to one side. So is the *posa,* a square building that holds the stele.' When I ask Mara for the dates of the ruins in Groups B, C and D, she throws up her hands.

'Impossible. So many re-buildings.'

51

Early on, the Chams were attacked and their temples burnt; even later when they built in brick, temples were destroyed by invaders. Succeeding rulers rebuilt and rededicated them, over and over again. As a result, it is impossible for archaeologists to say who built what, when. Only the stelae provide clues, when they are found.

'There were seventy-two buildings at Myson before the wars' (World War II, the French Indo-Chinese War and the American-Vietnam War, ending in 1975). 'Now there are only fifty buildings visible – but visible to me only because I know they are there.'

Then she tells us about the Polish archaeologist, Kazimierz Kwaitkovsky, who worked so arduously to restore Groups B, C and D. 'Patrizia Zolese arrived in Myson only months after he died in 1997. She was so disappointed, she had so looked forward to meeting and working with him.

'One thing, the *kalan* (main sanctuary tower) of B1 is the only building in stone and it may have been unfinished. Cham temples and towers are constructed of slim bricks. First they were built, then they were carved, the pillars, the alcoves, the figures, the faces and the decorations.'

On my earlier visit to Myson, I had stood longingly at the foot of a flight of log steps, taped off from the public.

Would it be possible to visit the site where the Italian team is now working?

'Of course!' and she leads us up the log steps into the secret world of archaeologists at work.

Around the central tower, it looks like a builder's yard, piles of bricks, to one side a standing stele and a curiously incised, narrow stone elliptical base.

'The base, possibly for a seated figure, the statue has been lost. We found the stele, marked by bullet holes. One thing I can tell you, Group G is the perfect example of a Hindu temple. It has five buildings: a *mandapa* (assembly hall), a *gopura* (gate), the *kalan* (sanctuary tower), a *kosagrha* (treasure house-library), a *posa* (stele house), surrounded by walls. The names for the buildings come from Sanskrit.

'Group G was built by King Jaya Harivarman I, rather late in the Cham era. We completely excavated the site. The (enclosure) walls are brick, faced with laterite. Group G is the only group that has laterite. The *mandapa* and *posa* are outside the walls.'

52

In 1145 the powerful Khmer king, Suryavarman, who built Angkor and who already controlled much of Thailand, had ambitions to extend his kingdom to the east coast of the peninsula. He attacked and defeated Champa and placed his brother-in-law on the throne. From the South, Jaya Harivarman rose up to defeat and rid Champa of the Khmers and reclaimed the throne as Jaya Harivarman I in 1147. He then undertook the restoration of Myson, looted and destroyed by the Khmers, as well as building this new temple complex.

Grotesque faces, *metopes,* grimace toothily from the base of the *kalan,* the main sanctuary tower. 'The *metopes* represent the terrifying Face of Glory' – fearsome mythical monsters, symbol of time and death, also of royalty.

'They guard the temple,' explains Mara – as well they might, against the vengeance of the Khmers.

At the beginning, the team was surprised to retrieve five thousand complete bricks from the rubble – thirty different types of bricks – three dimensions of brick. The team is reusing the original bricks, excavated and cleaned, each original brick marked with a number, now cut to the sizes required to restore the pair of stairways that lead from either side to the entrance of the *kalan.* When a brick is missing, they use a brick from the 'dumping', or new bricks made according to analysis in Milan, their composition as near as possible to the original Cham bricks.

'Instead of mortar, the Chams used the resin of a tree.'

Although there are many species of *dipterocarpaceae,* after many analyses in Milan, the resin used by the team is that most similar to the original. Mara runs her fingers admiringly over the old bricks at a point where they remain.

'They were so beautifully fitted together that you could not see the joins. First they built, then they carved, the columns, the decorations.' As horizontal scratch marks on the original bricks make plain, the bricks were rubbed against one another to smooth the surfaces and obtain a tight fit.

'The *gopura* is not yet restored. We are working on the sanctuary tower.'

And how long will the work go on?

'It is uncertain after this year (2010).' With a shiver, suddenly I feel the desperation Kwaitkowsky must have felt – were they to be forced to leave their work unfinished.

When Italian archaeologist, Patrizia Zolese, was first sent by UNESCO to examine the ruins, she was moved to record her initial impressions.

'I had expected visual impact; apart from some groups, I saw mostly ruins. Depressed, I returned to Hoi An. Preparing the report for Richard Englehardt (of UNESCO), I had a rethink: I felt that despite its state of conservation, this is an archaeologically and historically important site in South East Asia – and I thought about the bombing. The craters were dramatic. Group A was surrounded by piles of bricks; it was easy to imagine that the war had only finished a few weeks before.

'As I thought through things in Hoi An, I came to a decision: Despite the project's difficulty . . . I felt a responsibility to the site – the responsibility of a human being towards an important site of human patrimony, now abandoned by the international scientific community – and I wanted to do something. I felt offended by the destruction of masterpieces of human art.'

So Myson had beguiled yet another archaeologist, who found it impossible to leave the ruins in ruins.

Reluctantly at five, I leave Myson in order to get back to Hoi An before dark. The motorbike journey past cottages where red peppers, corn cobs and peanuts lay spread on mats to dry is enchanting, though these days, here and there a two-storey villa shatters the scale of a village. The smell of hot, dry, red earth mingles with the heavy scent of green vegetation. The heat is draining from the sun, leaving a red blotch low in the sky and settling into balmy, tropical twilight. To the passenger on the back of a motorbike, village life looks idyllic.

CHAM ISLAND

The scent of the sea rushes deep into the lungs. As the ragged fringe of firs gives way to water palms, the boat rounds the last tongue of sandy beach and the boat heaves with a wave into the open sea, the blinding sun igniting the water to quicksilver. Once out of the shallows, in the pilothouse the Vietnamese captain steers with one foot, eating a bowl of noodles. Ahead on the far horizon lies a double hump, violet behind filmy mist – Cham Island – roughly nine miles (15 kms), an hour and a half away.

What people call Cham Island is really a cluster of eight islands – Hon Ong, Hon Tai, Hon Lao, Hon Dai, Hon Mo, Hon La and Hon Kho, two small islands together. Bat Lao mountain rises over four thousand feet on the largest island, Hon Lao, where people live in Bai Lang hamlet, hugging their harbour. This fishing village is only three centuries old. Many people came there to escape during the wars; at the same time it became a military post. Now, about 2,500 people live there.

Caves riddle the cliffs along the eastern side of the island, as well as the cliffs of some of the smaller islands, where thousands of swallows breed, their nests providing a highly nutritious food and a valuable export.

I have hitched a ride in a diving boat, the divers attracted by the tropical fish and coral reefs lying off Kho, La, Tai and Mo islands: more than two hundred species of reef fish, two hundred species of hard corals and fifteen species of soft corals, amongst them three species of hydra, two thorn corals and one green coral. A framed picture of a vicious-looking fish hangs beneath the boat's tea caddy: Warning: Titon Trigger Fish.

Cham Island or islands, is one of the few places in Vietnam where primary jungle remains undisturbed – the largest tropical broad-leaf forest in Vietnam. In 2009, Cham Island(s) were recognized as a World Biosphere Reserve.

The forest harbours many precious trees: hard woods such as *quynh* and ironwood for building, rare types of rattan and medicinal herbs, as well as providing a habitat for twelve species of mammals and thirteen species of birds. More unexpectedly, the islands offer a home to one hundred thirty species of reptiles and five species of frogs; long-tailed monkeys and swallows are listed as protected species. One of the divers tells me that 'many small animals live in the jungle, but the people do not go into the jungle for fun, they go into the jungle to hunt for food.'

The captain steers toward the humps on the horizon, which slowly turn from grey to dusty green, then brighter green as we ease our way through the surface haze in the bright sunshine. As we draw closer, the humps divide into three islands and the water has turned to pale jade.

Just over a dozen divers are on board, apart from the crew: three Aussies, one Brit, one Japanese on a business trip on his one free day off, a Croatian couple, three French couples and a lone Frenchman. I laugh later when the girl from Devon leaps in without a wetsuit – she is accustomed to freezing water – while the rest don wet suits, one person even pulling on two.

As the others leap overboard to explore the underwater world, all goes quiet save the lapping of water against the boat, the boat gently rocking at anchor. I muse on the land left behind, sunk beneath the horizon. I well understand the lure of the sea, lost in a world reduced to a green heaving mass as far as the eye can see. For me, flying produces a similar euphoria, climbing through clouds into anonymous infinity, diminishing earthly attachments, anxieties and passions as the plane rises. It must be the same for sailors, afloat in an infinite sea.

On Hon Lao, sites of the earliest habitation go back three millennia. From deep down have came stone tools – axes, scraping blades and graters, pestles and grinders – glass, stone and agate jewellery of the Sa Huynh, and from slightly higher, ceramics and pottery from China and Champa. So the Sa Huynh lived here, before the Chams. In the upper layers dating from the ninth and tenth centuries have come shards of pottery from the Middle East.

That Cham Island was a stopover for international trade, where mariners replenished their supplies and took on water, has been well documented in early Chinese texts and later in the logs of Arab traders en route to China. The protected harbours on the lee-side of the mountain sheltered their ships from tropical storms and in more recent centuries, acted as one of the points for registering a ship's arrival and paying taxes for entering Hoi An.

The Chams built wells on Hon Lao, several of which still exist, recognisable by their distinctive characteristics: round at the top, a square ironwood frame at the bottom, wooden pillars at each corner. The Xom Cam well still provides fresh water for the local population of Bai Lang. Back in Hoi An, a famous old Cham well called Ba Le is tucked away in an alley a couple of turns off Tran Hung Dao Street. Hunting for the turn-off, a friendly Vietnamese girl I asked, invited me to hop aboard her motorbike and two turns down a narrow lane later, she deposited me right beside it.

Divers up and peeled out of their wet suits, we pass tiny rocking fishing boats. Soon a thin creamy line appears at the base of the largest island, Hon Lao. Thatch parasols and lounge chairs stud the beach where we scramble ashore, the sand scorching hot, even through plastic sandals. Past a grove of coconut palms, lunch is laid in an open, thatched pavilion: baby squid, steamed fish, pork, vegetables, French fries, rice, followed by watermelon.

Afterwards, we take a quick swim. From the water, the view of the beach – coconut palms, casuarinas and almond trees, parasols and hammocks – is a picture postcard hideaway, if you happen to like lying on a beach, doing nothing, but difficult for the local population to subsist. In the heat of the afternoon sun, a man is laboriously shovelling cement and laying hexagonal paving stones to improve the path to the restaurant, owned by the Vietnamese Government.

It is a hot climb up a steep, rocky path over the headland, and a bit over a mile to the village of Bai Lang. Having electricity from only six to ten in the evenings, there are no refrigerators on the island, so several families have pooled together to buy a generator to make ice. A natural spring tumbles down over vertical rocks behind the ice house. When the fishing boats come in, they fill their cold boxes with ice and take their fish to Hoi An market to sell. Without refrigeration, the only way the islanders have of preserving food is to dry it in the sun. We pass rack after rack of split squid, drying. Like the Chinese, the Vietnamese love to gamble and several small groups are gathered round tables, slamming down cards, shouting excitedly.

From the top of another hill, we look down over a sheltered bay where cargo ships still shelter during storms. Then it's down hill past a military barracks to Hai Tang pagoda where a huge white statue of Quan Am Te Am stares placidly out over rice paddies lined by new houses and a freshly paved road.

In the forecourt of the pagoda, women are raking dried tea leaves into a plastic bowl with their bare hands. For once, there is a sign in English stating that the pagoda was first built in 1758 in the nineteenth year of the reign of Cong Hung, that it originally stood at a site two hundred metres away, but having been heavily damaged by storms, the present pagoda was rebuilt in the first year of Tu Duc's reign, 1848. Helpfully, the sign identifies the rafters of the veranda as Hoi An style, *chong recong gia thu.* Would that Vietnam had more such signs.

A menacing temple guardian glares from the entrance, next to a Chinese general with two small helpers, one green-faced, one grey-faced, the grey holding tablets. I think I recognise the general from a pagoda in Hanoi – Duc Thanh Hien – a disciple of Buddha, whose responsibility in addition to keeping his two tiny attendants apart, is to deal with the 're-education of naughty children.' He also acts as a kind of fortune-teller, so during *Tet* people come to consult him about the New Year.

The story goes that he once held a great feast and invited all the wandering souls, poor things, who were so hungry that some of them stuffed themselves fit to burst and a few did – burst! To keep more souls from 'dying' – though I am a little unclear as to how a wandering soul between lives could 'die' – he charged his tiny attendants to drive them out of the feast and perhaps in desolation at his good deed gone wrong, asked that he himself be transformed into a general.

Beside him stands another benevolent Quan Am Te Am. The three Buddhas of present, past and future preside stoically over the central altar, seated side by side. In front of them stands a saffron-robed Buddha and below him, Sakyamuni, the Buddha as a child. An incense burner, a huge wooden knocker *(mo)* tapped during Buddhist prayers and an offering of bananas occupy the altar. Another vicious warrior with a stringy beard and a sword guards the entrance opposite; beside him a crowned figure sits unperturbed on a snarling lion.

On the veranda outside the pagoda, an old woman, grey-haired, wrinkled and missing a few teeth, serves us tiny cups of tea and offers very welcome second and third cups. She knows we have climbed the hills from the beach and the town. Through an interpreter, I ask her age – sixty-three – suddenly bringing home the harshness of life on Cu Lao Cham. We each give her a few thousand dong for her trouble and kindness.

Regrettably, there is no time to visit the Swallows Nest Ancestor temple where every year on the tenth day of the third lunar month, residents and birds' nest collectors mount a lavish ceremony to show gratitude to the founder of the birds' nest gatherers and pray for a good crop the following year. Nor is there time for Ong Ngu shrine, where fishermen worship the whale god, who protects them at sea.

And I would have liked to investigate the other white sandy beaches that line the western shore of Hon Lao: Xep beach, reputedly three small beaches where the rock caves are particularly beautiful and Chong, Bim and Huong beaches, backed by cliffs. At Bac beach, the rock caves are said to be particularly striking and at Ong, Lang and Huong beaches, terraces shelve the farm crops from the sea.

Feet dangle from the sun deck above. In the late afternoon light, the water has now turned from silver to turquoise, the sun a bright blur in a milky sky. The islands behind us fade from green to hazy grey. The horizon ahead breaks into a feathering of trees; the water smooths as the motor purrs. We round a sandy point where a lone, ramshackle fisherman's shack squats on the sand. Basket boats bob about between fish traps, as fishermen check their nets. In minutes the boat is pulling up to a wooden quay and we are back on dry land.

TO DANANG SLOWLY

At half past eight in the morning at the bus station, two Vietnamese men are lifting their T-shirts to fan themselves. The bus sets off with only ten passengers on board, several women still wearing the masks they wear on their motorbikes. Can the bus ride be *that* dusty?

Plastic flowers grace the dashboard beside a statue of the goddess of mercy, her head surrounded by twinkling red, green and yellow lights. Perhaps they were placed there by the driver's affectionate wife.

The bus creeps along at no more than ten miles an hour. Is it a broken-down bus or have I caught the slow bus to Danang? The conductress collects 30,000 dongs ($1.60); the Vietnamese pay only 10,000 (US 0.50). Throughout Vietnam, there is a two-tier price system: one price for locals, another for foreigners, based on the quite rational premise that foreigners earn many multiples of that earned by the Vietnamese.

Despite the slowness of the bus, we overtake a funeral. Family mourners in white sit alongside the coffin in an open lorry, a raucous band of oboe and drums in a lorry just behind. More mourners wearing white headbands bring up the rear on foot. The bus stops for petrol, then oddly, backs out of the petrol station. No explanation.

Open cafes under tin roofs, small cottage industries, a sawmill, narrow houses behind rows of potted kumquat trees – Vietnam's answer to *Tet* trees – now past their season, line the road. After twenty minutes of creeping, suddenly the driver shifts out of low gear, blasts an air horn that wouldn't go amiss on an ocean liner and I begin to hope that we might reach Danang, only eighteen miles (28 km) away before lunchtime. A hot breeze whips the knotted curtains. Houses begin to space out now with larger gardens in front.

Twenty-five minutes along, we stop for a passenger beside a house where a row of bird cages hangs from the eave. The driver shifts and we're off again in a roar. Now we are blazing along, wind-flapped curtains flailing. We flash past a picture postcard scene of pastoral life: a lone figure under a conical hat, sitting with a bamboo fishing rod beside a bamboo fringed stream.

It seems to be a three-tone horn: a deep, low-throated blast as a long distance, advance warning; a demanding, mid-tone bleep to rid the road of nearby bicycles and motorbikes and a high, piercing, hysterical screech to lift any slow-reacting motorbike into orbit.

The bus slows again to creep through what must be a village, hard to discern from the ribbon development. Forty minutes on, we stop for another passenger. Huge pipes lie along one side of the road awaiting proper burial. Vietnam is slowly replacing the old sewage systems installed by the French and where there were none, laying new pipes.

Suddenly, the two-lane road spreads into six lanes as the Marble mountains erupt from the flat coastal plain. During the Vietnam War, the Marble mountains hid a Vietcong anti-aircraft gun crew and a Vietcong hospital in one of its caves; a US marine base snuggled just beneath the mountains.

After a roundabout surrounded by large government and commercial buildings, sleek new, two-storey town houses spring up along the highway. We are now at the edge of Danang.

Inexplicably, the bus swings off the main road at a roundabout onto the bumpy, old road. The bus shudders and the windows jiggle as we rattle over the old bridge. Down river, small wooden boats with straw canopies float incongruously beneath a low, modern concrete bridge. In the far distance, a beautiful new suspension bridge gleams in the sun.

We blast our way through another roundabout and suddenly, we are in a city street. I strain to read a street sign and ask where to get off for the Champa Museum. My two nearby passengers become quite agitated – right here, it seems.

I am dropped virtually beside the wall of the Champa Museum of Danang.

A WALK-THROUGH HISTORY BOOK

Past three kiosks – one to sell tickets, one to sell books and postcards, one for the ticket collector – I stroll once again toward the squat, ochre, unmistakably French Colonial, villa-style museum completed in 1919, one of the original reasons for my coming to Vietnam thirteen years ago. Appropriately, the French named it the *Musée Henri Parmentier* in honour of the French architect who made that first monumental inventory of Cham ruins. Today in a fit of post-colonial correctness, it is called the Museum of Champa Sculpture.

Conceived as 'a sculpture garden', the museum evocatively faces the Han river as any honourable Cham temple, settlement or market place would have done, its vast windows open to the trade winds. Inside, the information board states that Cham monuments were created at Myson between the seventh and thirteenth centuries – preceding and exceeding by several centuries, the duration of Khmer temple building in the Angkor area of Cambodia from the ninth to thirteenth century. In fact, wooden temples were built at Myson, possibly as early as the end of the fourth century.

The central gallery is devoted to sculpture from Tra Kieu (Simhapura), the Lion City, upstream from Hoi An. It was through Lam Ap Pho – later, Hoi An – that Simhapura, 'capital' of the kingdom of Lam Ap, traded with the outside world. High walls eight miles (13 kms) in circumference protected Simhapura, according to Chinese sources. Although thought to have been one of the earliest Cham settlements, scholars generally agree that Simhapura emerged as the centre of Cham political power following the defeat and sacking of Khu Tuc near Hue by the Chinese in 446.

Reunified under the Sui dynasty by 589, the Chinese set out to consolidate their southern territories. After putting down a revolt of the Viets in the north, in 605 the Sui army pushed on to the south. Perhaps fired by memories of the great golden plunder of Linyi in 446, the Sui general, Liu Fang, again attacked a citadel in 605, this time in Chinese records called Quso (possibly north-west of Hue). After a further eight days march, the Sui army laid siege to what they called the capital of Linyi, almost certainly Simhapura.

Having been forewarned of the Sui army's approach, the Cham king vacated his capital, a strategy in early days when threatened by a more powerful enemy, followed by guerrilla warfare. Oh yes, guerrilla warfare in Vietnam goes back well over a thousand years.

The Chinese found the palace deserted, the treasure and ritual vessels gone. Only the royal archives and library remained, remarkably including eighteen golden tablets – how could anyone have forgotten them? – and 1,350 Buddhist texts in the Kunlun (Austronesian) language. The golden tablets and the Buddhist texts were all hauled back to China. Strange – that they were Buddhist texts and not Hindu texts. Another conundrum.

A different source tells a more dramatic tale – that General Liu Fang invaded Lam Ap and defeated the Chams by luring their war-elephants into booby-trapped pits where the Chinese massacred the Chams and captured the capital, Simhapura. Perhaps the Chinese had prepared the pits for the *returning* Chams? Or a tale by a self-aggrandizing Chinese general?

British archaeologist Ian Glover writes that the Chinese version in the *Sui Shu, (History of the Sui Dynasty)* relates how Linyi was subjugated at the beginning of the seventh century by an army of ten thousand Chinese cavalry and convicts and that the vanquished king of Linyi, Fan Zhi, fled and established a new capital. The Chinese then divided Linyi into three administrative districts, pursuing Fan Zhi and oddly or perhaps cunningly, installed him as ruler under Sui control.

And so, history is pieced together from various sources.

It is very difficult for scholars to discern exactly where all of these events took place; even the location of Linyi cannot be firmly established. And was Linyi the same place as Champa? At least one archaeologist is willing to say that the absorption of Linyi by Champa seems to have been complete by the early seventh century.

Fifteen years after the Sui attack, in 620 a wary Cham king sent a delegation to the newly established Tang Dynasty, asking to become a vassal. Whether this was the Cham king from Simhapura or from another Cham kingdom is not known.

British archaeologist Ian Glover describes a rather extraordinary dynastic crisis in the mid-seventh century when the Cham king, Prakasbhasdharma, died without male heirs. Glover suggests that rivalry must have been intense between two nephews, one who fled to Cambodia and Bhadreshvaravarman, who gained power but was assassinated by his chief minister in 645, along with all male members of his family – the usual method of ousting a dynasty in those days.

The cousin who fled to Cambodia married the daughter of Ishanavarman I, the Khmer – or perhaps a Chenla king? Their son, Prakashadharma Vikrantavarman (yes, two of these monstrous names), returned to Champa, having married 'the surviving daughter of this same king (Ishanavarman I) to legitimize his reign, thus reuniting the dynasty.' Glover points out that this manoeuvre emphasizes the importance of women to the succession, either through marriage or motherhood.

The Myson inscriptions dated 657 AD ordered by the returning son describe two new sanctuaries dedicated to Prabhaseshvara and Ishaneshvara, epithets of Siva, built in honour of the Cambodian king, Ishanavarman, 'his mother's father, that is, his grandfather, who was both the father of his mother and of his wife' – who would have been his aunt, probably the daughter of a different mother.

So the Chams were certainly kissing cousins, intermarrying with the Chenla or the Khmer in Cambodia in the pre-Angkor period – when they were not battling, as they did later.

Dominating the gallery is the colossal Tra Kieu altar from the seventh or eighth century. As a Westerner, I reel slightly at the magnitude of the towering lingum, the phallic symbol of Siva, standing boldly erect on a two-tiered, stone basin of lotus blossoms. Voluptuous full-breasted, slim-waisted *apsaras* dance round the base wearing nothing more than three-strand, beaded necklaces slung loosely over their slim hips and thighs. Beside them, a musician vainly attempts to play a broken lute or fiddle.

These erotic nymphs of Indra's heaven, the daughters of pleasure, dancing and singing, were romantic partners of the musicians in their love affairs. According to Hindu mythology, *apsaras* first appeared during the churning of the Milk Ocean (Milky Way) and because of their irresistible allure, the gods and the demons *(asuras)* both lusted after them, leading to war.

A few steps away, the bare-breasted Hindu goddess, Laksmi, the wife of Vishnu (seventh or eighth century), reborn during the churning of the Milk Ocean, holds in her hand a lotus, symbol of purity. The Chams considered her to be the mother of the world, the female personification of energy, the supreme being. As the goddess of good fortune, long disappeared for the Chams, she sits looking rather forlornly at an inexplicable world.

Quite how these numerous powerful goddesses rank, one against another is not easy to fathom. In a back gallery, the tenth century Cham goddess, Uma, legs splayed invitingly, perhaps dancing, also goes under the Hindu names of Devi, Parvati and Durga, depending upon the incarnation. As Siva's consort, she was considered to be a *Shakti* of female energy, 'the most powerful of goddesses.'

One stele from Tra Kieu describes the restoration of a temple dedicated to Valmiki, author of the great Indian epic, the *Ramayana*. I am unable to find what I recall as an elaborately carved sandstone pedestal depicting scenes from the marriage of Rama and Sita from the *Ramayana*. Perhaps it has been borrowed for an exhibition of Vietnamese artefacts currently touring New York and Houston.

An eleventh or twelfth century Vishnu waving four arms, wearing a high crown and multi-strand beads around his neck and waist, sits under a protective *naga*, a thirteen-headed sea snake from the underworld. Vishnu, the sun god and the god of preservation, rises from the sea where he sleeps during Brahma's night and strides the universe in three giant steps through the three phases of the sun: sunrise, high noon and sunset. Unhappily, his powers as the god of preservation failed him in protecting the Cham capital, Simhapura.

In one corner an eighth century lion from the Lion City roars silently. An exquisite stone pillar, curling vines covering every carved surface, stands propped in another corner.

Strangely, on the floor of a vestibule I find a portion of a famous altar base depicting carved riders on horseback playing polo – polo having been imported, indirectly perhaps, from Persia. Maybe it wouldn't fit into the packing crate for the travelling exhibition. A huge torso of Siva and a damaged dancing Siva (seventh or eighth century), and two stone elephants *(voi)* complete the exhibits from Simhapura, pathetically little to show from what once reigned as a wealthy and proud, walled city with grand palaces, temples and pagodas, the seat of Cham power for several centuries and the glorious capital city for the port of Lam Ap – Hoi An.

In the Myson gallery, I am drawn to a well-preserved pediment depicting a reclining Vishnu and the birth of Brahma from Group E1. My mind flies back to the tumbling-down brick tower braced by steel poles beneath a corrugated steel roof with its astonishingly undamaged white marble, lotus-shaped moonstone step at the bottom of the crumbling temple stairs.

A pediment displaying the birth of Brahma illustrates the Indian myth of the dawn of the lotus era – the present era on earth! Vishnu reclines in meditation on the seven-headed serpent *(naga)* of eternity. The world lotus sprouts from his navel and Brahma springs from it to create our new world. Still attached to the sprout from Vishnu's navel, Brahma sits cross-legged above the pediment, while an ascetic with a pointed beard looks on. Two figures with bird claws, resembling mythical garudas, grasp snakes. This beautifully preserved pediment has been dated by style to the last half of the seventh century – very early Myson.

Also from Myson's Group E and therefore, possibly early Myson, is a standing statue of Ganesh, 'the deity of Myson,' the label announces – there seem to have been a good many deities of Myson. Ganesh was the elephant son of Siva and Parvati. Having four arms, in his upper right hand he holds a rosary, in his left an axe, and in his lower left hand a bowl of sweets. His lower right hand, now broken, is thought to have held a fat leafy horseradish, which elephants especially relish – the sort of horseradish represented in North Indian statues of the seventh or eighth centuries, but not in Khmer art of the period – on such slim premises, pre-dating him to Angkor.

Also from Myson (E1) is an altar base from the central temple tower, which represented Mount Kailasa, the silver mountain whose summit was the abode of Siva. Its lingum has been lost, but carved scenes of mountains, forests and caves, peopled by ascetics, have been well preserved around the base of the pedestal.

An unusual small statue is striking: Siva's son Skanda, the god of war. It came from Myson (B3) where the Polish architect,

Kazimierz Kwaitkowski, worked so devotedly. A peacock squatting on clenched claws, displaying its tail feathers, backs the faceless deity. Skanda stands on the back of his mythical steed.

The kingdom of Linyi disappeared from Chinese annuls in 749, replaced by a new kingdom further south in the region of Phan Rang and Nha Trang, called by the Chinese, Huanwang. Chinese records report the death of the last king of Lam Ap, (Simhapura) in 756 – although Cham temple building went on for several centuries more.

The next gallery is dedicated to Dong Dzuong, the present-day village twelve miles (19 kms) south-west from Myson, built over the site of Indrapura. A stele inscription of 875 tells how Cham King Indravarman II founded a new capital, naming it after himself. Interesting, the early brick Khmer temples at Ruluos near Angkor were begun in 877, just two years after the founding of Indrapura. Although using brick, Cham building materials and methods, Indravarman II's complex of Buddhist temples and large assembly halls at Indrapura were reached through a succession of gates on an east-west axis, guarded by *dvarapala* (warriors), surrounded by brick walls – a Chinese-style layout.

For the first – and last – time in Cham history, Mahayana Buddhism became the state religion. The temples were dedicated to Laksmindra Lokesvara, a form of *bodhisattva* Avolokitesvara, *bodhisvattvas* being divine beings who have attained Nirvana but remain on earth to help others.

The religious art, sculpture and statues of Indrapura, combining the styles of Champa, India and China, are considered by certain art historians to represent the peak of Cham artistic creativity in their springy flexibility and robust energy of carving.

Italian archaeologist, Patrizia Zolese, in writing of the pioneer work of Henri Parmentier and Charles Carpeaux, tells how the two young Frenchmen had first worked at Dong Dzuong (Indrapura) before approaching Myson.

At break-neck speed – their presence was required at a conference in December of 1902 – 'work began on Sunday at 6 a.m. on the seventh of September, first with a work force of thirty, swelling to between a hundred-thirty and two hundred.

'During eighty-one days of excavation ending the twenty-sixth of November, more than 6,500 square metres were cleared, twenty-two monuments and numerous vestiges unearthed, cleared, cleansed, supported, described, measured, photographed and inventoried.' And this, during the monsoon season!

This 'archaeological feat' was later considered a 'rescue evacuation' Their work interrupted, they never returned. Nor did anyone else. Dong Dzuong lay neglected and 'degraded rapidly.' Sculptures disappeared and in the early thirties, turned up in European and American collections!

When I asked Federico Barocco if he had been to Dong Dzuong, he told me sadly that even three years ago, there was very little left to see.

In the Dong Dzuong gallery, a huge stone warrior guardian *(dvarapala)* leers protectively at a colossal stone Buddha, seated hands defiantly on hips in what is described as 'the European position'. Carved scenes from the life of Buddha – lions, princes and princesses, *dvarapala,* female followers and horsemen – circle the base.

During his reign, Indravarman successfully attacked China's southern trading territories and stoutly refused to support the Viets' revolt against Chinese domination. The Viets, having liberated themselves from the Chinese in 938, set up their capital at Hoa Lu, forty-six miles (74 km) south of Hanoi.

One source tells how in 979, the Cham king sent a fleet of ships to attack the Viets at Hoa Lu, but was thwarted by a storm. No doubt uneasy, the Viet king sent three ambassadors to the Cham court in 982. When they were detained, the Viets attacked. The Cham king, Phe Mi Thue, was killed, Indrapura sacked and looted. A hundred ladies of the royal harem, the Cham dancers and musicians, and an Indian monk were carried back to the Viet court at Hoa Lu.

It might be assumed that Simhapura, which lay on the route of march south to Indrapura, was also attacked. At this point, Cham political power again shifted further south. Although Lam Ap Pho (Hoi An) continued to function as a port, the importance of Dong Dzuong and Simhapura as centres of political power were at an end. But Myson, upriver from Hoi An, continued to serve as the spiritual sanctuary for Cham kings, wherever political power was centred.

Accorded a place of honour in her own alcove, a fine bronze statue of the *bodhisattva* Tara, the feminine aspect of compassion, stands alone. Bare-breasted and miniscule-waisted, wrapped in overlapping sarongs, the palms of her hands face outward in a *mudra,* said to be of reasoning, or argumentation. Her face certainly suggests anger; her thousand-year-old enamel eyes glare in fury at the intruder. The largest bronze Cham statue ever discovered (ninth century), local people found her as recently as 1978. It is thought that she might have been worshipped on the main altar of Indrapura's Buddhist monastery. Someone has reverently placed fresh orchids and one rose in a devotional bowl at her feet.

The yawning middle hall of the new extension contains and awaits further new discoveries. A display of photographs taken by the Italian team currently working at Myson hangs beside a photo of silver-bearded Polish architect, Kazimierz Kwaitkowski, who died at fifty-three, and touchingly, half a dozen of his sketches of the temples of Myson. Their elegance of line in no way betrays the difficult tropical conditions – the dust or the mud, the steamy heat, the insects – under which they would have been drawn.

The defeat of Indrapura in 982 was the beginning of a series of Cham defeats by the Viets, fought tenaciously by the Chams every battle of the way. Around 945, the Khmer army invaded the Cham kingdom of Kauthara (present day Nha Trang) further south and in 950, carried off the statue of the goddess from the temple of Po Nagar. The dates of what happened next differ, depending upon the source.

Champa suffered further attacks from Dai Viet, the newly independent Viet kingdom in 1021 and 1026, the Viets having moved their capital to Thang Long (now Hanoi) in 1010. In 1044, a catastrophic battle led by the Viet, Ly Thai Tong, resulted in the death of the Cham King, Sa Dau, and the destruction and sacking of the kingdom of Vijaya (present day Qui Nhon). The Viets captured elephants, musicians and even the Cham queen, Mi E, who preserved her honour by throwing herself into the sea as her captors carried her back to the North. For a time, Champa paid tribute to the Viet kings, sending a white rhino in 1065.

To avenge the defeat of 1044, in 1068 the King of Vijaya (Qui Nhon) invaded Dai Viet. Again the Chams were defeated and again the Viets captured and burnt Vijaya. Only a year later, Vijaya was burnt again when the Viet general, Ly Thuong Kiet, took a fleet, conquered and occupied Vijaya. The Cham king, Rudravarman III (known to the Vietnamese as Che Cu) was taken captive and eventually purchased his freedom for a ransom of three northern districts of his realm. Taking advantage of the power vacuum, another Cham leader set up an independent kingdom at Panduranga (Phan Rang).

In 1145, a Khmer army under King Suryavarman II, the builder of Angkor Wat, attacked and occupied Vijaya, destroying the temples of Myson. The Khmer were driven out by Jaya Harivarman I, who built temple Group G that the Italian team is working on at Myson.

Thirty years later in 1177, the Cham King, Jaya Indravarmadeva of Vijaya, retaliated by sacking Angkor. The Khmer King, Jayavarman VII, builder of the Bayon and Angkor Thom, in turn defeated the Chams and imposed thirty years of Khmer rule over Vijaya. Somewhat surprisingly, given the history of hostilities, in 1217 the Khmer and the Chams allied against and defeated the Viets to the north. Although the Khmer withdrew from the Mekong Delta, Champa did not again achieve independence until sometime around 1220.

Then 'the enemy of mine enemy is my friend' came into play. From the north, the Mongolian hordes of Kublai Khan – 40,000 of them – descended out of the plains of China, invading Dai Viet and Champa – three times – in 1257, 1284 and 1287. The Chams and the Viets joined forces to drive out the Mongols and became so close that in 1307, the head of the old Cham king turned to folly. Or did it?

Jaya Simhavarman III (Che Man), founder of the still standing temple of Po Klaung Garai in Panduranga (Phan Rang), in his last lust for the hand of a Viet princess, Huyen Tran, rashly ceded two northern districts to Dai Viet. Soon after the wedding, he died. The princess returned to her home in the North – to the national outrage of the Chams – to avoid the Cham tradition that a wife follows her husband in death. To add to the fury, the ceded Cham lands were not returned.

It was half a century before the Chams were revenged. Having united the Chams, Champa's last strong king, Che Bong Nga (reign 1360 to 1390) – known to the Viets as Che Bunga, the Red King – felt strong enough to attack Dai Viet from the sea in 1372, sacking and pillaging Thang Long (Hanoi). Five years later in 1377, he attacked Thang Long again. His last attack in 1388 was checked by the Viet general, Ho Quy Ly, founder of the Ho dynasty. This was the last serious offensive of the Chams.

In 1471, Champa's last ruler, King Tra-Toan, painfully repaid for Che Bong Nga's having sacked Thang Long. The Viets besieged and destroyed Vijaya after only four days of fighting on 21 March 1471, taking the Cham king prisoner and massacring the Chams. According to one source, sixty thousand Chams were slaughtered and another sixty thousand taken as slaves, thousands being forcibly moved to sparsely populated areas of north Vietnam. Those who escaped fled south or crossed into Cambodia. Cham cities were destroyed, archives and works of art burnt. After the defeat of 1471, Cham power was at an end.

Vijaya became completely absorbed into the Viet system, its independence never restored. Further south, the kingdom of Kauthara (Nha Trang) survived just, until 1653.

71

After 1697, all that remained of historic Champa was the kingdom of Panduranga (Phan Rang, Phan Ri and Phan Thiet). Under the 'protection' of the Viets, Panduranga preserved some small modicum of independence – the name Champa was retained. But Cham kings were reduced to being called 'lords' until Panduranga's final dissolution in 1832 by the Nguyen king, Minh Mang, ruling from Hue.

A concentration of Chams still inhabit Phan Rang and there are Cham villages in the Mekong Delta, but the glory days of Cham culture have long passed.

I catch a *xe om* to take me across the river to Cam Nam island to pass by Randy's book exchange, then to return a book to Steve at the Lazy Gecho bar. Steve is out, leading a motorbike tour. On the way back, the *xe om* driver, Hien, asks if I would like to see his wife's lantern shop – 'no pay.' The shop turns out to be a couple of pretty stalls, stuffed with a rainbow of silk lanterns across the bridge in An Hoi. I ask him where the lanterns are made and he volunteers to take me 'no money' to the factory, halfway out along the Cua Dai Beach road towards the beach, and off to the left.

The owner of the lantern factory, Linh and her husband Ha, have about fifty employees. Eight or nine women sit on the cement floor of the open shed, gluing the silk onto bamboo frames, then trimming the silk. The bamboo staves are wedged into notches, top and bottom.

For these particular lanterns, the red or white silk is glued over three staves, a quarter of the frame and trimmed along the staves. Another piece of silk is glued over the opposite quarter. Then the last two quarters are glued, after which the raw edges are trimmed along the glued ridges. To finish, the top and base are trimmed. It looks so simple in the hands of an expert, who has probably made thousands of lanterns.

Linh leads us to the back of the shed where the blocks of wood for the tops and bottoms are cut, turned and notched, where bamboo is split into staves and wedged into the notches to hold the lanterns rigid. Magically, the lanterns can be collapsed by simply releasing a spring at the top. Collapsible silk lanterns were invented in Hoi An – so that visitors can buy and pack them to take home.

PART II

EARLY TRADE

SECRET OF THE POTS

When China stopped exporting gold towards the end of the fifth century, direct maritime trade between China and India seems to have ceased. About that time, traders from the Persian Gulf started making long voyages, thanks to the magnetic compass – invented by the Chinese.

Champa is mentioned in two early Arab journals, both dated 850. One itinerary tells of a three-day journey from Qmar (Cambodia) to Sanf (Champa), before sailing on to Luqin (Hanoi) in the Red river valley. The second describes stops at Kadrang (possibly Panduranga-Phan Rang), then Sanf (Champa) to collect fresh water. They then sailed via Sundur Fulat (the island of Hainan) to the Gates of China at Guangzhou (near Hong Kong).

Tell-tale shards of indisputably Islamic ceramics have been found in archaeological sites at Bai Lan village on Cham Island where Arab ships paused to re-victual and to take on water from the Cham's wells.

Both Arab journals speak of the main product of Sanf (Champa) as *sanfi* (aloes wood), which the late ninth century Arab author, Ya 'qubi, thought the finest of aromatic woods, having the richest and most lingering perfume.

Sometimes called eaglewood, its fragrance comes from the resinous heartwood of *aquilaria agallocha*, this heartwood so dense that it sinks in water. The literal-minded Chinese called it sink wood *(chen mu)*. Much later in the seventeenth century, the Italian priest Cristoforo Borri, explained its appeal: 'As it is the custom in India for both Muslims and Buddhists to be cremated on a pyre of fragrant wood, huge quantities of aromatic woods were much in demand.'

When Chinese junks began once again to call at ports in South East Asia late in the eighth century, especially at Srivijaya (present-day Palembang on the south coast of Sumatra) and to travel again as far as India, Arabian and Persian ships no longer

73

had to travel all the way to China. They could buy Chinese merchandise in the ports of South East Asia.

About this time, the silver mines of Persia were worked out, so Arab and Persian traders began to bring silver from Europe for export to India and China, returning with cotton from Gujarat, pepper from South India and Sumatra, and silk and ceramics from China. For a time in the mid-ninth century, the rich Arab trade via the Malay peninsula, Java and Sumatra was disrupted by wars in southern China. The Chams, deprived of their usual trading partners in the north, turned to piracy, raiding the southern fringes of the Chinese trading territories, homeland of the Viets – bringing on the siege and fall of Indrapura (Dong Dzuong) and Simhapura (Tra Kieu).

Trade in Chinese ceramics between East and West is thought to have started in the ninth century. Chinese trade ceramics developed quickly during the Song dynasty (10-13th C) and the Yuan (Mongolian, 13-14th C). How did this affect Hoi An? In a quite intriguing mystery of the pots.

Over the years, Father Anton of the Catholic church in Danang collected shards of broken pots found in and around Tra Kieu, old Simhapura. In Sarawak (Borneo), unknown to Father Anton, a museum held similar shards and pots, thought to have come from half a dozen kilns up and down the length of China. It was a Chinese scholar passing through Sarawak, who began to unravel the mystery when he identified the museum's pots as the products of the Shiwan kilns of Guangdong Province in southern China, kilns that had revived the techniques and produced imitations of a dozen different glazes and styles.

Meanwhile in the late seventies, a burial site at Butuan on Mindanao Island in the Philippines – the same island where the intriguing lid of the Sa Huynh burial pot was found – yielded unbroken pieces of these same Guangdong ceramics from the Shiwan kilns: green-glazed pieces imitating the northern celadons of Shaaxi and Henan; copies of ceramics made in Zhejiang; white glazes reminiscent of those from Jiangxi and *gingbai* bluish-white glazes; brown monochrome and brown-painted pieces similar to those previously made in Changsha in Hunan.

The identification of the ceramics from the Philippines in 1978 by a scholar from Hong Kong, dating them from the eleventh or twelfth century, had a profound effect on the history of the Chams. This confirmed the controversial view that the Philippines had significant pre-Yuan dynasty contact with China. But what is most surprising, writes British scholar, Ian Glover, is that Chinese annuals state unequivocally that this contact was most certainly – through the Chams. Although not yet confirmed, the china in Father Anton's collection from Tra Kieu appears to be these same Guangdong ceramics, from which specialists conclude that the Chams were trading with the Philippines and Borneo during the peak of Simhapura's power, through the port of Lam Ap Pho – Hoi An – trade echoing back to Sa Huynh times.

Even more odd, again according to Glover, is that in Chinese annuls, names relating to the Philippines and Borneo always appear *under* Champa. Butuan (P'u-tuan) is described in the *Sung Shih, (Sung Hisory, Sung Dynasty 960-1179),* as a small country in the sea to the east of Champa, having regular communications with Champa, rarely with China. It might even seem that Champa was deliberately keeping the exact location of Butuan a secret from the Sung Imperial Court. Nothing in Chinese records suggests that the Chinese ever had direct contact with these settlements on the eastern edge of the South China Sea (known as the Eastern Sea in Vietnam for sensitive political reasons) – until the thirteenth century.

Glover writes that for four years starting in 1001, King Kiling (Ch'i'ling) of Butuan sent unsuccessful tribute missions to China and in 1004, the Sung imperial court went so far as to hand down an edict prohibiting the Butuan mission's export of Chinese goods. Again in 1007, King Kiling sent an envoy with a formal request for equal status with the envoy from Champa at the Sung court – his request denied on the grounds that 'Butuan was beneath Champa.'

In 1011, a new Butuan ruler once again sent a mission, but his time his request was engraved on a gold tablet. This concentrated the Chinese mind beautifully and the Butuan minister charged with the mission received the honour of a military title and a decree granting Butuan flags, pennons and armour 'to honour a distant land.'

It would seem that Butuan had at last achieved equal tributary status to Champa. But no. Having surmounted China's bizarre attitude towards trade, somehow inexplicably, Butuan seems to have been convinced (perhaps forcibly?) to abandon its quest for sending tribute trade missions to China.

A missing clue to the mystery was unearthed in an excavation at Butuan – a motive for Champa keeping Butuan a secret. The site produced astonishing evidence – that Butuan was a large-scale producer of gold! Champa's secret source of gold? Champa's secret from the Chinese?

That the ceramics collected by Father Anton were from Tra Kieu confirms that the Butuan-Cham trade *preceded* the fall of Indrapura and Simhapura in 982, pushing the three-cornered trade of the Guangdong ceramics from China to Champa to Butuan – back in time to at least the tenth century.

A SCENT FROM THE PAST

For some weeks I have been strolling past, thinking it to be some sort of weird, modern art gallery. Several tree trunks stand from floor to ceiling, their trunks hollowed out, peculiarly perforated, leaving them distorted and skeletal, as though some abstract artist has been busy at work, boring into the wood in search of his soul.

But no, Tram Hoi An, the last shop in Tran Phu Street before the Japanese Bridge, may be the only shop of its kind in Vietnam and just possibly in the world. For the shop specialises in products made from *agar,* a scented wood, its scientific name, *aquilaria* – the same scented wood sought more than a thousand years ago by the Arab and Indian traders to burn on funeral pyres, the wood they called *sanfi.*

The tree trunks look like they might have been through an acid bath, but this is not so, a pretty young assistant wearing an *ao dai* assures me. The object of the hollowing out is to take away the wood that has been damaged, the dead wood that retains no resin, leaving only the healthy wood.

Agar trees, now fairly rare, grow in the hinterland highlands, inland from Hoi An. The trees assume their twisted and knotted shapes as a result of weather, erosion, broken branches, damage caused by boring insects or by man, whatever perchance nature and fate bestow upon them. Sculptors do the rest, removing the damaged, light-coloured wood that contains no resin. The wood that contains the valuable resin is dark. This leaves a rather creepy, holey surface.

'A different kind of natural art.' Well, maybe.

The skeletal, sculptured tree trunks in the gallery somehow recall to memory the warped face of a patriotic Vietnamese war poet I met thirteen years ago, whose dark visage, furrowed by deep wrinkles, looked as if it had been wrenched and stretched vertically, leaving not so much a face as a graven image.

'To get the scent, you have to burn it,' the girl explains. 'The best quality wood you don't need to burn, but the best quality is rare. Every morning when we open, we burn *agar* in the doorway of the shop to keep evil spirits away and to bring good luck.'

This explains the small metal bowls I have seen in the doorways of shops and the huge baskets of small sticks for sale on the pavement in Le Loi Street.

'The scent of the wood is good for the health. It can be used in traditional medicine. We take the part that contains no resin away and keep the dark part.'

The girl leads me to the back of the gallery where a woman sits, placing fine slivers of bamboo into a machine, one by one, feeding the brown rosin paste in from the top – making joss sticks. 'It's quicker by machine than making joss sticks by hand. It smells like burnt wood while it's wet, don't you think?' she asks as she hands me a freshly turned joss stick.

Not surprisingly, Tram Hoi An also makes incense from *agar* rosin. In one corner a woman sits pinching the resin into cone-shaped nubs.

'Different scents. When it's dry, you have to burn it to get the fragrance.'

Upstairs, glass cases display tiny religious statues and carved medallions, some engraved with the Chinese characters for honesty and prosperity, Christian crosses and Buddhas – all made from the resin – anything the customer might require.

The eager assistant, now behind the counter, tells me that these charms can relieve insomnia and stress, and wearing the rosin helps to remove toxins from the body. Another showcase holds black necklaces and bracelets made of dried resin beads.

Tram Hoi An has even distilled the resin into perfume. The assistant squirts a drop onto my wrist and sure enough, it smells like burnt wood, which is fine if you happen to want to smell like burnt wood. While I am being rather sniffy about the scent of burnt wood, later I learn that *agar* is respected as one of the few natural fragrances, apart from ambergris, musk and rose, and that Yves St Laurent uses it in perfumes.

Of course, to burn the incense, naturally they sell incense burners. You can choose either a snarling sacred lion or a dragon. Both raise their heads to reveal small metal pots inside. 'The smoke comes out of his mouth. They are made of ebony wood.'

Ebony is also a product of this region, for centuries exported to China, India and the Arab countries.

Two girls sit threading black *agar* resin beads beside a window. A glass showcase holds beautifully crafted long, narrow wooden cylinders. I take them to be chopstick cases, but the girl opens one and carefully draws out the thinnest of incense sticks I have ever seen, made of pure resin.

The next showcase holds vials of powder. Powder?

'Put it on your hands or feet when they are hot and sweaty, and they dry.'

And of course, there are wood chips for burning.

It is a family business, she tells me. The Tran Quang Hiep family has been working with this wood for only two years. They also have an embroidery workshop on Le Loi Street – and silk worms to show to visitors.

Why am I vaguely riled by such overt commercialism? Hoi An has been a marketplace for over two thousand years.

Still in shopping mode, I wander up to the silk embroidery workshop-factory-atelier in Le Loi Street to watch the embroiderers.

On my first trip to Hoi An, I remember talking to an embroiderer, sitting on the pavement in front of her house, stabbing at a tablecloth. When I asked who had taught her to embroider, she said her grandmother. Apart from tablecloths, she embroidered cushion covers on which the embroidery covered every square inch of the cloth. When I asked her the price and how long it took to do the work, her earnings came to about a dollar a day. I wonder if things will have changed.

The pretty hostess wearing an *ao dai* at the door of the Fine Arts-Handcraft Workshop at 41 Le Loi Street is quite frank.

'We have been doing business for fourteen years in this location. We opened the business where visitors can come to see traditional handicrafts – embroidery, how to make silk and sleeping mats – so that when travellers come, they can see and do business.'

Twelve girls sit with needles and piles of colourful silk thread at embroidery frames. The firm employs forty-six girls in total. The embroiderers start at about eighteen, having finished high school, others after finishing college at twenty-two. The college graduates do the presentations. My pretty hostess, Ta Thi Phu, is a graduate from Danang University.

'It takes two years to train an embroiderer before they can do their picture,' she explains. 'Someone who is very skilled copies the design on the fabric and then they have to mix the colours. The embroiderers work eight hours a day. They start at about half past seven in the morning; they have a break at noon, one and a half hours, then start again and stop at six in the evening.

'How much they earn depends on how they work. They are only paid when the picture is finished. That picture' – a sampan silhouetted against sparkling water, calling for a myriad of subtle shades – 'will take three months and she has to make the date.'

So, the embroiders do piecework and work to a deadline.

'For that she will make one or two million Vietnamese *dong* ($52 or $104), depending on the quality' – for three months work. The same, already completed picture on display carries a price tag of $758 and took three and a half months to make.

Embroidered 'pictures' for sale plaster the walls of the shop from eye-level to ceiling: a woman with a carrying pole walking through a sunlit doorway, a shady alley, a fisherman with his butterfly net raised in black and white ($80), floating sampans ($175).

So realistic are the embroidered pictures that at first I had taken them for photographs: the face of an infant staring from the wrinkled arms of its granny, the Japanese Bridge, a black-and-white 'line drawing' of an old man wearing a black headband. Small embroidered pictures twenty-one by twenty-seven inches (55 x 70 cms) cost from $19, $24 with frames.

Girls are working on pictures of sampans lined up fishing; the back of a girl in an *ao dai*, mounting temple steps, a lotus blossom in her hand; a bowl of flowers; a street scene in Hoi An; a fisherman throwing his net.

In a small back room, a girl sits weaving silk on a hand-loom – a demonstration.

'She can weave two or three metres a day. This loom is quite old.' A newer, larger loom beside it dates from 1940. On my first trip to Hoi An, I remember passing a workshop where heavy cotton was being woven at hand-looms.

Upstairs, silk worms curl inside screened cages, gorging themselves. 'These worms are seventeen days old. The worms are fed mulberry leaves. It takes them twenty-three to twenty-five days to mature. When they are mature, they are placed in racks while they spin their cocoons. It takes about four days.'

On the opposite side of the room, nubs of white cocoons are embedded in vertical racks.

'To retrieve the silk, the cocoons are dropped into boiling water, the worms die and the cocoons are softened so that the silk threads can be gently unwound.' Mercifully, the boiling of the cocoons and the silk unravelling are not on view, nor the spinning of the thread, nor the boiling and dyeing, extremely hot jobs.

Last stop, inevitably, is the shop selling embroidered tablecloths and handbags, and in the front showroom, scarves and shawls, silk shirts, ties and suits for gents, dresses for ladies.

'We can make anything for you by tomorrow. Would you like to buy some souvenirs of Hoi An?'

MARCO POLO AND THE CHAMS

In 1271, according to Marco Polo's account, at the age of seventeen, accompanying his father Niccolo and his uncle Maffeo, he set out from Venice. Kublai Khan had conquered the Chinese Sung dynasty in 1260 and in 1263, founded Khanbalik, City of the Khan (Beijing). Kubli Khan handed over to his son Ogedai in 1279 and died in 1294.

According to Marco, the Polos remained in the court of Kublai Khan for seventeen years, the Great Khan sending him off on various quasi-diplomatic missions to far flung reaches of the realm. With Kublai Khan growing old, the Polos feared that their envied favour at court might become dangerous after the Khan's death, so they seized the opportunity to return by sea with three visiting 'barons' from Persia.

It seems that Queen Bolgana, the wife of Argon, Ikhan of Persia and ruler of the Levant, had died and in her will, stipulated that only a Mongol of her royal blood should take her place as her husband's wife. Therefore, three barons, named by Marco as Qulatay, Apusca and Coja, had come as ambassadors in search of a replacement bride. The lady Cocachin, of the same family as the deceased Queen Bolgana, was sent for.

'She was a maiden of seventeen, a very beautiful and charming person. On her arrival at court, she was presented to the three barons . . . they declared that the lady pleased them well.'

When the Persian barons, who had suffered greatly on their overland journey to the Mongol court, heard that Marco had recently returned by sea from India, they implored the great Khan to allow the three Venetians to return with them by ship 'on account of the great fatigue of that long land journey for a lady.'

In his famous travelogue, *Description of the World,* Marco Polo tells how he, his father and uncle set out from China on their return voyage homeward in 1292.

He recorded how thirteen ships, each of four masts, several of which carried two hundred fifty or more men, were assembled for the voyage. When they were ready to leave, Kublai Khan presented the Polos with 'two Golden Tablets of Authority, which should secure them liberty of passage through all of his dominions and by means of which, whithersoever they should go, all necessaries would be provided for them and for all their company' – rather better than VIP passports. They were also entrusted with letters from the great Kublai Khan to the kings of France, England and Spain. Written rather like a ship's log, Marco Polo describes the journey.

'When the traveller leaves Zaiton (Guangzhou, later Canton) on a course somewhat south of west, he sails for fifteen hundred miles (2,400 km) across a wide gulf called the Gulf of Cheynam (Hainan), which extends for two months sail. Within the gulf itself are many islands (Halong Bay), almost all of them populated. In these are found quantities of gold dust, recovered from sea water . . .

'After leaving Zaiton and completing the voyage across the mouth of this gulf, the traveller reaches a country called Chamba (Champa), a very rich country of wide extent. They have a king of their own, speak their own language and are idolaters. They render the Great Khan a yearly tribute of elephants and aloe wood, but nothing else. Let me tell you how this comes about.

'The fact is that in the year of our Lord, 1278, the Great Khan sent one of his barons named Sogatu with a large force of cavalry and infantry against this king of Chamba and launched a great invasion of his kingdom. The king was a man of great age and had not an army to match that of the Great Khan in battle, but he maintained a stout defence of the cities and fortified towns without fear of any foe. The open country, however, and the villages were all ravaged and laid waste. When the king saw the havoc that was being wrought in his kingdom, he was deeply distressed. He promptly summoned his emissaries and sent them to the Great Khan with a message such as you will hear . . .

'"Sir, the King of Chamba salutes you as his liege lord. He sends you word that he is a man of great age and has long ruled the kingdom in peace. He is willing to be your liegeman and to render you a yearly tribute of elephants and aloe wood. He begs you courteously, imploring your mercy, to recall from his country your baron and your forces, which are ravaging his kingdom."

'When the Great Khan had heard the old king's words, he took pity on him. He immediately ordered the baron and his forces to leave this kingdom and seek further conquests elsewhere.

You must know that in this kingdom (Champa), no pretty girl can marry without first being presented to the king. If he is pleased with her, he takes her to wife. If not, he gives her a sum of money appropriate to her station so that she may take another husband. I assure you that in the year 1285, Ser (sic) Marco Polo was in this country and at that time, this king had three hundred twenty-six children, male and female, including more than one hundred fifty men of an age to bear arms.

'The kingdom produces great quantities of elephants and aloe wood. There are also many groves of wood called bonus (ebony), which is jet-black and of which chessmen and pen-cases are made.'

Marco Polo's book, written before printing, was hand-copied and translated into many languages; there were at least one hundred forty different manuscripts of his book in a dozen languages. The manuscripts give various dates for Kublai Khan's conquests of Vietnam between 1275 and 1288. History records Kublai Khan's conquests of Vietnam as 1257, 1284 and 1287.

As the Polos began their homeward voyage in 1292 and as Marco states so emphatically that he visited Champa in 1285, we are left to assume that he visited Champa on a previous voyage – perhaps on his outward or return voyage from India. However, the supposed date of Marco Polo's visit to Champa differs in various translated manuscripts between 1280, 1285 and 1288.

When three years later, the Polos finally reached Persia and the three barons delivered the bride in Tabriz, they found that the ruler, Argon, had died, so the princess was handed over to his son, Cason. Moreover, Marco wrote that of the six hundred people who had set sail, five hundred and eighty-two had perished on the eighteen-month voyage, the three Polos and the Mongol princess, among those few who had survived.

But did Marco Polo really go to Champa? Did he ever go to China? Scholars have been asking themselves the latter for several centuries, which finally sparked a British scholar, Dr Frances Wood, Head of the China Department of the British Library in London, to gather all of the arguments for and against in a book aptly entitled, *Did Marco Polo Go to China?*

At the risk of over-simplifying her detailed, scholarly research and examination of the question, it is true enough that the Mongol ruler of Persia, who died in 1265, was a cousin of Kublai Khan; sharing a grandfather, Genghis Khan. She notes that Marco's father and uncle on an earlier journey arrived in Constantinople in 1260, then travelled from the Volga to the Caspian Sea to the territory held by the Mongol ruler, Berke (ruled 1257-67). Finding themselves unable to return to Constantinople because of war between Berke and Hulegu, the Mongol ruler of Persia (who died 1265), they indeed met the great ruler, Kublai Khan, with whom they discussed Christianity.

If that sounds unlikely, the Mongol Hulegu had a Nestorian wife and his mother had been a Nestorian Christian. The Nestorians had been evicted from China in 845! So Christianity was not unfamiliar to the Mongols. Kublai Khan gave the Polos letters to deliver to the Pope, requesting that he 'send a hundred learned men of the Christian religion to argue the cause of Christianity.' He also asked the Polo brothers 'to bring back oil from the lamp that burns above the sepulchre of God in Jerusalem' and sent one of his men to accompany the Polo brothers on the first part of their journey, providing them with a tablet of gold on which it was written that they should be given all the lodging they might need and horses and men.

Having returned to Venice, the Polo brothers set off once again almost immediately in 1271, this time taking Niccolo's son Marco, but as the Catholic church was between Popes, they obtained no papal response for Kublai Khan, although they did manage to obtain the holy oil. In Karakorum once more, the Polos were welcomed by Kublai Khan, who used young Marco as an emissary. The Mongols had taken the North of China in 1260, but the South, not until 1279.

Dr Wood's research revealed that the Venetian Polos, indeed, had been traders for generations. Marco the elder (an uncle of Marco, the writer) had a house in Constantinople and a house in Soldaia (Sudak) on the Crimean coast of the Black Sea. In his will of 1280, Marco's uncle left the Crimean house to the Franciscans.

In his *Description of the World,* Marco Polo claims to have governed the city of Yangzhou for three years. Dr Wood writes that there is absolutely no Chinese record of Marco Polo in Yangzhou gazetteers. One Chinese scholar suggests by way of explanation that Marco's use of *sejourna* might have been miscopied as *governa.*

Dr Wood notes that numerous Christian missionaries had already written about the Mongols. One John of Montecorvino, Petrus de Lucalongo (1247-1328), who travelled with the Bishop-to-be of Peking from Tabriz to Peking in 1291 – while the Polos were supposedly in China – had later provided funds to build the first Catholic cathedral in Peking, complete with bell tower in 1299. He even organised choirs of little boys to sing hymns for the Khan!

Other sceptics have pointed out that Marco Polo, despite his self-professed powers of observation, neglected to note the Great Wall of China, the tininess of Chinese women's bound feet – or even tea. The same Chinese professor staunchly defends these omissions, saying that Marco was surrounded by Mongols, who didn't drink tea and had little to do with the Chinese and in any case, as China's cloistered women were secluded from the public, he might well be excused for not having noticed this particularly Chinese phenomena. As for the Great Wall . . .

Dr Wood surmises that Marco Polo's book was probably written in 1298, while he was imprisoned in Pisa for three years alongside a writer of romances, one Rustichello or Rusticciano, who had, incidentally, written a romance of King Arthur. Sometime after Marco's return to Venice in 1295, he took part in a conflict between Venice and Genoa and was taken prisoner. Dr Wood suggests that he and Rustichello, as gentlemen, might well not have been walled up in a dungeon, but instead, have passed their confinement in a private house in Pisa with a useful library.

Marco Polo's account, even the spelling of place names and terminology, follow closely the history of China as described in the *World History* of Rashid al-Din.

'Even where there are mysteries or mistakes, Rashid and Polo run parallel. The earliest foreign eyewitness descriptions of China were almost all Arabic,' writes Dr Wood. But then, in his prologue Marco Polo does not claim to be reporting the truth, the whole truth and nothing but the truth. Quite the opposite, he states quite clearly that he is setting out to entertain: "In the year of the Nativity of Our Lord Jesus Christ 1298, while he was in prison in Genoa, wishing to occupy his leisure as well as to afford entertainment to readers, he caused all these things to be recorded by Messer Rustichello of Pisa, who was in the same prison."

Dr Wood has written a very even-handed analysis. She comes to two conclusions.

'Marco Polo stands accused of retelling well-known tales, like the invasion of Japan or of the Wang Zhu's uprisings, and the delivery of the princess to Ikhan of Persia. Yet if Marco Polo was *not* in China, there is, unfortunately, nothing to prove he was anywhere else between 1271 and 1295.' She goes on to say that in his uncle Maffeo's will of 1310, there is a passage relating to the still outstanding loan to Marco of money, jewels – and a gold tablet from the Great Khan.

86

In Marco Polo's own will of 1324, the foremost evidence of any contact with the East is the grant of freedom and a small legacy to Peter, his Tartar slave, whose own will was registered in 1329, in which he was referred to as Petrus Suliman.

Dr Wood concludes: 'Whilst I include to the view that Marco Polo himself probably never travelled much further than the family's trading posts on the Black Sea and in Constantinople, and was not responsible for Italian ice-cream or Chinese dumplings, this does not mean that the *Description of the World* does not remain a valuable source of information on China and the Near East, in particular. His usefulness as a recorder of information otherwise lost is similar to the case of Herodotus (c 484 to c 425 BC), who did not travel to all the places he described and who mixed fact with fantastic tales, but shoe work is nevertheless not to be discarded lightly . . . The contents of *Description of the World,* used critically, remain important, and can be regarded as an example of the type of world geography which was beginning to become popular in the fourteenth century.'

Marco Polo – or whoever wrote the source from which he drew – penned an absorbing description of the boats of Champa in the late thirteenth century.

'Mostly built of fir and pine, on one deck there can be as many as sixty little rooms or cabins, sometimes more, where a merchant can stay comfortably . . . They have one good sweep or helm, which in the vulgar tongue is called a rudder, four masts and four sails and they often add to them two masts which are raised and put away every time they wish, according to the state of the weather.'

Some ships, the larger ones, he wrote, have thirteen holds or divisions, 'on the inside made with strong planks fitted together, so that if it happens by accident that the ship is staved in any place, namely that either it strikes on a rock or a whale fish striking against it in search of food staves it in. And this often happens; for if the ship sailing by night making the water ripple, passes near a whale, the whale seeing the water glisten as it is moved, thinks that there will be feed for it, and moving quickly forward, strikes against the ship and often staves the ship in some part of it.'

The sailors would then empty the merchandise out of the staved hold to another. 'For the water cannot pass from one hold to another, so strongly are they shut in . . . for they are all lined, that is, they have two boards, one above the other' – the entire ship had a double skin – 'in the common speech of our sailors, caulked both outside and inside and they are well nailed inside and outside with iron pins.'

Then he divulges the Chams' secret of shipbuilding. The ships 'are not pitched with pitch, because they have none of it in those regions; but they oil them in such a way as I shall tell you, because they have another thing which seems to them to be better than pitch. For I tell you that it becomes sticky and holds like birdlime. And with this thing they smear their ships, and this is worth quite as much as pitch' – the same tree resin that the Chams used to glue the bricks of their temples and to seal their basket boats, even now.

What then surprised me was how big these Cham ships were.

'Moreover, I tell you that these ships want some three hundred sailors, some two hundred sailors, some one hundred fifty sailors . . .They also carry a much greater burden than ours. And formerly, in times past the ships were larger than they are now at present; because the violence of the sea has so broken away the islands in several places that in many places water was not found enough for those ships so great, and so they are now made smaller; but they are so large that they carry quite five thousand baskets of pepper . . . But I tell you, too, that they take forty, fifty, some sixty, some eighty, some one hundred sailors and these go with oars and with sails – when there is opportunity. And often again they help to tow the great ship with ropes, that is, hawsers, when they are moved along with oars . . .

'They take two and three of these large tenders, but the one is larger than the other. And of small ships which we call boats, also they take quite ten, to anchor and to catch fish and to wait upon the large ship in many other ways. And the ship carries all these boats through the water lashed to her sides outside and when necessary they put them in the water; but they tow the two large ones astern, which each have their mariners and their sails and all that is needed for themselves and for them. And again I tell you that the said two large tenders also carry small boats.'

And then, he tells the most extraordinary tale of how the Chams repaired their ships.

'Moreover I tell you again that when the great ships wish to be decorated, that is to be repaired . . . they nail yet another board (skin) over the aforesaid original two all round the ship, without removing the former at all, and then there are three of them over the whole ship . . . and then, when it is nailed, they also caulk and oil it with the foresaid mixture, and this is the repair which they do. And at the end of the second year, at the second repair, they nail yet another board, leaving the other boards to that there are four. And in this way, they go each year from repair to repair up to the number of six boards (hulls), the one nailed above the other.

'And when they have six boards, the one upon the other nailed, then the ship is condemned and they sail no more in her on too high seas, but in near journeys and good weather, and they do not overload them; until it seems to them that they are no more of any value and that one can make no more use of them. Then they dismantle and break them up.'

A little latter, he goes quite fanciful, or is it fanciful?

'Cipingu is an island in the sunrising (east), which is on the high sea fifteen hundred miles (2,400 km) distant from the land of Mangi . . . the people of it are white, fair fashioned and beautiful and of good manners. They are idolaters and keep themselves by themselves, that is, they are ruled by their own king, but pay tribute to no other, and have no lordship of any other men but of themselves. Moreover, I tell you that they have gold in very great abundance because gold is found there beyond measure. Moreover, I tell you that no man takes gold out from that island, because the king does not easily allow it to be taken from the island and therefore no merchant as it were, nor other man, goes there from the mainland, because it is so far, and ships are rarely brought there from other regions, for it abounds in all things.'

It is quite likely that whoever wrote the above had not actually been to Cipingu or Mangi. Might Cipingu have been the island of Butuan in the Philippines that Marco was describing – Champa's secret source of gold? Certainly, if the Chams had kept their secret from the Chinese until the thirteenth century, neither Marco Polo nor passing Arab nor Persian ships would have been there either, though a rumour might well have drifted over the waves.

OF POTS AND BOATS

On my first trip to Hoi An, I climbed abroad one of the colourful awninged excursion boats to putter along the shore of the Thu Bon river to visit Kim Bong, the boat-building village. In those days, the boat had two wooden throne-like armchairs painted marine blue and I felt like a minor potentate in my elevated position.

The boat floated out along the quay, crowded with second-hand clothes stalls, past a ferry about to depart, stacked with bicycles on the roof. We rounded a sand bar where small boats were beached for repairs, past a flock of dizzy white ducks swimming slowly in a circle. From my throne, I had a grand view of thatched and tile-roofed, wooden houses nestled under fluttery groves of bamboo along the shores. We passed men standing hip-deep in the water, vigorously pushing sticks into the river bed – 'raking for clams, very hard work,' said Hoa, the guide.

Children splashed in the shallows and flocks of fluffy ducklings, hemmed in by bamboo fences planted in the shallow water, skittered at the sound of the boat engine. At the river's edge, a man scrubbed a sleeping mat. A little further on, heavy logs had been dragged up on the river bank near where a wooden fishing boat was being built. A tiny shrine clung precariously to a tree trunk. Smoke rose from a brick kiln.

Looking back towards the land, the sky was a filmy wash of slate blue, swathes of clouds flung carelessly like fine, diaphonous white silk over the mountain tops. To seaward, the violet outline of Cu Lao Cham lay smudged against the sky. A wobbly-looking platform on stilts in the middle of the river supported a winch to raise a huge square fishnet, draped like golden gossamer on poles above the water to dry. For the first time, I noticed that the boatman had lost an arm below the elbow. In those days, one saw a few amputees in Hoi An, who while scavenging for scrap metal, had accidentally stumbled upon mines. These days, fewer people lose limbs; they have been educated to be cautious.

We stopped at the village of Thanh Ha, where a crowd of small children besieged us, each carrying a basket chock-full of clay whistles shaped like fish, turtles and birds. So this was where they came from. The children clamoured all over us like puppies, so eager to sell that it was difficult to walk, even slowly. This pottery village, first called Cam Ha, dates from the seventeenth century. Nowadays, few potters remain. Understandably, young people refuse to take up the craft because the pay is so low, but it is sad to witness the decline of traditional crafts.

Clay had always been brought to the village from elsewhere and we walked past great grey mounds of it, waiting to be worked. When I shied away from a barking dog, Hoa laughed, quoting a Vietnamese proverb.

'Barking dogs don't bite.'

The children followed us through the narrow, dusty lanes between wood and thatch houses until we came upon a young man standing over a heap of dry clay, little by little, carefully stirring the dry clay into a puddle of water in the centre, like mixing cement. In some of the courtyards, rows of roof tiles lay baking in the sun; another courtyard held the round perforated charcoal bricks used in the flower-pot cookers.

In another courtyard, a young woman energetically threw wet clumps of clay into a square mould and deftly sliced off the excess with a metal wire, rather like a horizontal cheese-slice – a highly labour-intensive way to make floor tiles. In another courtyard, a team was using a similar method to mould bricks, the method probably unchanged for centuries.

Eventually, we came upon a young woman in an open thatched hut, patting a mound of clay on a rough board while turning a potter's wheel with one foot. Beside her an older woman squatted on a two-inch (5 cm) high stool, shaping a pot. Around a bougainvillea-draped corner, we found another team, this time sisters at work making bowls. Their courtyard was choked with earthen bowls drying in the sun, awaiting the kiln. Picturesque as it was and though many occupations in Vietnam require equally hard or harder labour, it was difficult not to wish these women a better life.

Beside the riverbank as we were leaving, I noticed a small thatched hut under a tree. A man had come to the hut, a pig sty, to feed the pig, who led an idle life in the shade of a tree, catching any cool breeze from the river, a considerably easier life than that of the people living in the village.

Ensconced once more on my floating throne, we passed a woman washing her laundry in the river, who gave us a big smile and a wave. Standing atop a boat cabin, a boy concentrated fixedly on his bamboo fishing rod. A dredger sucked up river water and strained out at least some of the sand before it gushed back into the river. As we headed towards more gleaming fishnets looped between poles over the water to dry, a butterfly flitted across the bow.

A beautifully polished wooden boat under construction stood propped on the river bank. Carved, arched-back, wooden carp served as pillars between the cabin windows. A fortune teller would be consulted before it was launched as an excursion boat, Hoa explained. At the time, it stirred romantic daydreams of idly floating along the river's backwaters, hopping off to visit villages along the way.

Our boat drew into Kim Bong, the village of wood carvers and boat builders, who through the generations have carved the altars of Hoi An's pagodas and temples. In an attempt to preserve their craft, UNESCO had financed a workshop and the master carver, Huynh Ri, had fifteen apprentices in training.

The project in hand was a headboard destined for Europe, the open fretwork teaming with peacocks, foliage and carved grapes. Including transport, it would cost four thousand US dollars. Woods used in the workshop were the local hardwoods, *kim kieng,* mahogany and jackfruit from the Central Highlands.

Nearby, quite ordinary wooden doors were being assembled. Along the riverbank, boat hulls stood braced in various states of construction. We came upon a fishing boat, propped up on planks with men underneath, busily trampling wood shavings with their bare feet as Europeans used to tread grapes – to soften the shavings to be used for caulking the cracks.

Outside her thatched home, a woman squatted with a large knife, splitting canes to weave baskets. At first, she slit the end of each cane, leaving it on the knife blade. Then when she had nine or ten split reeds lined up on the blade, she grasped them in one hand and pulled hard, slicing them simultaneously, a triumph of Vietnamese time and motion.

This time in Hoi An, I think I saw once again the boat with the carved carp – that or one very like it – propped up, dry-docked on the river bank, old and retired from sailing. It made me feel unspeakably sad.

MYSTERY OF THE VASE

The salvage of a shipwreck off Hoi An in the year 2000, radically changed Vietnam's history of trade. From the mid-eighth century, Chinese merchant vessels laden with silk, porcelain, classical texts and Buddhist scripture in Chinese translation had traded in Japanese ports. In exchange the Japanese traded swords, handicrafts, fans and copper containing silver, which the Chinese turned into coins.

However, the hungry Japanese market suffered from an imbalance of trade, having insufficient export merchandise to satisfy the home market's lust for Chinese silk and porcelain. As a result, early in the twelfth century, Japanese merchants turned to piracy along the coasts of Korea and northern China.

Partly to rid himself of these troublesome Japanese pirates, the Ming emperor slammed shut the doors to China in 1371, limiting maritime trade to the Chinese imperial fleet and to those allowed to come bearing tribute. Chinese merchants were forbidden to go abroad by sea. Amongst those few permitted to continue trading were the Chams and the Viets to the north. This Chinese ban on sea trade held for nearly two hundred years. It was not lifted officially until 1567, although in the latter years, Chinese merchants slipped out clandestinely to trade. During this Closed Door Policy between the years of 1371 and 1567, Vietnam very profitably filled the vacuum left by Chinese exports, particularly in supplying fine quality ceramics and silk.

Although the fifteenth and sixteenth centuries are considered to have been the peak of Vietnam's export of ceramics, fragments of blue flowered Vietnamese ceramics have been found at a tomb in Dazaifu, Japan, dated 1330. And early Vietnamese ceramics have been discovered in some thirty sites around Japan and South East Asia – even as far away as the Middle East, in the Sinai Peninsula and in Egypt.

Until fairly recently, it had been assumed that most of Vietnam's ceramics for export were produced at Bat Trang, a village just outside of Hanoi, still functioning today as a pottery village. Monochrome wares of jade green, brown and yellow glazes for export were produced in the South at Binh Dinh, two provinces south of Hoi An, the latter in all probability shipped out of Hoi An.

The salvage of a shipwreck off Hoi An in the year 2000, dashed the assumption that most ceramics for export were produced in Bat Trang. An astonishingly fine collection – 2,316 pieces – was salvaged from a fifteenth century shipwreck that the auctioneer's catalogue dubbed *Treasures from the Hoi An Hoard*. All of the salvaged ceramics had come, not from Bat Trang, but from kilns in Chu Dau between Haiphong and Hanoi. To give some notion of the quality, the tiniest piece of the salvaged china sold for more than a thousand US dollars.

A few years ago, long before I had heard of the salvaged shipwreck or the auction, I spied a beautiful piece of china in an antique shop in Oxford, a tiny blue and white scent phial – and was astounded at the price. It might well have come from the shipwreck off Hoi An. Amongst the ceramics from Chu Dau brought up from the sunken ship, almost undoubtedly would have been pieces made by a woman whose kiln was at nearby Quang Anh on the Dinh Dao canal. Her name was Bui Thi Hy and like me, she was born in the year of the Tiger – in 1420. Unfortunately, the international auction dispersed the entire collection, piece by piece, into the hands of personal collectors and museums throughout the world.

That Bui Thi Hy became a potter seems almost an accident of the historical circumstances in which she found herself. Extremely rare for a woman in the fifteenth century – most women were not even allowed to learn to read – she developed a talent for writing and drawing. More bizarrely, she practised marshal arts and disguised as a man, passed the first two royal examinations to become a mandarin before being exposed and expelled. This last achievement is remarkable – very few men mastered the Confucian classics sufficiently to pass these examinations.

Diverted from becoming a mandarin, she married a wealthy man, Dang Si, who owned a ceramics business in Chu Dau. Bui Thi Hy took an interest in her husband's business and showed great skill as a potter. She and her younger brother, Bui Dinh Khoi, set up a kiln in 1452 on the Dinh Dao canal from where they could transport their ceramics by boat to Chu Dau and on, along with those from Chu Dau to the royal court in Hanoi. The family business also exported ceramics to 'the north country' (China), to Japan and to the West – quite how far west we are left to ponder when it turns out that a graceful, long-necked, blue and white, round-bellied vase with intricately entwined flowers in the Topkapi Saraji Museum in Istanbul

94

bears the inscription: 'The eighth year of Thai Hoa reign (1450), Nam Sach District, sculptor Bui Thi Hy but.'

For a long time, Han Chinese scholars argued that the signature could be translated two ways: either that a male potter named Bui, joyously wrote the character Hy (joy) in a fit of light-hearted whimsy, or grudgingly, that a female sculptor named Bui Thi Hy might have fashioned the vase and inscribed it. They refused to concede that the vase was fashioned by a woman.

The mystery of Bui Thi Hy's Topkopi vase was finally resolved in 2007 when descendants of her family produced not only the written family history, but a terracotta sculpture of a young terracotta lion bearing the inscription: 'Made by Bui Thi Hy at Quang Anh fief in the first year of Quang Thuan reign.'

A further find proved the case conclusively, this time dredged from the family's pond located on the site of the former kiln. A broad shallow saucer, discarded because it had been improperly fired – the glaze hadn't taken – bore the inscription: 'Made by sister Bui Thi Hy, brother Bui Khoi, at Quang Anh fief, Gia Phuc District in the first year of Dien Ninh (1454).'

Then the plot moves a step closer to Hoi An. It is recorded that Bui Thi Hy's husband, Dang Si, died in a shipwreck on the Eastern Sea (South China Sea) – just possibly the shipwreck salvaged off Hoi An in 2000. From the inscription on her tombstone, we learn that Bui Thi Hy carried on her husband's shipping business, operating her own ships at a time when there were very few Vietnamese *men* running ships. Foreign merchants controlled most international trade.

Her devoted second husband, Dang Phuc, dedicated the inscription on her tombstone to: 'The wonderfully talented wife named Bui Thi Hy . . . She led the business to Japan, China and the West to trade special wares. In the night of the twelfth day of the eighth month of the Year of the Goat (1499), there was a typhoon with heavy rain, lightning and thunder. She lay behind a screen glowing with a rose-coloured light like an ascending dragon. Then she passed.' It would have been her eightieth year – a long and productive life in the fifteenth century.

So far, only these three signed ceramic works by Bui Thi Hy have come to light: the Topkapi vase, the young lion and the large saucer found at the bottom of the pond. Oddly, there is no explanation for the absence of inscribed ceramics for over a century following the Topkapi vase. Nor were Bui Thi Hy's the first inscribed Vietnamese ceramics. Amazingly, there is a wide-mouthed Vietnamese jar dated 149 AD, inscribed with the name Ly, amongst the Huet Collection in Belgium's Royal Museum of Art and History in Brussels.

So inscriptions began much earlier, but why did they stop? A further mystery for art historians to solve. And how many more of Bui Thi Hy's pieces lie unrecognised in collections and museums around the world?

The story doesn't quite end with her tombstone – which has perished or been lost. The message on Bui Thi Hy's tombstone had been copied in Han Chinese onto a round copper tray by a relative, Bui Duc Nhuan, many generations later in 1932, who rightly feared that in turbulent times, the original stone stele might be lost. The copper tray, treasured and handed down as a family heirloom, indeed, survived destruction of the family house during the French Indo-Chinese War when coals fell on its rim, thankfully leaving the message intact. After that, the family buried the tray in a terracotta jar for safekeeping. The last words on the copper tray read: 'Even if times change, the original stele of the Great Aunt kept in the sacred land forbids any breaching.'

Until the recent emergence of the tray, it had been thought that only foreign trading vessels had called at Chu Dau to ship goods. The tray proved not only that Viet vessels had taken part in this foreign trade, but vessels, moreover, controlled by a woman, who headed her own shipping fleet. It is only by the grace of Vietnam's tradition of ancestor worship that we have discovered Bui Thi Hy, not only an extraordinary woman in her own time, she would have been an exceptional artist and potter in any era.

Inside the door of Hoi An's Trade Ceramics Museum (80 Tran Phu Street) is a huge wooden model of a sixteenth century boat – perhaps not unlike the one that floundered with its cargo of pottery from Chu Dao, possibly with Bui Thi Hy's husband on board. I overhear a tour guide telling a French group that the house was rented by the Dutch East India Company (VOC) – a bit unlikely, however beautiful this old house, as I later learn that the Dutch had left Hoi An well before the house was built in the early nineteenth century. But I am in search of Bui Thi Hy's vases.

The second room holds ceramics found on Cham Island: Yue Zhou glazed ceramics of the ninth and tenth centuries and shards of glazed turquoise Arab pottery, also from the ninth and tenth centuries.

Glass cases beside the door to the courtyard hold pretty blue and white china – a Chu Dau vase with a lid and a bowl, sure enough, salvaged from the shipwreck off Cham Island, part of the Hoi An Hoard! Another cabinet holds more Chu Dau ceramics from the ship wreck off Cham island: a wispy bird painted like a watercolour in the bottom of a bowl; leaves of foliage in another; and in a third, a sassy bird, his tail up and his beak open, still squawking after half a millennium. I think of asking the museum curator to open the case, then realise that even if the vase and bowl were signed by Bui Thi Hy, neither he nor I would be able to read the Han Chinese characters. Who painted them must remain one of Hoi An's secrets – at least for the present.

Several times I pass by the house at 80 Nguyen Thai Hoc Street, its display windows full of dusty, blue and white plates and vases and the enticing sign: Hoi An Hoard.

A kindly young man, Nguyen Duc Pho, has offered to act as my translator between jobs. When I tell Pho that I would like to visit the house with the ceramics collection, he says that everyone in town knows Sung Senh, the richest man in town, at least by reputation. One evening when I happened to find myself having supper in a restaurant opposite, a man had appeared at the door with no shirt on – at thirty-seven degrees centigrade (98F), who could blame him. He spat on the dirt road, retreated and closed the broken wooden latticed doors. A hole at the bottom might have been to give a cat access – or a very small dog.

When Pho inquires at the house, the same man tells us that the owner of the house is not at home. It seems to both of us that Pho may be speaking to the owner, but Pho has an idea. He knows that the brother of the man he spoke to is a photographer, living a few doors away, so he goes off there to inquire. Happily, the photographer agrees to meet us the following day – in the pot house.

Thai Te Thong is seventy-seven years old, he has close-cropped grey hair, slits for eyes when he laughs, crooked teeth and the square-jawed face of a Chinese. Wearing a pair of khaki trousers and a short-sleeved blue shirt, from his general appearance no one would guess that he or his brother are among the wealthiest men in Hoi An. He invites us to sit at a high rectangular table. Two carved antique chairs face two identical chairs opposite – four-square, balanced, Confucian. Along the walls, more antique chairs brace themselves against glass display cabinets, floor-to-ceiling, brimming with blue and white ceramics, the entire length of the room, both sides. The family alter occupies the back wall.

He hands me a card with his name printed in Vietnamese on one side, in Chinese on the reverse.

'I was a photographer for sixty years, I started at sixteen. I became interested in photography through my father. He was also a photographer, so I started young, always with a camera. I closed the studio in 2001.'

Mr Thong's library holds several thousand photographs, 'Not only portraits, landscapes, everything.' He brings out a German magazine, or rather, his brother brings out the magazine, *Geo Special,* and shows me street scenes of Hoi An with no traffic, pre-motorbike, pre-car, maybe even pre-bicycle, it looks so quiet – another world. The photos were published two years ago for which he tells me proudly that he was paid two thousand euros.

'They asked for the negatives, they also invited me to attend the exhibition.' Mr Thong has had two major exhibitions and his photographs have also been published in *Gap Vietnam* and *Heritage* magazines. He brings out another photo album of old Hoi An: the streets utterly empty, a photo of the last rickshaw taken in 1945, a shot of the flooded streets in 1964 – the worst flood in history when the water reached to just beneath the eaves.

I ask if his family remained in Hoi An during the Second World War.

'Oh yes, I used to go out taking photos with a German photographer,' he says cheerily.

Thai Te Thong was one of twelve brothers and sisters, 'Half boys and half girls. They all live in Hoi An, except for the five who have died, leaving seven.'

It is his younger brother who lives in this house. Thai Te Thong has been married for sixty-one years; his wife is the same age as he. He is the father of five boys and one girl. They are all married and have produced eight grandchildren.

With a touch of humour, he says, 'According to Chinese tradition, when the children become adults, they can live by themselves. Their parents don't have to support them anymore – not like the Vietnamese.'

I ask about the photographs that surround the family altar, pointing to a large photo of two young girls in white, one standing stiffly beside the other, sitting in a chair, portraits from a more formal, genteel past, long past.

'My mother – she would have been a hundred, but she died in 1996 – with her sister as young girls. Her sister died in 1994.'

On the left is a photograph of three children, again wearing white. He points to one brother.

'He died at eighty-three, just a few months ago, living in Los Angeles. The other two are younger sisters of my mother. One uncle was killed by the Japanese in World War II.

'Another of my mother's younger brothers, my uncle, is a professor of philosophy in Ho Chi Minh City. He graduated from the University of Thanh Hoa (Ching Hoa) in China.'

I point to a photograph of a dapper-looking dandy in a white suit with a cane, who looks as though he might be stepping out for tea at Hong Kong's Peninsula Hotel.

'My grandfather.' And on the left? 'My grandmother – who built the house during the Qing Dynasty.'

Another portrait of a studious-looking young man with round-framed glasses is 'my grandfather in 1911,' his name, Tan Hoi, printed in Roman letters beneath the photograph.

'My family migrated to Hoi An around 1856 from Fukien, Canton. Mine is the fifth generation in Hoi An.'

For a moment, he thinks I am pointing to the lacquer panels with gilt characters.

'The one on the right translates as "True prices, true commodities"; the one on the left as "The same prices, the same quality" ' – the inference being that prices and quality are the same for everyone, rich or poor, child or adult, Pho explains.

His grandfather dealt in herbal medicines; his own father was in many different kinds of businesses, amongst them lubricants, which explains the antique Shell sign that hangs outside. Many people have wanted to buy it, but Mr Thong has always refused.

The inscribed mirror bearing Chinese characters at the top of the family altar was an award bestowed upon his grandfather in 1934 by Bao Dai, Vietnam's last emperor, along with a medal 'congratulating him as leader of the Chinese community in Hoi An.'

Slightly higher than the gold Buddha under glass on the altar, and perhaps ranking slightly higher in the family's esteem, stand three china statuettes representing 'happiness, longevity and luck' – three prerequisites for a fulfilled Chinese life.

I ask where all of the ceramics came from, where they were purchased? Were they all brought up from shipwrecks?

It seems that both his grandfather and his father, born in 1907, collected china.

'Most of them were bought in China, at the time, ordinary utensils in the house, but now antiques.'

My heart leaps when he brings out the thick, expensively produced Butterfields auction catalogue from 2000, *Treasures of the Hoi An Hoard.* More than three hundred pages illustrate the ceramics offered for sale, no lot with a reserve price lower than $2,000. The auction took place simultaneously in San Francisco and Los Angeles.

He opens a cupboard holding at least sixty dainty, blue and white powder pots with lids, and there are as many more in the shelves opposite. He hands me a tiny perfume phial with a hole in the top, not unlike the one I saw in the antique shop in Oxford.

'Medicine pots, powder pots, the tiny cups contained poison medicine. The top mandarin would tell you, "You have to drink from this cup." They are all from Chu Dau village in (North) Vietnam.'

So, many of them were bought from the Hoi An Hoard. I ask if he has any signed by Bui Thi Hy.

'I have heard of her, but I don't think so.'

A large sandalwood statue of Quan Diem stands in front of the display cases – 'New,' he says dismissively.

Displayed on a small stand is a truly amazing sight – a clump of old metal coins moulded together by time, which had been buried in a vase, so vase-shaped. They were, indeed, discovered in Vietnam, but not near Hoi An, he says.

'Ninth century Chinese, Tang dynasty, a thousand years old. Many coins stuck together.'

Mr Thong explains that in troubled times, a rich family, especially the wife, might have buried the coins in a vase for safe keeping. 'But when she died, nobody knew where the family fortune had been buried.'

In leaving, I notice attached to the second-floor terrace of the house, a huge painted, wooden cut-out of the fat Buddha of the future – and prosperity.

PART III

HEYDAYS

EASTWARD HO!

Asia was rumbling with tectonic political changes in the fourteenth, fifteenth and sixteenth centuries. The upstart Thai kingdom of Ayuthaya overthrew the kingdom of Sukhothai in 1376 and in the early fifteenth century, founded Malacca on the Malay Peninsula as a vassal state. Not long after, with the support of Chinese admiral Zheng He, Malacca threw off Siamese rule and became in turn, a vassal state of China.

Zheng He's fleet of thirty enormous vessels – his ships three times the size of Christopher Columbus's later Santa Maria – manned by a total of thirty thousand men – called repeatedly at Malacca during his voyages to Sri Lanka, Aden, and Africa between 1405 and 1430, once even bringing a Ming princess to wed the local Sultan, Manshur Shah.

Zheng He (1371-1435), a Muslim and a eunuch, to say the least an outsider in Confucian China, mounted seven major maritime trade expeditions. When the Chinese fleet stopped calling after 1430, Malacca again fell under the yoke of Ayuthya, but succeeded in expelling the Siamese with the support of local Muslims, after which Islam was adopted as the state religion.

The Siamese then turned on Cambodia, defeating and looting Angkor in 1431, marking the end of the glorious era of temple building and the Khmer as a political force.

Malacca, occupying a pivotal position on the Straits of Malacca between East and West, became an important entrepot in maritime South East Asia. Here ships from India and the Middle East met those from the East. Muslim merchants had set up trading posts and small communities under Muslim rulers in Ayuthaya, Pegu (Burma), Malaya and Java, converting people to Islam along the trade route. The Cham ports of central and southern Vietnam maintained active commercial and religious ties with these Muslim city states.

When the Viets definitively defeated and destroyed Vijaya in 1471, the Cham king sent one of his sons off to Malacca and another to Aceh (Indonesia).

After the Turks took Constantinople in 1453 and disrupted trade in the eastern Mediterranean, the race was on to find a new sea route to the spice islands of Asia. A Papal Bull of 1493 obligingly divided the world: east of a line drawn north-south through the Atlantic went to Portugal, west of the line to Spain.

Prior to the fifteenth century, Arab and Chinese records make no mention of military obstacles to trade in the East – only pirates. Marco Polo, Ibn Batula, Persian Abdur Razzac, Venetian Nicolo de Conti, Genoan Stanto Stefano, all found the Indian Ocean a scene of thriving, openly competitive trade.

All that was to change when Portuguese Vasco de Gama rounded the Cape of Good Hope at the tip of Africa and reached India under sail in 1498 – breaking the monopoly of Arab and Venetian spice traders. With the arrival of the Portuguese in the East, trade became the object of fierce military conquest, jealously and bloodily defended. The Portuguese hastily constructed forts to protect their trading posts established along the coasts of the Persian Gulf, India and East Africa, their ultimate goal to reach the Moluccas before the Spaniards. Under royal patronage, Jesuit missionaries always travelled on board Portuguese merchant ships, proselytizing in these new settlements. As early as 1505, Portugal declared a royal monopoly of the Moluccas spice trade. Royal decrees and reality, however, sometimes differ. Arab and Indian traders continued to evade the Portuguese and to carry highly prized spices destined for Europe back through the Red Sea.

In 1509, a small fleet of the Portuguese Viceroy of India, Alfonso de Albuquerque, dropped anchor in Malacca and attacked; the Portuguese were smartly repelled. Again in 1511, this time with reinforcements from Portugal, although still with only eleven hundred men against the Sultan's estimated twenty thousand – folly to attack – Albuquerque managed to capture and occupy Malacca through collusion with local Chinese merchants. The defeated sultan and his court moved off to Johor to form a new kingdom opposite present-day Singapore.

The first European recorded to have called at Hoi An was Portuguese Antonio de Faris, aboard his ship, the Albuquerque, in 1535. Hoi An, then called Faifo on Portuguese navigational maps, 'would be of as much interest to his compatriots as Malacca or Macao,' de Faris declared, after which Portuguese ships began to call regularly at Hoi An.

The Portuguese were allowed to set up a trading post in Hirado (Nagasaki) in 1550. However, the Chinese did not allow them to create a permanent settlement in Macao until 1557 – as a reward for helping to expel pirates.

By the mid-sixteenth century, the Portuguese held a semi-monopoly over the spice trade. Local traders were forced to pay a tax to the Portuguese on exports, although traders from Aceh, Oman and India continued to flout their authority.

In China, pressures against the Ming ban on maritime trading were building up. So strong were the demands for pepper and cloves from Java and Sumatra, for copper to mint coins and for silver to circulate as bullion that seafaring merchants, operating from various islands in the South China Sea, began to flagrantly ignore the Chinese trade ban. These seafaring merchants, although of diverse nationalities, were referred to as Japanese pirates. This flouting of trade policy finally forced the Ming Emperor to end China's Closed Door Policy in 1567, officially opening trade to private seafaring merchants. Interestingly, it had been aboard the junk of one of these so-called Japanese pirates that the Portuguese had first 'discovered' Japan in 1543.

Meanwhile, in Latin America, the Peruvian silver mine at Potosi had opened in 1545, sending vast quantities of silver via the Spaniards to Europe, who established their settlement in Luzan (Philippines) in 1571. For a time, the Portuguese-Spanish monopoly on silver in the East remained impregnable. (Spain and Portugal were united from 1580 to 1640).

In Japan, because of internal political upheavals, no tribute missions had been sent to China since 1549. Although China lifted its trade ban in 1567, still chafing from Japanese piracy, China refused to allow Japanese ships into Chinese ports. Desperate for Chinese silk, Japanese shogun Toyotomo Hideyoshi sent a doomed military expedition from Japan to Korea in 1592 to try to force the (Korean) Yi dynasty to grant permission for trade with the Chinese (sic) emperor. No permission was granted and China was furious. Determined to expand trade, Toyotomo Hideyoshi then attempted unsuccessfully to establish diplomatic relations with the Portuguese viceroy in Goa and the Spanish governor in Malina (Manila).

Political stability returned to Japan with Tokugawa Ieyasu (1542-1616), who seized power on the death of Toyotomi Hideyoshi and initiated the task of suppressing Japanese pirates. Ieyasu devised a brilliant scheme to thwart the pirates and at a stroke, to break the Portuguese trade monopoly with China, thereby guaranteeing silk for the Japanese market – by licensing certain ships, allowed to visit only designated ports. These licensed ships called *shuinsen,* sailed under an official red seal or charter, loaded mostly with silver and copper, the production of silver having increased dramatically in Japan after 1580. The *shuinsen* ships sailed south to meet Chinese merchants carrying silk and ceramics – far beyond the nearby Chinese mainland – thereby setting up indirect trade between Japan and China by creating a new triangular, international maritime trade route.

And where did these Japanese and Chinese ships rendezvous? Largely in Hoi An.

With the creation of this new trade route, China's supply of silver now came via two routes: from the New World via Portugal or Manila and from Japan via Hoi An. The Portuguese monopoly of the silver trade was broken.

The same north-east trade winds that bore the Chinese junks, bearing the silk and ceramics so coveted by the Japanese, blew the Japanese *shuinsen* ships loaded low in the water with silver and copper, south to Hoi An. Thanks largely to Japanese silver and copper, Hoi An became the wealthiest port along the entire coast of Vietnam in the early seventeenth century. Silk and ceramics from China were sold to Japan and Europe; silver and copper from Japan were eagerly bought by the Chinese; silk, ceramics, sugar, cinnamon and aromatic woods from Vietnam were exported to Japan, China, India and Europe. The merchants of Hoi An flourished.

Rather surprisingly, the story of the Japanese and Portuguese in Hoi An is inextricably intertwined with that of an English sailor.

Further political rumblings closer to home were to deeply affect Hoi An. Nearly a century after the defeat of the Chams by the Viets in 1471, the Viets in the North set about establishing tighter control over their new southern, formerly Cham territories.

For several generations in the Dai Viet capital, Thang Long later Hanoi, (the Nguyen pronounced, Win) clan had been active in royal court and military affairs under the Le dynasty, always in fierce competition with another family, the Trinh.

The story goes that during the reign of King Le Tang Tong (1533-1548), Nguyen Hoang (1525-1613) heard a rumour that his brother-in-law, Trinh Kiem, was plotting to have him assassinated. Hard on the deaths of both his father and brother in battle – rumour had it they had been stabbed in the back – the assassination rumour seemed all too plausible. To escape the court intrigues, Nguyen Hoang managed to get himself appointed governor of the frontier southern region, then known as Dang Trong and in 1558, moved South with his clan, his father's army and a good many artisans to the village of Phu Xuan, near Hue.

Nguyen Hoang quietly worked away, ostensibly to develop the Dang Trong region, while gradually building up his military power and establishing an administrative structure, mirroring the royal court in the North. In 1570, he was appointed governor of an additional southern area, Quang Nam, which included the Thu Bon river and Hoi An. This gave him even more land and he busily settled more emigrants, who either volunteered or as often as not, were forced to move to the new territories.

However, the friction between the two families, the Trinh and the Nguyen, continued and towards the end of the sixteenth century and early in the seventeenth, Nguyen Hoang's son, Nguyen Phuc Nguyen, the second Nguyen lord to assume power as governor in the South, felt strong enough to challenge the dominance of the Trinh in civil wars. The Nguyens ceased to pay tribute to the northern court after 1627, tantamount to declaring themselves independent.

The early Nguyen lords, seeing trade as a source of revenue, took control of the old Cham ports, encouraging foreign traders. Not only were there gains to be made by collecting harbour duties and a portion of each cargo as a tax, more importantly to the Nguyen, foreign trade provided a means of obtaining Western military weaponry, useful in their conflicts with the Trinh.

In time, the Nguyen lords came to control the numerous small ports dotted along the central coast of the Indo-Chinese peninsula, south around the Mekong delta and up to Ha Tien on the Gulf of Siam near the Cambodian border. Yet thanks to its favourable position as a gathering point for produce brought both by land from the rich hinterlands, down river and by sea, Hoi An was by far the largest and most prosperous of these ports. It was, after all, a well-established Cham port, having traded with Chinese, Malays, Javanese, Thai, Indian and Arab traders for centuries – and now the Portuguese.

Had the rumour of the assassination plot not reached Nguyen Hoang in the first place, he would never have moved south and the Nguyen would never have developed a sufficient power base from which to challenge Trinh power in Hanoi.

Nor would there have been, much later, a Nguyen dynasty in a city called Hue, Vietnam's last feudal capital.

A LIMEY IN JAPAN

The first Englishman to set foot on Japanese soil, William Adams, was to have a profound effect on distant Hoi An. His swashbuckling tale inspired James Clavell's novel, *Shogun,* and later the film.

Born in Gillingham (Kent), Adams was apprenticed at twelve to a shipwright in Limehouse. After twelve years of learning the trade of shipbuilding, astronomy and navigation, in 1588 he joined the Royal Navy and served as master of the *Richarde Dyffylde* under Sir Francis Drake against the Spanish Armada. He then set sail for the Arctic in search of the north-east passage in an unsuccessful, two-year expedition. Plainly, a young adventurer.

When 'the Indish (sic) traffic from Holland began . . . I was desirous to make a little experience of the small knowledge which God had given me.'

At thirty-four, he set sail in 1598 as 'pilot major' (navigator) of a fleet of five ships, sponsored by a company of Rotterdam merchants that pre-dated the Dutch East India Company. The fleet's wildly ambitious mission was to sail to the coast of South America where they would sell their cargo for silver – then only if this first mission failed – head for Japan, where they would obtain silver, add spices in the Moluccas and return to Europe.

It proved to be a horrific voyage. The ships were driven onto the coast of Guinea. From West Africa, they struck out across the south Atlantic for the Straits of Magellan. Only three of the five ships made it through the perilous straits at the tip of South America. The *Blijde,* disabled by rough weather and set adrift, was captured by the Spanish, scuppering any hopes of obtaining silver from them. The *Geloof* possibly mutinied before clearing the Straits and returned to Rotterdam in 1600, bearing only thirty-six of the original crew of a hundred and nine. The *Hoop* and the *Liefde* arrived at the meeting place, Floreana Island off the coast of Chile, but the captains of both ships, as well as Adams's own brother Thomas and twenty sailors, were killed in a clash with natives.

The two remaining ships set sail from Floreana across the Pacific. The *Liefde* and the *Hoop* made landfall at several islands and hardly surprisingly, eight sailors deserted. Tragically, the *Hoop* sank in a typhoon with all hands aboard in February 1600, leaving only the *Liefde,* alone in the Pacific to persevere on the voyage.

Much later, the *Trouw,* the missing third ship that had not made it to Floreana, turned up in Tidore (Indonesia), where the crew was murdered by the Portuguese. International trade was zealously defended to retain exclusive markets, nowhere more viciously than the lucrative spice trade in the Moluccas.

After nineteen months at sea, the *Liefde* finally dropped anchor off the island of Kyushu (Japan) in 1600. Only twenty sick and dying men out of an original crew of a hundred waded ashore. They were greeted by locals and Portuguese Jesuit priests, who claimed to the Japanese that Adams was a pirate and clamoured for him and his crew to be crucified. The *Liefde* was seized and the crew imprisoned in Osaka Castle on the orders of Tokugawa Ieyasu, then daimyo (lord) of Mikawa.

Adams and his crew were saved by an interpreter who spoke Portuguese, through whom Adams was able to explain their friendly intentions, showing his map of the world to an incredulous Tokugawa Ieyasu, who could hardly believe they could have travelled so far. Ieyasu asked Adams if his far away country had wars and when Adams said yes – with the Spanish and the Portuguese – Ieyasu decided in Adams's own words, that 'as we as yet had not done to him or to none of his land any harm or damage; therefore (it was) against reason or justice to put us to death . . . with which they (Portuguese priests) were out of heart that their cruel pretence failed them.'

When Tokygawa Ieyesu, the future shogun – in feudal Japan, the power behind the throne of the emperor – learned that Adams was a shipwright, he forbade him to leave Japan and ordered him and his seamen to build Japan's first Western-style ship, an eighty-ton vessel, which was used to survey the Japanese coastline. In 1603 by then shogun, Tokugawa Ieyasu commissioned a second, larger ship of a hundred-twenty tons.

Through the ship-building and as Adams learned Japanese, he gained the ear and the confidence of the shogun, eventually replacing the Portuguese priest, Valentim Carvalho, as Ieyasu's official interpreter and advisor on all matters Western and foreign.

From his very arrival, as an English merchant seaman and a Protestant, the Portuguese had seen Adams as a rival. At first, the Jesuits had attempted to convert him, then secretly offered to bear him away from Japan on a Portuguese ship. That the Jesuits were willing to flagrantly disobey the orders of Tokugawa Ieyasu – Adams was forbidden to leave Japan – showed the degree to which they correctly feared his influence.

Meanwhile in Hue, Lord Nguyen Hoang also had been plagued by Japanese pirates. According to conflicting reports, in 1585 he sent his sixth son in a squadron of ten ships to Thuan An on the coast near Hue – to deal with them. There his son destroyed two ships and captured Kenki, a genuine Japanese merchant, mistaken for a pirate. Not until sixteen years later in 1601, did Lord Nguyen Hoang finally send Kenki home with his first official letter to the Tokugawa Shogunate, apologizing for attacking Kenki's ships and expressing amicable friendship between the two countries.

Very possibly with this incident in mind, Tokugawa Ieyasu wrote to the Supreme Military Commander of Annam in 1601 – Lord Nguyen Hoang – stating: 'In future, ships visiting your country from our country are to be certified by the seal shown on this letter, and ships not carrying the seal should not be deemed lawful.' These *shuinsen* seals, in effect trade licences, were only issued by the shogun to the noble families of Japan, presumably people he could trust not to turn pirate. Legally, only red seal *shuinsen* ships were permitted to make foreign trading voyages.

Eighty-seven *shuinsen* ships called at Cochin (Central Vietnam), thirty-seven visited Tonkin (North Vietnam) during the shuinsen period that lasted until 1636.

As early as 1604, Adams was able to negotiate for the *Liefde's* captain and treasurer to be sent on a Japanese red seal *shuinsen* ship to Pattania (southern Siam on the Malay peninsula) to contact the Dutch East India Company's trading 'factory' (trading post), established there in 1602 – in an attempt to break the Portuguese monopoly on Japan's foreign trade with the West. The Jesuits had been right to fear Adams's intentions.

As a mark of his respect and high esteem, Tokugawa Ieyasu presented Adams with two swords representing the authority of a samurai in a ceremony that decreed that William Adams the pilot was dead and that Miura Anjin, a samurai, was born. This effectively rendered Adams's wife in England a widow and his English children orphans. Sometime later, Adams took a Japanese wife, Oyuki, daughter of the harbour master who had taught him Japanese, with whom he had two more children, Joseph and Susan.

The Dutch Government granted the newly combined Dutch East India Company (VOC), formed in 1602, virtually a monopoly of trade in Asia – if they could but oust the Portuguese! The VOC was granted the rights to maintain an army and a fleet, to declare war and to negotiate peace in the region – the VOC was literally entrusted to act as the official representative of the Dutch Government in the East.

Outmanoeuvring the Portuguese, the Dutch set up their first trading post in Bantam (West Java) in 1603 and by 1605, they were competing against the Portuguese in the spice trade.

By the mid-seventeenth century, the Dutch had nearly replaced the Portuguese in controlling the spice trade, still hotly challenged as the Portuguese before them had been, by traders from Aceh, Oman and India.

The Dutch in Batavia (Jakarta) set up a network of fortified trading posts from India to China, from Japan to South Africa. Portuguese Malacca fell to the Dutch in 1641, who held it until 1824 when it was ceded to the British East India Company. From 1826, Malacca was ruled as a Crown Colony.

In 1605, Adams succeeded in what he had hoped to do – he obtained a letter from Tokugawa Ieyasu, formally inviting the Dutch to trade with Japan. When the first two Dutch ships arrived in Japan in 1609, bearing a letter from Prince Maurice of Nassau to the court of Edo, one of Adams's former shipmates, Melchoir van Santvoort, was appointed to establish a Dutch trading factory in Hirado, the western most point of Kyushu, Japan's southern island.

Quite satisfied with his efforts, Adams wrote: 'The Hollanders be now settled (in Japan) and I have got them that privilege as the Spaniards and Portugals (sic) could never get in this fifty or sixty years in Japan.' That privilege, thanks to Adams, was free trading rights throughout Japan – the Portuguese were limited to trading in their 'factory' at Hirada and required to sell their goods at fixed, negotiated prices.

In 1611, twelve years after his departure from Holland, Adams learned of an English settlement in Bantam (Indonesia) and managed to send a letter, asking that news of him be forwarded to his wife and family in England. He also urged his contacts in England to set up trade with Japan: 'The Hollanders have here an Indies of money.'

111

In 1613, an Englishman named John Saris of the British East India Company (EIC) duly sailed into Hirado on board the *Clove*, looking to establish a trading factory alongside those of the Portuguese and the Dutch. On arrival, Saris noted, perhaps enviously, that Adams personally had 'reselling rights' in Edo (Tokyo) for the cargoes of foreign ships.

Adams presented Saris to Ieyasu's son, Hidetado, by then nominally shogun, although Ieyasu still retained power. On his departure, Hidetada entrusted Saris with two valuable varnished suits of Japanese armour as a gift for King James I of England, today displayed in the Tower of London.

With the arrival of Saris, Adams requested and at last received Tokugawa Ieyasu's permission to return to England. Ultimately in what must have been an intensely moral soul-searching, Adams decided to stay in Japan.

'The reason I would not go with him (Saris) was for diverse injuries done against me, the which were things to me very strange and unlooked for.'

Despite the call of his homeland, his English wife and family, facing another long and treacherous journey, very possibly at the mercy of a man who might well be judged an enemy, in the end seemed too much of a risk. But from 1613 onwards, Adams sent letters and regular financial support to his English wife and family through the Dutch and English trading companies.

In 1613, Adams accepted a position in the newly opened post of the British East India Company at Hirado for an annual salary of one hundred English pounds, more than double the usual salary of forty pounds earned by other factors at Hirado. During the ten-year activity of the company (1613-1623), apart from the *Clove*, only three further English ships brought cargoes directly from London to Japan.

The trade that supported the East India Company factory at Hirado was that between Japan and South East Asia, mainly undertaken by Adams buying Chinese goods for Japanese silver. In 1617, Richard Cocks of the British East India Company, wrote in his diary: 'Were it not for hope of trade into China, or procuring some benefit from Siam (Pattania in lower Siam) and Cochin China, it were no staying in Japan, yet it is certain here is silver enough and may be carried out at pleasure, but then we must bring them commodities to their liking.' There was not much demand for woollen vests from East Anglia in tropical South East Asia.

Both the Dutch and the English tried to enter the Macau-Nagasaki trade, but were unable to compete with Portuguese and Japanese *shuinsen* ships – their objective in coming to South East Asia from the beginning of the seventeenth century having been to break the monopoly of the Portuguese and Spanish.

Influenced by Adams and the social problems being caused by numerous Catholic converts, Tokugawa Ieyasu expelled the Jesuits from Japan and demanded that Japanese Catholics abandon their faith. When the Jesuits were expelled from Japan – with the help of Adams and the Dutch East India Company in 1614, where did they go? They went to Hoi An.

Christianity and Catholicism were first introduced to Vietnam in Hoi An. Following their expulsion from Japan in 1614, the Macau-based Council of Bishops sent a mission of Jesuit priests to Dang Trong (Vietnam's South) to establish a permanent mission.

Hoi An was already known to the Jesuits. Portuguese traders had always carried Jesuit missionaries on board their ships. Early on, the priests had only come with the ships and stayed over in Hoi An for three or four months, preaching through interpreters while the ships were in port, leaving when the ships were loaded.

This new permanent mission consisted of an Italian priest, Francesco Buzomi and a Portuguese, Diego Carvalho (perhaps a relative of Valentim Cavalho, who had called for the crucifixion of Adams and his crew in Japan) and three friars, two Japanese and one Portuguese. Cavalho stayed for only a short time. Buzomi stayed for twenty-four years, built a church in Danang and another in the provincial town of Quang Nam. Among his early converts was a woman of the aristocracy. Encouraged by this success, in 1617 the Macau Council of Bishops sent a younger Portuguese priest, Francesco di Pina, who learned Vietnamese quickly and began to preach without an interpreter. Francesco di Pina was the first European to speak fluent Vietnamese.

A year later, Macau sent a second mission, this time an Italian priest, Christoforo Borri, and Pedro Marquez, a half-caste Japanese-speaking chaplain. Borri had been trained to go to China, but following the expulsion from Japan, was sent instead to Hoi An. He stayed in and around the town from 1618 to 1622 and became the second Western missionary to speak fluent Vietnamese.

Christoforo Borri's memoires make it clear that in early seventeenth century Hoi An, there were distinct Japanese and Chinese districts – what we now know as Chinese Street and Japanese Street – each with its own *tong tran* (governor) and regulations. Borri considered them to be two separate towns. Japanese documents, including a stele inscription, refer to the Japanese district as Japanese Palace *(Nhat Bon Dinh)*. These two independent towns were unique in seventeenth century Vietnam; there were no other autonomous towns – nor had there been before, nor since.

114

On seventeenth century Portuguese and later French maps, Hoi An is indicated as Faifo or Feifo. Where the name Hoi An came from is open to scholarly surmise. One stele reading *Hoi nhan nhu hoi thuy*, translates as 'human gathering is as propitious as water accumulation' – or in a stretch, 'near a market (human gathering) near a water current (river).' Interestingly, *hoi* is a Chinese word that can mean 'gathering' or 'reunion'.

Although Portuguese was the language then used in trading with Westerners, the Jesuits realised very early on that they needed translators. In the early stages of the Hoi An mission, there were always a few Japanese priests. Christoforo Borri was assisted by a half-caste Japanese-Portuguese named Pedro Marquez. This was because the Japanese priests could read and write Han characters, necessary for their correspondence with the Vietnamese lords – and Chinese merchants. Equally important, through Japanese priests, the Jesuits could rely on obtaining inside information on Vietnam's political and economic scene from the Japanese residents in Hoi An.

For the Japanese had already begun to settle in Hoi An before the Jesuits appeared. Japanese traders, perhaps some of them pirates, came to Hoi An and stayed at least part of the year during the several months long trade fairs between monsoons. Many took Vietnamese wives, who proved to be extremely useful in business as translators and negotiators with local tradesmen and farmers. And they looked after the business while their husbands were at the other end of the trade run in Japan.

The Portuguese priests noted that di Pini's preaching in Vietnamese was far more effective than that of the priests using interpreters. There was nothing for it; all of the priests would have to learn Vietnamese. Christoforo Borri and Francesco di Pini set to work on a dictionary. First came the phonetic transcription of Vietnamese into Romanised script. A number of words were transcribed according to Borri's Italian pronunciation; others followed the rules of di Pini's Portuguese. For some time the transcription was not governed by a consistent set of rules.

Borri observed that 'the language they speak daily differs a lot from the one they teach and read while studying.' This was because of the relationship – or lack or it – between Vietnamese and Chinese; they do not belong to the same language family. That the Vietnamese used Han Chinese characters *(chu nom)* to write their language was merely because the Viet nation to the north, without a written script of its own, had borrowed the written language of its neighbour for use in documents and literature, while using its own language for everyday communication. To cope with this complicated situation, the priests made use of their experience in transcribing Chinese and Japanese into Romanised script. Despite Christoforo Borri being Italian, the diacritical markings indicating pronunciation and tones of their transcription were mainly Portuguese.

Back in Europe, a year before his death, Christoforo Borri published in Rome in 1631, *An Account of the New Mission of Jesuit Fathers in the Kingdom of Dang Trong*. The book, now preserved in the Library of the Vatican, was the first written by a Westerner, giving detailed descriptions of many aspects of Vietnam and Vietnamese life: its boundaries, climate, flora and fauna; its traditions, customs and costumes; its language, religions, family and social structure. In it, he favourably compares the Vietnamese to the Chinese, describes elephant and rhinoceros hunting, the custom of a guest washing his feet before entering a Vietnamese house and the civility of a host in sharing with guests whatever food he may have, however meagre.

The book was immediately reprinted in Milan. Three French translations followed in Paris, Lille and Rennes and in the following two years, it was translated into Latin, Dutch, German and English.

In Borri's Romanised Vietnamese *quoc ngu*, there was only one accent, namely a falling tone, an accent that occurs in Italian. This may have been because the Jesuits had not yet sorted out a full system of diacritical markings – or simply that the printers of Rome in 1631 had not yet cast *quoc ngu* printing types. Borri's book carried only a few short, simple sentences in *quoc ngu*, considered by later scholars to be rather rudimentary.

Christoforo Borri's departure from Hoi An in 1622 was followed in late 1624 by the arrival of a new French missionary, Alexandre de Rhodes. After a year spent learning Japanese in Macau, poor man, he was then faced with learning Vietnamese.

'I must confess that when I first arrived in Dang Trong and heard the natives speak, especially women, I thought I was hearing birds chirping and I lost all hope of learning the language.' But learn it he did, sufficiently by 1627 to be given the important mission of taking Christianity and Catholicism to the northern part of the country where he was to establish a mission in Dang Ngoai (Hanoi). After Francesco di Pini and Christoforo Borri, Alexandre de Rhodes was the third Western missionary to speak Vietnamese fluently.

116

De Rhodes recalled how a little native boy in three weeks had taught him the different sounds of Vietnamese, although the child knew not a word of French and de Rhodes not a word of Vietnamese. He also related his misadventures in the language. Once when he asked his cook to buy fish, *ca* in Vietnamese, the cook returned with a basket of aubergines – the difference in pronunciation being in the tones. He also recalled ordering his men to cut down some bamboo, *chem tre* in Vietnamese – and all the children ran away. In his mispronunciation of *chem tre,* he had ordered the men to 'kill the children!' What so baffled the missionaries was not just the pronunciation, but the tonality of Vietnamese – six different tones in the North, five in the South.

For a long time, the French credited the monumental task of developing *quoc ngu* to Alexandre de Rhodes alone, as it was he who published a French-Latin-Portuguese-Quoc Ngu dictionary and the catechism in 1651. Subsequent scholars unanimously agree that *quoc ngu* was undoubtedly created, developed and refined as a continuing, cooperative effort by Portuguese, Italian and French priests and was certainly not the work of any one individual.

From the brief excerpts included in Christoforo Borri's book to the books published by Alexandre de Rhodes, *quoc ngu* had made a great leap forward to a systematic, theoretically based script. The diacritical markings of de Rhodes's *quoc ngu* are very similar to those of present-day *quoc ngu.*

A JAPANESE BRIDGE

At the end of Tran Phu Street stands an old, arched, covered bridge. You step over the humble beam of the threshold as you might enter a pagoda, which serves the modern function of prohibiting motorbikes inside the darkened, almost hallowed space, not unlike a chapel. In the early morning or late at night in the dark after the tourists have gone, you might have stepped back into the sixteenth century.

A pair of sculpted stone dogs sits obediently inside the entrance, a pair of monkeys beside the exit to Nguyen Thi Minh Khai Street. The story goes that building of the Japanese Bridge began in the Year of the Dog and ended in the Year of the Monkey, sometime in the 1590s. The old bridge has been restored and rebuilt at least six times in the past four hundred years.

In the warm, brown gloom of old wood, especially if the doors are closed, it is easy to overlook the tiny temple, hidden in the central span on the north side of the bridge. The Vietnamese script over the temple door, Lai Van Kieu, translates as Bridge for Friends from Afar, a reference to Confucius: 'Friends coming from afar, isn't that a pleasure.' The Nguyen lord, Nguyen Phuc Chu, named it Lai Van Kieu in 1719, but somehow the name never quite caught on with the locals, who still call it Chua Cau, Pagoda Bridge.

This being Vietnam, building the bridge was based around a legend. A *mamazu,* a monster so huge that its head was in India, its body in Vietnam, its tail in Japan, was known to bring floods and earthquakes to Japan. The bridge, rather like a sword in his back, was meant to pin down the monster, so that Japan would be protected from earthquakes and Hoi An from floods and other natural disasters. The tiny temple is dedicated to the god against floods and drought, Bac De Tran Vu, both of which have afflicted Hoi An over the centuries. The monsoon season in Hoi An is sufficiently serious for Hoi An's roof tiles to grow velvety green moss and for colour postcards to show people in boats, rowing through the streets, the water reaching half way up their doors.

Every year during the rainy season (October to January), Hoi An floods once or twice. A glance at the surrounding countryside answers the question of why they didn't just move the town to higher ground – there is no higher ground, unless they had moved inland to the mountains and they were seafaring people, needing to be near the port for trade. As for why they didn't build their houses on stilts like the Chams, well, as they weren't Chams, they didn't build like Chams, they built in their own tradition.

Enshrined among the treasures of present-day Jomyo Temple of Gencho San in the town of Tsusui (Nagoya, Japan) is a stone statue of Avalokitesvara, the Buddhist goddess of mercy, and a famous scroll from the Edo period, describing a voyage to central Vietnam made by Chaya Shinrokuro Masachika in the time of Tokugawa Ieyasu. The scroll has come to be known as the Sea Map – Trade with the State of Jiaozhi (the Japanese name for Hoi An). Most of what we know about the Japanese in Hoi An is taken from the notes made by Shinrokuro on his scroll. Chaya Shinrokuro, who died in 1698, was a Nakashima, one of the three wealthiest families in Kyoto; the Chaya of Nagoya was a branch of that family. Chaya Shinrokuro made several voyages from Japan to Jiaozhi between 1615 and 1624. Whether Shinrokuro drew the scroll, his pictorial travelogue, while he was in Hoi An or from memory, is not known.

The Sea Map contains not only his map and notes on the trade route, but drawings of Japanese vessels leaving Nagasaki, his arrival at what is now Danang and his ship being towed up the Tra Co river by three pilot vessels. He drew the straw huts on stilts he observed in the Tang (Chinese) sector, described as 'the quarter of neighbouring people, who made a living by towing Chaya ships from Danang to Jiaozhi.' Most interesting of all, towards the end of the scroll are his drawings of Japanese Street in Jiaozhi – Hoi An – as it looked in the seventeenth century. I was delighted to find a copy of part of the Sea Map in Hoi An's Museum of History, illustrating not only Hoi An's Japanese houses, but a large Japanese junk being towed by three long boats manned by oarsmen.

In the early, upper part of the scroll are sketches of two-storey houses and five people, possibly members of the Chaya family, bidding him farewell in Nagoya. Further along, a house in Nagasaki serves as the backdrop for a man, perhaps Shinrokuro and four youths, chatting to foreigners. For some time, Nagasaki was the only Japanese port into which foreign ships were allowed.

As depicted on the scroll, Jiaozhi's Japanese Street was about three blocks long, close to a river and unlike the Tang sector, consisted of ornate, two-storey houses, built on the ground, very close to one another with overlapping roofs. Naturally, the Japanese built houses in the same style as the homes they had left in Japan, houses that served as homes, offices and warehouses. Two of the houses have three stories, elaborately built in the Kyoto style, suggesting that they might have been meeting places for the Japanese community in Jiaozhi. Most of the Jiaozhi houses face the street with verandas or covered arcades to shield people from the sun or from being drenched by monsoon rains. The draughtsmanship of Japanese Street is exceedingly detailed. Pillars on the upper and lower stories have been very carefully drawn, very straight.

The houses of Nagoya and Nagasaki at the beginning of the scroll depict exactly the same style of architecture as the houses on Japanese Street at the end of the Sea Map, the only architectural departure being the verandas supported by pillars in Jiaozhi. What the houses of Nagoya, Nagasaki and Japanese Street have particularly in common is their rafters, *udatsu* in Japanese, lifted up to allow heightened elevation of the roofs, for commercial warehousing.

Udatsu is a term that appears in several Japanese proverbs: 'High rafters, good business' *(udatsu ga agaru);* 'trying without being able to get higher' *(sapari udatsu ga agararei)* – so there were glass ceilings, even in sixteenth and seventeenth century Japan.

In describing the forty-day, eighteen hundred nautical-mile (2,880 km) voyage south of his *shuinsen* ship, Shinrokuro tells how during the voyage he felt quite lost in an endless sea. When a storm broke, the wind tearing at the sails, huge waves tossing and swamping the vessel, poor Shinrokuro, terrified and fearing disaster, prayed aloud, beseeching Avalokitesvara to come to their aid. At once, the sea calmed.

On his arrival in Jiaozhi, Shinrokuro tells how he presented the king of Annam – by then the Nguyen lords called themselves kings – with a multi-coloured robe from Japan, which pleased the king extremely well. He hosted Shinrokuro to good wine and Hue's delicate rice cakes and politely asked him about his country. Did the Japanese believe in Buddhism? Shinrokuro confirmed that Buddhism was Japan's predominant religion and Avalokitesvara, its most sacred deity. He then related to the king his experience of the terrifying storm at sea and how praying to Avalokitesvara had saved them. The king was very moved and presented Shinrokuro with a gift: 'Take this statue of Avalokitesvara. It is from India, its beauty is matchless, take it together with our respect.'

On the return voyage the ship again was struck by a storm and had to drop anchor for a day and a night, the fog so thick that nothing could be seen. An old man on board came forward to tell a story: 'Once a ship was sailing from Japan to China with a valuable cargo including gems. As the sea god had a liking for gems, he raised a big storm. So the cause of this present storm may be the statue of Avalokitesvara.' Once again, everyone on board prayed aloud and once again, the storm calmed and the ship returned home safely. It is this same statue of Avalokitesvara that now resides in Jomyo Temple of Gencho San in the town of Tsusui (Nagoya, Japan).

During their early years in Hoi An, while China's Closed-Door Policy remained in force, the Japanese hunger for fine silk and ceramics was partially satisfied by Vietnamese exports. The Japanese ceramics industry remained relatively undeveloped and only began to develop in the sixteenth century, their techniques far behind those of Vietnam where celadon and white porcelain had been produced since the eleventh century. Quite a few Vietnamese ceramics were brought to Japan during the fifteenth and sixteenth centuries, valued and revered by the Japanese as exotic *objets d'arts* from abroad. It was about this time that the tea ceremony was coming into vogue in urban Japan, demanding fine quality ceramics.

Apart from silver, the Japanese exported tons and tons of copper coins. Worn out, poor quality, privately minted Japanese coins called *bitasen* were removed from circulation in Japan and sold abroad by enterprising Japanese merchants in Hoi An at a high multiple of their value in Japan. In Hue, they were melted down and converted into cannons by the Nguyen lords – a very useful cargo – to use against their enemies in the North, the Trinh. The prominent feature of Nagasaki coins was the large square hole in the centre (some of them in Hoi An's History Museum).

The mystery and controversy that raged for years concerning the location of Japanese Street and Chinese Street has finally, and only recently, been solved by scholars. Tran Phu Street, east of the Japanese Bridge, was Japanese Street; Chinese Street was on the far, west side of the bridge, Nguyen Thi Minh Khai Street.

When the Japanese announced their Closed-Door Policy *(sakoku)* in 1636, *shuinsen* trade was banned and Japanese residents in Hoi An were ordered home to Japan or be 'excommunicated'. Most returned to Japan, but the record of a Japanese merchant's contribution to a Buddhist temple in Hoi An in 1640 proves that at least a few Japanese stayed on. And a few Japanese graves dot the rice fields just outside of Hoi An.

When the Japanese left Hoi An in 1636, they consigned their trade in copper coins to the Dutch East India Company (VOC), whose trade with Japan multiplied exponentially as they took over the trade of the *shuinsen* ships. What a pity that William Adams (died 1620) never lived to see it. The Dutch maintained a factory (warehouse) in Hoi An from 1636 to 1741, Dutch factors, like the Japanese before them, often marrying Vietnamese wives. Dutch VOC records relating to Vietnam – the North (Tonkin) and the South (Quinam) – run to some seven thousand pages, handwritten in early Dutch, which today only scholars can decipher. A few headings of these VOC reports addressed to their superiors in Amsterdam give some idea of the swashbuckling nature of trade in South East Asia in those days and of just how dangerous seafaring remained.

– Diaries of the ship *Keijser* sailing from Taiwan to Batavia and sunk in Pandodang Bay off the shore of Champa, 18/1/1637

And what looks very like a report of Dutch piracy –
– Statistics and evaluation of goods obtained from Portuguese boats off the shore of Champa, 2/2/1637

Then a string of records reporting disasters –
– Copy of the letter by Dutch prisoners from Quinam sent to Paulus Traudenius, 19/7/1642
– Copy of the declaration by Corporal Juriaem de Booden on the barbarities of the Portuguese from Macau towards 50 Dutch people addressing the King of Quinam, 2/7/1643
– Copy of the letter sent to Dutch prisoners in Quinam, 30/3/1647
– Letter of merchant Gerrit Voogt and his second-in-command Pieter Kesteloot sent to the Governor in Batavia, written in Faifo, Cochinchina, 31/1/1716
– Manifest of the crew of the ship *Arion* leaving Japan but sunk in the middle of the trip and of those still alive in Cochin China, 22/2/1716
– Letter from the King of Cochin China sent to Mr Blom (including) two permits and bonus from the King sent to the boats and personnel of the Company.

– Account by merchant Gerrit Voogt on victims of ship *Arion* who have returned by Chinese boat and on events since the ship left Japan as well as sufferings after the ship was sunk, 14/3/1716

– Information from a Chinese named Kiqua about four Dutchmen and one black boy on the *Arion* seen staying on Paracell Islands, 12/4/1717

– Report by deputy head merchant Pieter Lestekoot related to the information by a Chinese named Kiqua coming to Batavia in 1717 from Cochin China saying that two persons, probably Europeans and two aides, died in Cochinchina, 12/4/1717

In the seventeenth century, the Dutch East India Company (VOC) was riding high. The Dutch had replaced the Portuguese in the Moluccas spice trade. In India they took Surat in 1612, Madras in 1629, Bombay in 1668, Pondicherry in 1674, Calcutta in 1698, and they gradually overshadowed Portuguese Goa. The VOC had seized Malacca from the Portuguese in 1641. The Spaniards were in Manila, the Portuguese in Macao.

In 1661, the VOC lost Formosa (Taiwan) to Koxinga, last of the seafaring adventurers of the South China Sea, born of a Chinese father and a Japanese mother – in fact, related to the Ming. The Qing dynasty, having defeated and succeeded the Ming in 1644, again closed China to trade, this time not against Japanese pirates but against Koxinga! Following Koxinga's surrender in 1681, the Qing government reopened China and once again admitted foreign ships.

The VOC's trade between Hoi An and Japan continued until new regulations, restricting first the export of silver as mines in Japan were worked out, then copper in 1715, were imposed by Japan.

OLD PAGODAS AND TEMPLES

The crumbling, yellow and white gate stands deep in long grass, mouldering in the humid climate, the paint on the wooden doors of the three arches long faded. A sapling grows out of the top. But at least they have kept the gate to what is considered to be Hoi An's earliest pagoda, Chuc Thanh. Obligingly, Pho has brought me on his motorbike a couple of miles north of Hoi An to visit it.

Anticipating an old pagoda, I am disappointed to find Chuc Thanh glittering with colourful embellishments, pristine in detail, a wide, low building on a grand scale behind its formal courtyard almost glowing in the mid-afternoon sun. It could be a state monument to Buddhism.

What I have forgotten is that unlike stone cathedrals in the West, which people continued building through several centuries before completion, then left them to accrete a patina of age, in a hot moist climate where construction is of wood, brick and tiles, when buildings deteriorate quickly, often they are torn down and completely rebuilt. To a Westerner accustomed to sombre cathedrals, Vietnamese pagodas and temples can appear to be almost frivolous in their extravagantly colourful decorations. At Chuc Thanh, a colossal white statue of Quan The Am stares down implacably over the courtyard from boulders to one side. Rapacious dragons ripple along the ridge line of the central hall of worship; defiant phoenix sparkle from the eaves. Inside, two monks in saffron robes are chanting prayers, alternately striking a gong and tapping a wooden *mo,* carved in the shape of a carp.

'Because the carp never sleeps, always watchful and aware, to keep out evil,' Pho explains.

Buddhism has long thrived in the Thu Bon valley. Although Buddhism became the state religion for a brief time in ninth century Indrapura, possibly under the influence of Chinese monks, after the fall of Indrapura, Cham rulers further south reverted to Hindu Saivism, the worship of Siva.

Archaeological finds testify to there having been a Chinese presence in Hoi An since before the dawn of the Christian era, Chinese administrators and traders. Furthermore, a number of old tombstone stelae bear witness to the existence of a community of Chinese living in and around Hoi An by 1437. Most probably, this Chinese community lived in Cam Pho hamlet along Nguyen Thai Minh Khai Street, later known as Chinese Street, on the far side of the stream – before the Japanese Bridge was built.

With the lifting of China's trade blockade in 1567, historians note the rush south of Chinese traders to the ports of central Vietnam, without saying whether or not they came to settle or merely to trade. What is known for certain is that the fall of the Ming dynasty in 1644 brought waves of immigrants fleeing south to Hoi An from several provinces of southern China – to escape persecution. The present-day Chinese community of Hoi An commemorates as its ancestors, ten Ming mandarins who fled, the Ten Great Fathers, their clan names Khong, Nhan, Du, Tu, Chu, Hoang, Truong, Tran, Thai and Luu.

This community of Ming immigrants founded Minh Huong village, located in what are now Le Loi and Tran Phu Streets. Minh translates as Ming, Huong means homeland. In the seventeenth century, Minh Huong became virtually synonymous with Faifo, the name for Hoi An that appears on early Portuguese navigational maps. It is thought that after the Japanese departed from Hoi An in 1636, that many Chinese residents of Cam Pho moved across the Japanese Bridge into what had been Japanese Street, Tran Phu Street.

A Chinese Buddhist monk, Thich Dai San, recorded his impressions in 1693: 'Hoi An is a big seaport, a meeting place for merchants from many countries. The main road, three to four leagues long, runs along the bank of the river; it is bordered on both sides by closely built houses inhabited by people who came from Fukien. They wear the clothing of the previous (Ming) dynasty. The street ends at the Japanese Bridge, in other words Cam Pho; on the other bank at Tra Nhieu, foreign vessels moored.'

The Viets in those days for the most part did not live in Hoi An, but in the surrounding villages and countryside, working as farmers and craftsmen. One contemporary Hoi An resident asserts that eighty percent of the old quarter of Hoi An, formerly Minh Huong, was Chinese until very recently – as recently as 1975, after which there has been a rebalancing in the Chinese-Vietnamese population of the Old Town. Also, many surrounding areas where the Vietnamese were living have been incorporated in the new official boundaries of Hoi An – Cham Island(s) were only added in 1975. Having said that, the Chinese in Hoi An have become so integrated with the Vietnamese, having married Vietnamese women for many generations, that many today do not even speak Chinese, only Vietnamese.

On the 26th day of the first month of the Year of the Pig, 1695, a Chinese monk named Minh Hai travelled to Hoi An. In 1697 he built a modest hut in which to worship Buddha, which he called Lam Te. Through successive rebuildings, it has became known as Chuc Thanh pagoda and each year at the beginning of *Tet,* Vietnam's New Year celebration, a ceremony is held here to honour the anniversary of the death of its founder, Minh Hai.

An arched, covered bridge approaching kitsch is wedged between the main hall and the temple behind – to shelter the monks during the monsoons. Orchids bloom from hanging baskets. Yet somehow, despite the chanting monks, Chuc Thanh feels a bit soulless, exuding more of an aura of prosperous rectitude than of piousness. Adding to this feeling is the absence of worshippers. I console myself with the thought that come the first and fifteenth of the lunar month, crowds of the faithful will throng the hall of worship, falling to their knees, lighting joss sticks and raising their prayerful hands three times to their deities, sending up the perpetual pleas of humanity – for a bit more money, for a child, for better health, for a loved one.

We then putter off on Pho's motorbike to Van Duc pagoda, roughly three miles north-west of central Hoi An. Centuries ago when there was a sea entrance from Danang to the port of Cua Dai (Hoi An), ships travelled inland, behind a long slim island that ran parallel to the coast, along the Han river, then the Co Co river to a huge lake where they moored. From old maps, it looks as though Van Duc pagoda, founded in the late seventeenth or early eighteenth century, might have been sited near this lake, the lake now much diminished. Perhaps the pagoda even stood on the lake shore.

When I first arrived in Vietnam, as an inveterate temple tramp, I had wondered if the old religions would have survived the current political regime. I need not have worried. As Vietnamese scholar, Huu Ngoc, so elegantly put it, 'Lying dormant in the subconscious Vietnamese mind is an inclination towards Buddhism, which has been the basis for religion in Vietnam for eighteen centuries. The Vietnamese are attracted by the preaching of universal compassion rather than karma, non-self and nirvana.'

Confusing to the Westerner, pagodas *(chua)* are for Buddhist worship – and not to be confused with temples. And there are three different kinds of temples: *den* to honour historic, mythical or even local heroes and heroines, who have been deified; *dien* for Taoist spirits and immortals; *van tu* or *van chi* for the cult of Confucius.

None of them have convenient signs out front to tell you which they are. Village community halls *(dinh)* and the Chinese assembly halls of Hoi An perform the same functions as temples, as well as providing space for more secular activities – in the case of the Chinese, for business. A pair of ferocious temple lions guards the courtyard and the entrance to Van Duc pagoda. A young monk, looking not unlike a Buddha himself, offers to show us around. Dragons curl round the columns marking the triple entrance of the central hall. The monk obligingly translates the gilt Han Chinese characters on the three lacquer panels above: 'This is a place of peace and quiet; the name of the pagoda, Van Duc; and the souls of monks live in close relationship to the Buddha.'

Colourfully painted panels depict scenes from the life of Buddha: 'The first place where Buddha taught, Buddha attaining enlightenment and Sakyamuni as a new-born baby.'

A gargoyle-faced lion cradles a sturdy, spoked wheel in the centre of the roof ridge: 'The circle of life, symbol of the wisdom of Buddha, pouring out to the living.'

Dragons ripple at the extremities of the ridge line. At first, I have to smile when the monk says that the dragons are merely decoration, then corrects himself, remembering that dragons represent the symbol for power. A crane, 'symbol of long life,' peers out from a decorative panel to the left of the entrance; sparrows flutter amongst bamboo on the panel to the right. 'Sparrows are the symbol for those who take advantage of others.' So many strange symbols, an alien religious lexicon.

'Van Duc pagoda was most recently rebuilt in 1995,' volunteers the monk. This explains why it feels so brand spanking new. 'Each time the pagoda is rebuilt', he explains, 'it is built anew, changing, enlarging.' Very possibly, the old, extravagantly carved canopies, their paint flaking, that frame the life-sized, guardians with bulging eyes, glowering with raised swords beside the entrance, are the only survivors from an earlier period. A white elephant lopes across a lintel above one door – reminding me that Hoi An was elephant country, a lion above another door.

Inside, the three golden Buddhas of past, present and future sit side by side, unmoved, indifferent to the world, behind multi-coloured pennants fluttering from the beams. Parallel sentences hang from the columns. Unlike many pagodas, which are often dark, here an appealing painting of delicate wisps of bamboo against a pale blue sky lights the back wall of the hall of worship.

'Bamboo is the symbol of a good person, strong and flexible,' explains Pho. A solitary monk kneels, chanting, tapping his wooden carp. The scent of burning rises from several rows of lit candles.

'Each candle represents a dead person,' says Pho. 'The first of March is the time when many people come to celebrate ceremonies for the dead in order to give them a peaceful death in the next world.'

Round one side of the hall of worship, past a headily fragrant frangipani tree, the five holy mothers have been crowded together above a small altar in an open shed beside the old temple that formerly housed them.

'They had to be moved,' the monk explains, his brows knitting. Seeing the condition of the holy mothers' old temple, tumbled down, its tile roof sagging in a perilous state, brings home the precariousness of keeping pagodas – any buildings – in good nick in this hot, damp climate.

Beyond is a temple dedicated to notable monks. The young monk points to the portraits above the central altar, as he might to the portraits on a family altar.

'Two monks who came from China and built a small pagoda here more than four hundred years ago.' Photos of more recent monks flank the altar above glass-front cabinets containing Buddhist texts. Beneath each photo, a tablet records the monk's name, birthplace, date of birth and death – instead of tombstones – in red lacquer and gilt.

Behind the temple dedicated to the monks, potted bonsai stand in a rigid grid beside a community of stupas, the burial place for monks. Beyond, a miniature town of pastel-painted tombstones rises in contrast to the austerity of the stupas, a cemetery for ordinary mortals. As a vagabond, I muse on how satisfying it must be to know where your bones will be gently placed when you die.

So peaceful and quiet is it, you would hardly guess that you are only a few miles from the centre of Hoi An. The motorbike ride back passes bamboo swathed cottages and dense green paddies, their grain heads now tinged with gold, past a lake, beside a river.

Pedalling towards us comes a country bike tour of foreign visitors. For Hoi An's luxuriant pastoral beauty, their route has been well chosen.

Early next morning, before the marshalled battalions of tourists behind their flag-waving guides appear, I stroll along Tran Phu Street, formerly Japanese Street, where ironically, most of the Chinese community assembly halls have been sited. When the Japanese left Hoi An in 1636, the Chinese moved into their vacant houses, 'because they appreciated the higher standard of building of the Japanese,' explains one resident.

A Westerner, confronting Hoi An's old buildings – pagodas, temples, Chinese assembly halls and merchant houses – can feel slightly overwhelmed by so much busy, unfamiliar architectural detail, a concentration of baffling symbology: finials of beams carved in the form of a dragon's head, a squirrel, a cluster of grapes, a carp; peaches representing longevity and triumph over evil spirits; custard apples and pomegranates symbolizing fecundity; a plethora of carp, crabs, shrimp, serpents, monsters, the eight sacred weapons, fishermen, woodcutters, farmers, the four seasons.

The peculiar round wooden objects, always in pairs, attached to the lintel above an entrance are door eyes, the soul of an old house or public building: eight-petal chrysanthemums; bats, the Chinese symbol for happiness or the character for longevity; black and white yin-yang surrounded by a pair of dragons, the upper adoring the sun, the lower paying homage to the moon – the total representing the sun, the cosmos and the evolution of the world.

Opposite the market, Quan Cong temple, also known as Chua Ong, is one of Hoi An's oldest, thought to have been founded in 1653. Quan Cong was a Chinese general who lived during the Thuc Han dynasty at the time of the Three Kingdoms in the third century AD. Held in high regard throughout Vietnam for his valour, loyalty and sense of justice, people striking a bargain, even today, often meet and swear before his statue as we in the West might sign a contract. Quan Cong's statue stares out from the central altar, flanked on the left by a trusty general, on the right by his adopted son. The carved white horse that looks as if it might have leapt off a carousel was his steed.

Behind Quan Cong temple, Hoi An's Museum of History and Culture (now moved to the corner of Nguyen Hue and Tran Phu) was originally a Buddhist pagoda dedicated to the *bodhisattva*, Avalokitesvara, the goddess of mercy. Also known as the Quan Am temple and the Minh Huong temple, its date of founding is thought to have been sometime between 1753 and 1783. In the courtyard, a mynah bird chortles raucously at visitors from a cage beside the rock garden. It has to be said that a rock garden in Vietnam is quite something else from what a Brit or a Japanese might imagine, dangerously approaching gnome-land. It starts as a lump of rock or several rocks placed artfully together to form a mini-mountain. So far so good. Into the crevices all manner of small plants and orchids are introduced. This is never quite enough. Invariably, tiny plastic storks, frogs, a miniature temple, a tower, an arched bridge must be added to produce an extravagant three-dimensional miniature fantasy-land, a play-table for adults and usually, the centrepiece of a courtyard.

The Fukien Assembly Hall, first built in 1697 as the Kim Son temple by the people who migrated from Fukien province, belies its age. Painted monsters on the old gate 'represent two vampires, who were so impressed by the pure goodness of a young girl seeking medicine for her sick mother in the terrifying dark mountain forests that they were converted into – good monsters,' the guide told me on my first visit. Through a modern pillared gate under a green tiled roof with turned up corners, I find myself in a courtyard where stone lions guard a flight of stairs – a miniature version of the approach to the royal palace of the Purple Forbidden City in Beijing.

The temple behind the assembly hall is dedicated to the Tao goddess of the sea, Thien Hau, protector of those first waves of Chinese refugees fleeing to Hoi An. 'Thien Hau's magical powers enable her to travel on a flying mat above the waves with her assistants to rescue sailors and fishermen. One of her assistants has the power to see for a thousand miles, those in need of help, the other assistant to hear for a thousand miles.'

The temple also commemorates six commanders, loyal to the Ming dynasty, who fell in battle. The Six Families are honoured here every year at a festival held in the second lunar month.

'The high threshold forces people to bow their heads reverently.' Inside is a large wooden replica of a Chinese junk, exactly the kind of boat that brought the waves of Chinese immigrants from Fukien to Hoi An. Atop its masts, carp weathervanes – the symbol of abundance and expected success – provide a good omen for seafarers.

'The temple is popular with young couples, wishing for a child. The altars are dedicated to ancestors, to prosperity and to the goddesses of birth, the twelve midwives' – giving a fair indication of Chinese priorities.

The rather grand Duong Thong Assembly Hall, also known as the Five Chinese Communities Hall, was built with the combined contributions from the Fukien, Zhao Zhou, Canton, Hainan and Jiain communities in 1741 – as a place for fellow countrymen to meet and help one another in business. A stone stele from the same year, the Duong Thuong Rules, laid down the ten principles for the Chinese doing business in Hoi An. One of these rules stated that all Chinese who marry Vietnamese women must register the marriage at the community hall and the name of each child as it was born, like church registers of marriages, births and death.

Exquisitely carved filigree clings to the beams above the gate. The curling green wrought iron railings of the side pavilions, alongside a courtyard blooming with potted oleander bushes, might have been lifted from New Orleans.

Past two vicious black-skinned guardians, constrained in glass cases beside the entrance, the main hall is dedicated to the female deity, Thien Hau, the same Tao goddess honoured in the Fukien Assembly Hall. Here she wears a square, golden crown and holds a candle, surrounded by four female attendants. Two carry fans on long poles, another a box that looks like a present with a bow on top, the fourth, what might be a roll of silk. The statues form a life-sized group beneath a gilt canopy of carved cranes, bamboo and birds in flowering trees. A smaller version of the same goddess sits on a red lacquer and gilt dragon altar, this time wearing an elaborate beaded silkrobe embroidered with a red, pink, blue and green phoenix. I wonder if it was bequeathed by a silk merchant.

Once your own cultural associations slip away – no blood-dripping St Sebastians, no crucified Redeemer – you realise that Buddhism and Taoism are, indeed, much gentler religions. To one side, another boat model perhaps ten feet long, carries two sails, tiny altars aft and mid-deck, a miniature kitchen complete with minuscule terracotta pots – a replica of the kind of boats that bore the immigrants fleeing China. As they are folded, at first you don't notice the beautifully carved and painted doors into the main hall until you are leaving: cranes, deer, birds and phoenix. A Chinese paradise.

131

The stone temple dogs guarding the entrance to the Hainan Assembly Hall have proved utterly ineffectual against the hat and bag shop set up under the gate. The shops have even crept into the courtyard: piles of necklaces, lanterns on shelves, well-established shops. Then again, perhaps this is how the Chinese community halls were originally used, as shopping centres.

A trouserless toddler kicks a ball with other little boys in the paved courtyard. Potted pink oleanders, jasmine and areca palms stand in straight ranks forming an avenue to where two topiary deer stand nose to nose at the entrance to the hall. Carved ebony, antique chairs with round inset marble backs line the sides of the vestibule. Gleaming red lacquer pillars stride the hall towards the impressive gilt altar, three hundred years old – an intricately carved and lacquered, three dimensional court scene, protected under glass. The gilt canopy provides a roost for cranes in pines, musicians and men with bird cages amongst flowers. Another Chinese paradise.

The Hainan Assembly Hall was built in 1875 to commemorate more than one hundred Hainan merchants killed in error by retainers of the Nguyen king, Tu Duc, who took them for pirates. In guilty retribution, Tu Duc donated funds to build this assembly hall in which the fallen merchants have been deified.

The red columned gate under a green tiled roof of the Cantonese Assembly Hall might have been built yesterday. In fact, it dates from 1885. A king-sized dragon, his chipped ceramic scales sparkling, romps in the rock pool of the courtyard. Flowering vines gush from the roofs of the two open side halls where tawny dragons creep round the red pillars. A dozen spiral joss sticks burn from the beams of the main hall of worship, amongst red silk lanterns. Carved foliage clings to the beam between the central pillars and above the carved, gilt altar. Here the Cantonese revere Confucius and the holy mother, again the Tao goddess Thien Hau, Quan Kung and of course, their ancestors – if you can get past the militant ticket checkers at the gate!

Every day I walk along Nguyen Thi Minh Kai Street on the far side of the Japanese Bridge, my favourite street in Hoi An because the people here seem to retain such a close knit community. They sit at the doors of their shops, chatting to one another and unlike Tran Phu and Nguyen Thai Hoc Streets, the people here have stayed for the most part in their ancestral homes and not rented them out, but keep shop themselves.

In this street, what looks like a pagoda turns out to be Cam Pho Community Hall, 'built a long time ago and restored in 1817.' Whenever I stop by, there is never anyone about, compared to the hordes in the Chinese assembly halls.

Open-sided meeting halls to left and right form an inverted, square U-shaped building. Into the wide courtyard, paved with homely Bat Trang bricks, extends an open, central vestibule, a study in heavy hardwood pillars resting on lotus shaped 'vases', their beams supported by coloured china ceramic braces, their huge china finials forming lotus buds.

Rollicking dragons dance across half the ridge line of the roof; in the centre, a cluster of clouds supports the sun – or moon – the turned up eaves embellished with flamboyant phoenix and a bird, possibly a crane, flapping its wings about to take off.

Artful collages composed of ceramic chips form a colourful cornice under the eaves: yellow and white flowers on a branch, birds perched in a flowering peach tree, cranes and deer among pines.

Inside, each of the three alcoves holds an altar, above which hang gilt Han Chinese characters, framed by more carved red lacquer and gilt. Here, the wooden altars bear painted tableaux: a pheasant amongst chrysanthemums, a phoenix paired with a flying dragon, a pheasant amongst flowers. Truly, one of Hoi An's most enchanting, rarely visited examples of local folk art.

Above the shop at 83 Tran Phu Street hangs a wooden panel announcing Calligraphy. I am led inside and introduced to Su Chan Quan, a sturdy man with salt and pepper hair wearing square, metal framed glasses, an open-neck white shirt and white knee length shorts. He is sitting at a desk, black framed samples of calligraphy hanging on the surrounding walls.

Mr Quan obligingly translates his samples: 'Success, Virtue, Heart, Patience, Happy Birthday, Love, Be Happy, I Love You, Hope, Longevity, Wealth, Happiness' – reflecting the wishes of the numerous patrons who have passed by his door: $2 each.

Su Chan Quan is the third generation of a Hoi An Chinese family. His grandfather dealt in Chinese medicines, which he imported from Hainan Island, himself having migrated from Hainan. His son, Mr Quan's father, carried on the business.

'But I didn't. I studied pedagogy at the university in Hue and taught in Hoi An High School – Vietnamese literature. I am now retired.'

Su Chan Quan has five brothers and five sisters, now living in Danang and Ho Chi Minh City. His children live in Danang and work in computers.

Had his father or grandfather taught him Chinese?

'No, from the age of seven until I left to go to university at sixteen, I attended Hoi An's private Chinese school, supported by the Hoi An Chinese community. There I learnt calligraphy. The school accommodates just over a hundred pupils.'

I ask him about the calligraphy.

'Also people's names, written in Chinese.' He gets out a folder with more samples of calligraphy. Slightly larger samples carry short poems: *Tranquillity, Love, Zen* – $15 a poem. What a choice.

COME TO THE FAIR

Every year during the sixteenth and seventeenth centuries, they came. When Chinese and Japanese merchants wished to trade, they made a date for the Faifo fair.

Come the north-east trade winds of January, merchant ships from China, Japan and Portugal (Macau) would set sail south, bound for Faifo. The north-easterly winds blew from January to March; the dry months from February to August provided ideal conditions for a long, open-air trade fair held on the banks of the Thu Bon river.

Towards the end of the trading season in July or August when the winds swung round to blow from the south-east, the merchant ships would lift anchor and set sail northward for home, hoping to beat the typhoons. The Portuguese priest, Carvalho, noted, 'People saw the Chinese merchants bringing much silk yarn and silk there and the Japanese bought it all to take home!'

Italian priest Christoforo Borri noted the typical trade pattern in Faifo: 'Trade with Dang Trong (Cochin China-Annam) was chiefly done by the Chinese and the Japanese at a nearly four month long fair . . . The Japanese used to bring in 40,000 to 50,000 *taels* of sterling silver. The Chinese came on sailing boats together with numerous vessels which they called *sommes,* bringing a great quantity of fine silk, silk yarn and other goods.'

In the words of Chinese writer, Thich Dai San, visiting Faifo in 1695, 'Along the coastline, the rocks are rugged, monkeys gambol in the trees, there are wild flowers and fruits of every colour everywhere. Seen from afar, the shore resembles a forest of masts and one learns that these are junks transporting supplies, anchored, awaiting the wind. Mostly, the women take care of the commercial dealings. Many Chinese residents have married local women in order to facilitate negotiations.'

Thich Dai San also observed that carts and people with bamboo poles carry heavy loads to the market from before sunrise. 'All day people buy and sell vegetables, fish, fruits and shellfish. Here one can find medications that do not exist in the capital . . . The city is close to the sea on three sides . . . A type of garrison to defend against foreigners is about ten leagues from the city.'

135

Faifo's trade was closely related with the commercial town of Thanh Ha, which lay closer to the Nguyen authorities at Phu Xuan (later Hue). Although the Nguyen lords were eager to receive gifts, commodities and port fees from visiting merchants, for reasons of security, only a limited number of foreign vessels, mostly Chinese, were permitted to call and dispose of their goods at Thanh Ha, then allowed to proceed to Phu Xuan for an audience at the Nguyen lord's palace. Ships from elsewhere, especially Western ships, were compelled to anchor at Faifo.

Consequently, goods sold in Faifo were always more diverse and less expensive than those in Thanh Ha. In fact, many foreign traders preferred to trade in Faifo where there were looser controls and lower duties. Moreover, since the country had been divided since 1627, trade between Dang Trong (Cochin China, the South) and Dang Ngoai (Tonkin, the North) was illegal – and conducted by traders from the North, who slipped into Faifo to sell goods, then smuggled bronze coins back to the North.

Full of wonder in 1776, the historian Le Quy Don wrote: 'The products (in Faifo) are so abundant that even one hundred large junks would not be sufficient to load them all at one time. The goods are quickly sold; there is no leftover inventory. The goods imported (by the Chinese) are quite varied and the exchanges fulfil all requests.'

Le Quy Don listed Chinese exports as gauze (silk), satin, multicoloured brocade, hundreds of pharmaceutical ingredients, gold and silver leaf, gold and silver chains, perfume, paper of all sorts, ink, needles, buttons, furniture, objects made of copper and pewter, porcelain – the list seemed endless.

He also described the formalities: 'When a foreign ship comes to Quang Nam for commercial purposes, either by the sea mouth of Dai Chiem to go to Faifo or through Danang to go to Buy Lau, it must offer products of its country (to the Nguyen lord) and pay the stated import-export taxes.' Foreign vessels were most heavily taxed, based on their greater volume:

Western countries	8,000 *quan*
Macau (Portugal) and Japan	4,000
Shanghai and Guangdong, Fukien	3,000
Siam and the Philippines	3,000
Hainan (China) and Cuu Cang (Singapore)	500
Ha Tien (Vietnam) and Son Do (Vietnam)	300

The Nguyen lords exercised strict control; they held virtually a monopoly over trade in and out of Central and South Vietnam. Le Quy Don explains how the feudal system worked.

'It was the old stipulation by the Nguyen lords that all the regions pay tribute in gold, silver, sandalwood and tortoise shell for the royal consumption . . . salt, fish sauce, refined sugar, granular sugar, green beans, white linen, Thuan Thanh mats, paper, rhinoceros horn, earthenware, elephant tusks, *buon* leaves, black wood, bronze bells, are to be sent to the royal storehouses.'

Doing business in Hoi An carried with it certain risks. As well as paying port duties on arrival, ship owners were required to present themselves in a ceremony and chance having their goods confiscated. If the Nguyen lord wished to buy any goods, he would order his mandarin in charge of the ship to place the goods in the State warehouses for purchase. The captain and the pilot would follow them to handle the scales and only the goods the lord did not buy could be sold in the market!

Two chief mandarin controlled foreign trade; only they were permitted to buy foreign goods for the Nguyen lord's consumption and to sell gold, iron and ivory to foreigners. The State exercised a strict monopoly over the purchase of certain foreign goods such as metals – bronze, zinc alloys and ready-made weapons.

The Nguyen lord and the high-ranking mandarin themselves were speculators, profiteers, and sometimes producers of false goods and even counterfeiters. Though the Nguyen lord bought goods early in the year, the sellers had to wait until June for the lord to pay. The mandarin also bought goods, but deferred payment until the end of the trading season when the ships were ready to leave port. And then, now and again the merchants had to accept forged coins or worse, occasionally traders received no payment at all by the end of the trading season when their ships had to leave.

In a win-win arrangement for the Nguyen lord, those merchants who wanted to buy goods from the lord had to pay for them in advance and when the end of the trading season came, the lord or his mandarin might fail to supply sufficient goods.

Despite these complications, relations between the Nguyen lords and the Japanese proved to be quite profitable and therefore cordial. Lord Nguyen Phuc Nguyen, the second Nguyen lord, even married one of his four daughters to a Japanese merchant, Araki

Shutaro and in 1619, wrote welcoming him into to the royal family under the name of Nguyen Taro Hien Hung. Building on his father's earlier encouragement to foreign trade, the second Nguyen lord, Nguyen Phuc Nguyen, was without doubt the architect of Hoi An's prosperity. As a young prince entrusted with the administration of the markets of Quang Nam, he had paid great attention to the ports. Of the thirteen known letters between the Nguyens and Japan, twelve carry his name and title: *thuy quoc cong,* King of Annam.

Produce was funnelled through Faifo down river from the hinterland and from the southernmost regions of Central Vietnam by boat and by horse drawn cart. Silk topped the list of Hoi An's exports. All of the villages along the rivers of Quang Ngai and Quy Nhon to the south planted mulberry bushes and raised silk worms.

According to French traveller, Pierre Poivre in 1774, 'Dang Trong (Cochin China-Annam) silk products surpass Chinese products in quality and delicacy of design. The best come from Quang Ngai. Chinese merchants buy up a lot and make ten to fifteen per cent profit from sales.'

Pierre Poivre also noted 'stocks of twenty to eighty *quintals* of sugar that would have required eighty junks to transport.' Sugar was sold in various processed forms: powder, spongy lumps or candy.

Sea swallows' nests, highly prized by the Chinese and later by Japanese and Western merchants, originally collected from Cham Island(s) off Hoi An and from other offshore islands, were a delicacy reserved for delivery to the Nguyen authorities – for export only.

Le Quy Don goes on to excaim, 'It is impossible to list all the pharmaceutical ingredients (for traditional medicines), which number in the hundreds, as well as nutmeg and cardamom, rhinoceros horn, deer ligaments, shark fins, dried shrimp, sea turtle shells and elephant tusks.' Exportation of timber, rhinoceros horn and elephant tusks drew the highland tribal people into the export business. Aromatic woods, sandalwood and *aquilaria* – the *sanfi* of the Arab traders – were also valuable hinterland products, transported down river from the mountainous forests.

'The most valuable privilege granted by the local seigneur to the skipper of the *Malacca* is the right to trade in *tram huong,'* wrote Christoforo Borri. 'This sandalwood' – confusingly, he then proceeds to call it *calamba* – 'where it is gathered is valued at five ducats the pound; yet at the port of Cochin China (Hoi An), it yields more and is scarcely to be had for under sixteen ducats the pound; and being

138

transported to Japan, it is valued at two hundred ducats the pound . . . with a piece of such greatness that a man lay his head on it as on a pillow, the Japanese will give three hundred or four hundred ducats to the pound.'

The people of Tra My in the hinterland south-west of Hoi An, specialized in producing cinnamon, as well as the province of Quang Ngai, south of Hoi An. Other products exported through Faifo included dried areca nuts, pepper, fine furniture and ceramics.

Moreover, Faifo's prosperity as a port spurred the production of pottery for shipping containers at the nearby village of Thanh Ha and wooden boxes from the village of Kim Bong to transport cinnamon and the thousands of tonnes of sugar. Then as now, Kim Bong built boats and ships, in those days ranging from sixty to two hundred tonnes.

The passing British trader, Chapman, declared, 'Dang Trong is gold country,' gold coming from the Tra No and Tra Te mountains at the source of the Thu Bon river in the Duy Xuyen district, as well as from Thang Hoa, south-west of Hoi An.

Mining rights were strictly controlled. Historian Le Quy Don mentions a man named Giang Thuyen, who bought the rights to mine gold in the mountains at the source of the Thu Bon river, 'who recorded taking no less than a thousand *hot* to Hoi An to sell.'

Once through the port procedures when your entire cargo might be confiscated – bought by the Nguyen lord or his mandarin – trading in Faifo was fraught with a tangle of seasonal prices and business being conducted in numerous currencies. There were agreed prices, 'coerced' prices and black market prices. The prices quoted to the Nguyen lords were cheaper than those for the mandarin; prices for the mandarin were cheaper than those charged in the free market.

There were trading season prices and roving season (the dead season) prices. In 1744, the price of gold bullion (ten *taels*) during the trading season was worth 130-136 *quan,* at times up to 150 *quan.* By the end of the trading season, the price had dropped to 100-110. There were also net prices, which seem to have been the wholesale prices, the price paid at source, and exchange prices.

Black market prices appeared when the *thien minh* currency was minted, the state stipulating that it was equivalent to the old currency – whatever the old currency might have been.

As the value of *thien minh* currency devalued, the black market value sank to only a third that of a zinc coin. There came a time when no goods at all could be bought in the market with *thien minh* currency. Foreign merchants absolutely refused to accept it, demanding gold, silver or merchandise.

The Japanese brought in pure sterling silver, ten-*liang* pieces with a Japanese hallmark and offered them as presents to the Nguyen lord twice a year – at the New Year *(Tet)* and on the lord's birthday. The *schuitje* currency, eighty-two per cent silver and coins made of Japanese bronze were also in circulation in Faifo.

Silver was the preferred currency; then came gold and coins. Apart from the ten-*liang* silver piece, there was silver bullion. Foreign merchants used Japanese and Chinese silver to buy goods. During the seventeenth century, when the price of a ten-*liang* silver piece in the market was sixteen *quan,* the Nguyen lord befuddled the exchange rate by ordering a selling price of twenty *quan,* whereas the purchase price was only fourteen *quan.*

To add to the perplexity, there were bronze coins, zinc coins and several foreign currencies circulating: Thai *binh* currency right up to the eighteenth century; *khang hi* currency and the *khai nguyen* currency of the Tang; the currencies of *thuan hoa* and the *tuong phu* of the Sung dynasty, these fine bronze coins so treasured that people tended to hoard them.

Den coins, which Dutch merchants brought to Faifo, also brought a good exchange rate. In 1637, the Dutch shipped in 13.5 million *den* coins and made a tremendous profit because *den* coins were made of Japanese bronze, which the Nguyen lords bought to melt down to make weapons! Mexican and Spanish silver coins were also in circulation, along with English and later, French *piastrs.*

The Portuguese tended to trade from the decks of their ships. Travelling Chinese merchants used their assembly halls for trading, as they were built. Resident Chinese, Japanese and Vietnamese traders conducted business from their enlarged merchant houses called hotels; the front was used to sell goods, the back and upper floor for storage and sleeping.

Much trade was done from small wood and bamboo craft, conducted by Vietnamese traders carrying goods to ports up and down the coast, the boats built in Kim Bong (Cam Kim) and Tra Quan (Cam Thanh) villages. This Cochin China fleet of coastal vessels distributing goods up and down the country in 1763, numbered four hundred forty-seven.

Merchants having less capital, mostly Vietnamese women, traded in betel and areca nuts, assorted cakes, flowers and incense, sometimes as retailers, grocers or as roving traders, although amongst them were traders with capital, who acted as mediators and distributors of goods – or lenders, charging high rates of interest. The business skills of these small traders were much admired by their foreign customers.

Foreign merchants who wished to order goods of high quality for the following year's trading season sometimes left secretaries or hired intermediaries, mediators or representatives to negotiate and purchase goods. To facilitate purchases and sales, the Chinese, Japanese and Dutch nearly all married Vietnamese women, thus eliminating the middleman or woman. These intermediaries – Vietnamese wives – would approach the production units of silk yarn, sugar, cinnamon or whatever, placing orders with prepaid payments, often putting long-term investment of capital and technology into the production units. As many producers ran short of capital, they had to borrow the merchants' capital, effectively rendering themselves employees of the merchant. Profits always went to the merchants.

Following the mass exodus of the Japanese back to Japan in 1636, the Dutch set up a factory, taking over the rich *shuinsen* trade. The British East India Company, coming rather late to the fair in 1695, sent Thomas Bowyear on board the Delphin to propose that British merchants be allowed to set up a factory. The negotiations failed, despite the fact that a merchant named Peacock had been trying on behalf of the company since 1613.

The baffling assortment of currencies, swindling, deception, downright lying and the use of false scales, all were a danger. Frenchman Pierre Poivre remarked rather acidly: 'When I conducted business with people of this country, they never told the truth once. Today, they confirm this and tomorrow they deny their agreement. They thought the more they deferred business, the more profit they could get. The more gifts they were given, the more they were eager to get.' The worst was that a number of Hoa (Chinese) merchants gave forged coins in exchange for gold and other precious metals. In the early nineteenth century, Frenchman de la Bissachere painted a black portrait of the local merchants: 'Almost every Chinese merchant has got two scales, one is used when buying and the other when selling.' Suddenly, Thai Thi Thong's grandfather's sign declaring 'True prices, true commodities' clicks into perspective.

141

In spite of the nerve-racking risks of trading, Faifo was probably no better nor worse than Macao, Malacca or Batavia. Faifo's annual fair served as a showplace for the oriental world's merchandise. Each year, the ships of foreign merchants came bearing new novelties – weapons, mirrors, wool, leather, cosmetics – to please the Nguyen lords or the mandarin in charge of foreign trade.

In exchange, the Nguyen lord often presented the merchants with expensive gifts. Sandalwood and silk were two items much favoured by the Japanese. In 1628, Lord Nguyen Phuc Nguyen sent a fine piece of sandalwood and ten lengths of white silk to Japanese merchant Chaya Rojiro and in 1635, he sent Chaya Shiro Jiro a kilo of prized sandalwood and four lengths of silk.

Delighted by the array of goods on offer, year after year the foreign traders returned. Faifo promised such a bounty and diversity of goods – they had to come.

Riding high in Hue, the Nguyen lords were teetering on the brink, had they but realized. The French had been relatively late in coming to Faifo (Hoi An), their East India trading company having been founded in 1664 – half a century after the founding of the Dutch and English companies. Belatedly in 1742, the French had sent Pierre Poivre to survey the prospects for Faifo and Turon, variously spelled Touran, Tourane and Touron, the French name for Danang, which at the time was totally unsettled.

Another Frenchman named Friell, supported by the director general of the French factories in Pondicherry (India), had been warmly welcomed in 1744 by Nguyen Lord Phuc Khoat, who granted him a commercial license and permission to build a warehouse in Faifo. Pierre Poivre returned in 1748, this time hoping to set up a business to establish a monopoly on exotic, precious aromatic woods. Not surprisingly, Frielle refused to share with him the licence granted by the Nguyen lord in 1744.

Poivre came again to Turon in 1749, then on to Hoi An, where he reported: 'This is where all the merchandise from China and other countries is warehoused.' In his view and perhaps he was the first to say so, Hoi An was not a suitable place for establishment of a trading post – 'because the port would engender additional costs to transport merchandise from Turon to Hoi An.' He therefore recommended Turon.

Trade was still thriving – the sixteenth and seventeenth centuries were Hoi An's heydays – the town having grown rich, thanks to China's Closed Door Policy in the sixteenth century and on the Japanese trade in silver and copper in the seventeenth.

Poivre proceeded to Hue, paid tribute to the Nguyen lord, who received him appropriately, but following a dispute, Poivre left hurriedly, taking a Vietnamese interpreter along with him. He was pursued and as punishment, the Nguyen lord expelled the French missionaries; only his French doctor was allowed to stay. Poivre's misadventure put pay at least temporarily to the French East India Company's efforts to establish commercial relations in Dang Trong.

However, the French were determined. In 1750, Dupleix in Pondicherry sent a missionary, Father Bennetat, who at first was cordially received by the Nguyen lord, although he was subsequently arrested and sent to Macau. Dupleix, refusing to abandon his goal, dispatched yet another representative, named de Rabec, who obtained certain privileges from the Nguyen lord: freedom to trade, housing, a warehouse. However, Dupleix by then having been recalled to France, de Rabec was obliged to return to Pondicherry.

Back in Paris in 1768, Pierre Poivre was stirring up trouble for the Nguyen. He managed to find the ear of one of Louis XV's influential ministers, Choiseul, and suggested an armed attack on the Nguyen lord's citadel in Hue. Fortunately for the Nguyen, the plan never materialized because of Choiseul's downfall.

Meanwhile in Dang Trong, the populace was chafing under heavy Nguyen taxation. When a poll tax was levied in 1773, a popular uprising erupted, led by three brothers, a general, a merchant, and a priest from the village of Tay Son near Qui Nhon, south of Hue. Their revolt became known as the Tay Son Rebellion (1773-1788). First, the Tay Son chased the Nguyen court in Hue to south of Gia Dinh (Saigon) where they assassinated the Nguyen lord and as many members of his family as they could lay hands on – the custom in those days for toppling a dynasty.

Faifo (Hoi An), perceived by the Tay Son as the source of armaments and the financial life support of the Nguyen lords, was besieged and burnt to the ground in 1773. The resilient people of Hoi An picked through the ashes and over the years, rebuilt their houses in much the same style as before. Hoi An's historic merchant houses of today are those rebuilt houses, dating from the late eighteenth and nineteenth centuries.

Elsewhere in the country, Tay Son trials and executions took place. Recognizing that there was strong support for the Nguyen in the South, the Tay Son brothers marched their peasant army to Gia Dinh (Saigon) where the city walls were destroyed and twenty thousand inhabitants put to the sword.

The Tay Son then attacked the North, where first they defeated the powerful Trinh clan, the power behind the throne in Thang Long (Hanoi). In Thang Long, the Le king remained at least nominally a vassal of China, so following the first engagement, he fled north to seek military assistance from the emperor of China, who obligingly – one need not wonder at his motives – ordered the viceroy of Canton to proceed south immediately at the head of an army of a hundred thousand men.

The Tay Son, hearing of the Chinese advance, laid waste the towns and villages along their route, destroying the source of provisions for the advancing army. The Chinese were forced to fall back, long before they reached the frontier of Tonkin – at least, that is one version of the story, as recorded by a French naval captain, employed by the Nguyen court at the time of the revolt.

In Hanoi, the story reads rather differently. Invaded by the Chinese, who thought they had detected a moment of weakness after the defeat of the Trinh, the battle culminated in the Tay Son army vanquishing the Chinese army in the Dong Da district of the capital, Thang Long (Hanoi). In the North, the Tay Son brothers have been deified as folk heroes, who unified half the country for the first time from Qui Nhon to Hanoi, freeing the Viet people from the worst excesses of feudalism – and the troublesome Nguyen.

In both versions, the Tay Son brother, Nguyen Hue, crowned himself Emperor Quang Trung in 1788. He was to rule for only four years before he died (1792) at the age of forty. It is thought by some that had he lived to rule, say for twenty years, that the country would have remained united, its capital in Thang Long or possibly in Quy Nhon, his family seat, two hundred miles (320 km) south of Hue.

At first unbeknownst to the Tay Son brothers, a French missionary, Pigneau Behaine of Adran, usually referred to as Adran, had aided the last surviving Nguyen 'prince', the young fifteen-year-old Nguyen Phuc Anh, to escape.

For months the young prince and the priest hid on an island in the Gulf of Siam near the Cambodian border, Pulo Wai, now known as Phu Quoc. The people of the South flocked to his support, crowning the young 'prince', king of Cochin.

Finding one French ship, seven Portuguese vessels and a number of junks in Saigon harbour, this fleet was hurriedly hired to make a surprise attack on the Tay Son fleet. But when the French vessel ran aground, the Portuguese vessels fled to Macao, forcing the young 'king' to make a hasty retreat to Pulo Wai (Phu Quoc) This failed attack brought down the wrath of the Tay Son brothers, who when they discovered his hiding place, determined to march against him. Wisely, Nguyen Anh fled the island and the country, throwing himself under the protection of the king of Siam.

As it happened, Siam was at war with the Burmese. Nguyen Anh offered his services against the Burmese; the King of Siam accepted. Having learned a few European tactics, Nguyen Anh led his small army of about a thousand men, attacked the Burmese only from commanding positions, throwing obstacles in the enemy's path and harassing him continually – manoeuvres unknown to the Burmese, who sued for peace on Nguyen Anh's terms. He returned to the Siamese capital in triumph and the king rewarded him with presents of gold, silver and precious stones.

Relations quickly soured, however, after Nguyen Anh's sister not only refused the Siamese king's proposal to take her as a concubine, but snubbed his increased offer to make her his queen. Added to this rejection, when Rama I, king of Siam discovered that Nguyen Anh had also appealed to the Portuguese for military aid – Rama I considering himself to be Nguyen Anh's protector – suddenly, the Siamese court seemed a less friendly place, hostile even. Nguyen Anh and his followers, about fifteen hundred people, decided to flee under cover of darkness, commandeering whatever Siamese and Malay vessels lay in the harbour. They reached the island of Pulo Wai (Phu Quoc) safely, which Nguyen Anh then fortified as best he could against attack, threatened now by both the king of Siam and the army of the Tay Son brothers.

While in Thailand, Adran the priest had conceived a plan to appeal to Louis XVI of France for support in replacing the 'lawful heir' to the throne in Hue on terms that would be acceptable to the young Nguyen lord – and highly advantageous to France. Later, in a letter from Pondicherry, he wrote, 'I met with the unfortunate monarch in a very wretched situation, accompanied by a few faithful friends on one of the small islands in the Gulf of Siam . . . his soldiers were subsisting on roots which they dug out of the earth.'

Nguyen Anh must have been feeling utterly desolate, fearing the worst, an attack not only from the Tay Son army, now also from Siam. It was at this time that he committed his four-year-old son to the care of the French missionary, earnestly entreating him in the event of any misfortune befalling himself, to act as a father and a friend to his little son, continuing to advise and assist him, instructing him never to lose sight of his lawful dominions of which his father had been deprived by violence and usurpation.

Accepting the charge, Adran set sail with the little prince for Pondicherry and from there, aboard a vessel bound for Europe. They arrived in Paris in the year 1787. The young prince was presented at the Court of Versailles where he attracted much attention and was shown due respect.

The Treaty of Versailles, dated 28 November 1787, was drawn up and signed by Adran, the newly promoted Bishop Pigneau Behaine on behalf of Nguyen Anh and by the French Foreign Minister on behalf of King Louis XVI. The third clause read: 'The king of Cochin China is waiting for the support that his majesty, the very devout Catholic king will be pleased to accord him. He is willing to concede to his majesty and the royal family of France, the right of ownership and sovereignty over an island called Hoi An, which offers two main ports in Cochin China and which is called Touron by Europeans.'

The poor scribe seems to have been befuddled by the geography and to have had trouble with the name, Hoi An. In some clauses, mention is made of Hoi Nan (sic) Island. In others, it was called Danang, 'an island with Cua Han in the North and Cua Hoi in the South.' This portentous agreement, which France never honoured, served later as the justification for France's official interference in Vietnam's affairs.

Not only did the king honour Adran with the title, Bishop of Cochin China, he was also appointed Ambassador Extraordinary and Plenipotentiary to the Nguyen Court – yet to be established. At the time, the French monarch had other matters weighing on his mind. The extravagant French court was in financial straits and the French Revolution was barely two years away. The promised military support for the Nguyen cause was not forthcoming. Funds to mount a modest military fleet were mainly raised by the newly appointed bishop and ambassador, Adran, mainly on his return voyage – from the community of French merchants in Pondicherry.

Despite the French king never honouring the Treaty of Versailles, it was taken that in exchange for the financial support to mount an attack against the Tay Son by the Pondicherry merchants, that the French would be permitted to establish a trading post through which they were allowed to trade freely – and build a garrison.

With the funds from the Pondicherry merchants, Nguyen Anh mounted an attack on Hue in 1801. By then, the Tay Son king, Quang Trung had died of a brain disease, some said by poisoning. The throne was nominally occupied by his young son. After much jockying back and forth, Nguyen An proceeded north and took Thang Long (Hanoi) in 1802. In doing so, he established a new – and Vietnam's last – dynasty, indeed uniting the entire country from the Mekong delta to the border of China for the first time.

147

Nguyen Phuc Anh crowned himself King Gia Long, the first of a dynasty of thirteen Nguyen rulers, Vietnam's last feudal dynasty, his capital in Hue.

In Hoi An, at first the French built colonial style, ochre-painted houses of two stories, houses with terraces on the upper storey, several still standing, scattered, and at the eastern end of Nguyen Thai Hoc Street. But as time passed, the French were drawn to the deep harbour of Turon (Danang).

THE BRITISH COME TO TEA

In 1792, Lord George Macartney set out as British Ambassador to the Imperial Court of China, along with his secretary, Sir George Staunton of the British East India Company. Accompanying them was a useful young man named John Barrow, who had learnt Chinese and who kept a chronicle of their journey. Subsequently, he published it as *A Voyage to Cochinchina in the Years 1792 and 1793.* Much later, he served as Under-Secretary of the British Navy – for some forty years.

Their ships dropped anchor in Hoi An and spent sufficient time in port for young Barrow to pen an eyewitness account of the town and the adventures of the ships' crews. Thirteen years ago in Hoi An's History Museum, I came across a watercolour and beneath it the words, John Barrow. The original watercolour has now been removed, but a photocopy of it remains, showing Hoi An's harbour, the painter having taken the trouble to carefully illustrate the numerous kinds of craft he saw before him.

Not only did John Barrow describe in colourful and occasionally, wryly humorous terms all that he saw, he also gained access and permission to translate and copy the historic memoirs of a Captain Barissy, a French naval officer, 'who, having several years commanded a frigate in the service of the king of Cochinchina and being an able and intelligent man, had the means and the opportunity of collecting accurate information.'

Quite which 'king' of Cochin China the French naval officer served is not known, doubtless one of the Nguyen lords (governors) preceding the Tay Son Rebellion, who called themselves kings when dealing with foreigners. At the time that the British ships called in Hoi An, Nguyen Anh would have been hiding in the South, preparing for his return to power. The Tay Son king, Quang Trung, had only just died (1792), and Barrow refers to the young king, Quang Trung's son, on the throne in Hue. From his account, comparing the Vietnamese with the Chinese, it must be assumed that he wrote at least part of his journal on his return journey from China.

The more serious purport of John Barrow's chronicle was to impress upon the British East India Company, not only the commercial advantages of establishing a presence in Hoi An, but more importantly, as an obstruction to the French naval establishment in Danang, which he saw as a serious threat to Britain's valuable China trade. So the French had installed themselves at Danang immediately after Adran's return from France, sometime after 1778.

After terrifying a poor fisherman into piloting the British ships into the harbour, the British found that they were arriving not long after the Tay Son Rebellion that had all but destroyed the town. At first the people of Hoi An were highly suspicious and wary, having been warned by a Portuguese trader, 'who sought to protect his exclusive and lucrative trade,' that the British were up to no good. The market closed, troops and war elephants were assembled, but as the people of Hoi An came to realize that the British merely sought to buy provisions, relations between the ships' company and the people of Hoi An thawed.

Before long the hospitable and entrepreneurial people of Hoi An had constructed a bamboo shelter in order to serve those ships' officers who might find themselves in Hoi An at mealtime during the day. Then as today, a row of little tables was laid with benches to sit upon to accommodate twenty-odd officers. In China, Barrow observed, it was customary to cover the little tables completely with dishes. Here in Hoi An, the Cochin Chinese not only covered the tables, they piled up the bowls in rows three or four deep.

'I suppose that we seldom sat down to a fewer number of bowls than two hundred, exclusive of the cups of rice, which were handed round in place of bread. Each person is laid a spoon of potter's ware and a pair of porcupine quills or small sticks of bamboo, sometimes tipped with silver,' then as now. The dishes held 'beef, pork, fowls and fish, cut into small pieces, mixed with vegetables and dressed in soups and gravies variously seasoned. We had neither wine or spirits, nor fermented liquors of any kind, not even water, were served round during the time of eating; but when dinner was over, Chinese *seau-choo* was handed about in little porcelain cups.

'The governor or general commanding at Turon did not indeed condescend to sit down with us, but usually on these occasions, lay stretched on a mattress spread on a mat at the end of the room, smoking tobacco, or eating his areca nut and betel pepper, while two tall fellows fanned the air the whole time with large fans made of the wing feathers of Argus pheasant.'

The British company returned the hospitality. 'Some of the leading men daily visited the ships, where notwithstanding the very little relish they seemed to feel for our cookery, they usually dined, they neither admired our beer nor our wine; but their avidity for raw rum, brandy, or any kind of spirituous liquors was so great that after their first visit, it was found expedient not to leave the quantity to their discretion, as the whole party went out of the ship in a state of complete intoxication.'

As the British ambassador had not yet visited Turon, it was decided that his visit should be the occasion of his Majesty's birthday on the fourth of June. The Portuguese captain, who originally had tried to mislead the party, decided to redeem himself by offering a European style meal – as best he could in the circumstances.

'Thus by his misplaced zeal, a good Cochinchinese entertainment was entirely marred by a bad Portuguese dinner.'

The British on arrival at the dinner rather disgraced themselves by making polite bows to the representative of the governor and taking their seats. It had been expected that they would 'make the traditional nine protractions (kowtowing) to a yellow skreen (sic) of silk bearing in large painted characters the name of the young (Tay Son) prince at Hue, for the general commanding at Turon, who sat cross-legged on a bench as proxy for his master, observed that having made our bow, we filed off and took our seats regardless of the yellow skreen (sic), appeared to be greatly disconcerted and could hardly be said to recover himself the remainder of the day.'

They were entertained by a theatrical company, probably performing traditional *hat boi* folk opera, described by Barrow as a 'relation of histories. The voices of the women were shrill and warbling, but some of their cadences were not without melody . . . whose slow melancholy movement breathed that kind of plaintive softness so peculiar to the native airs of the Scotch.'

When the British band in turn was brought ashore to entertain, 'the Cochinchinese had no ear for the soft and harmonious chords of European music.'

Walking across the village green, the British observed 'a dozen young fellows playing at football with a bladder . . . displaying their agility in leaping over an horizontal pole . . . a noisy group amusing themselves in fighting cocks . . . young boys in imitation of their elders, training quails and other small birds and even grasshoppers to tear each other in pieces.' The British were most impressed by 'a party of young men keeping a shuttlecock up in the air by striking it with the soles of the feet.

151

'A seaman of the Lion, having quarrelled with one of these people, insisted on making a ring and boxing it fairly out. While the sailor was squaring his arms and manoeuvring and looking for the exact spot where he should hit his antagonist a knock-down blow, the Cochinchinese, while grinning in his face, very coolly turned up his heel and, giving him a hard and totally unexpected kick in the jaw, walked away with great composure, leaving the astonished sailor to the laughter and merriment of the crowd.'

There were jugglers and conjurors, 'and those who did not openly practice juggling as a profession were equally as expert in the art of picking pockets. Scarcely a day occurred in which some of the party did not return to the ships without the loss of pocket handkerchiefs, an article for which they seemed to have a particular liking. We found them all, from the highest to the lowest, most importunate beggars, craving without the least ceremony for every thing that might suit their fancy. Neither were they satisfied with a simple denial, nor with obtaining what they asked, becoming generally more urgent in their demands in proportion to the liberality of the giver, and what they could not obtain by begging they usually endeavoured to procure by stealing. This disposition to stealing was so general that it was even found necessary to watch narrowly the officers of government who came on board the ships.

'The houses in general near Turon Bay consisted only of four mud walls, covered with thatch', built on the ground, or near rivers 'raised upon four posts of wood or pillars of stone to keep out vermin as well as inundations.'

Despite the thieving, Barrow compared the people of Hoi An very favourably to the Chinese. Clearly, he liked them and enjoyed his visit immensely.

'The Cochinchinese are, like the French, always gay and forever talking, the Chinese always grave and affect to be thinking. The former are open and familiar, the latter closed and reserved.'

He went on to contrast their differing attitudes to women. 'A Chinese would consider it as disgraceful to commit any affair of importance to a woman. Women in the estimation of the Cochinchinese are best suited for and are accordingly entrusted with the chief concerns of the family. The Chinese code of politeness forbids a woman to talk unless by way of reply, to laugh beyond a smile, to sing unless desired and, as to dancing, she labours under a physical restriction (bound feet) which makes this kind of movement

152

impossible. In Cochinchina the women are quite as gay and as unrestrained as the men.' In China, he goes on to say, 'women are condemned to the most degrading and laborious task of dragging the plough, whereas in Cochinchina, we observed them day after day and from morning till night, standing in the midst of pools of water, up to the knees, occupied in the transplanting of rice.

'They even assist in constructing and keeping in repair their mud-built cottages; they conduct the manufacture of coarse earthen ware vessels; they manage the boats on rivers and in harbours; they bear their articles of produce to the market; they draw the cotton wool from the pod, free it from the seeds, spin it into thread, weave it into cloth, dye it of its proper colour, and make it up into dresses for themselves and their families.

'Almost all the younger part of the males are compelled to enrol themselves in the army; and such as are exempt from military service employ themselves occasionally in fishing, in collecting swallows' nests . . . felling timber; building and repairing ships and boats . . . for they are not by any means of an idle disposition.'

A Cochin Chinese man was allowed to have an unlimited number of wives or concubines, he explained, and the parties could dissolve a marriage or a liaison by breaking one of their copper coins or far easier, a pair of chopsticks, before proper witnesses.

In his observation of women's behaviour in Hoi An society, Barrow fervently hoped that the 'general character of the nation may not exactly correspond with that which prevails at one of the most frequented of its sea port towns. Neither the husband nor the father seems to have any scruples in abandoning the wife or the daughter to her gallant', he observed, 'the indifference on the part of the men for the honour and chastity of the sex . . . by no means confined to the common people; they apply indeed more forcibly to the first ranks in society, the officers of government.

'It is evident indeed, from the whole tenor of their conduct, that the men, even in the common ranks of life, consider the other sex as destined for their use; and those in a higher station, as subservient to their pleasures.' He was astounded 'of the facility with which they are disposed to transfer their women to strangers, our party had several curious instances.

'An officer of the Lion was one day sent on shore to purchase a couple of bullocks for the use of the ship's company. As the price had previously been fixed at ten dollars a head, the officer had only to count down the money before the magistrates of the place, and receive his bullocks. The mandarin, taking up the dollars, dispatched a couple of his attendants, who shortly returned with a fine young girl, whom the magistrate handed over to the officer.

'Whether this gentleman's modesty was too much shocked at so barefaced and indecent a transaction, or whether he had not a sufficient sum of money to make up the price of the bullocks, is immaterial to the purpose; it is enough to observe that he preferred his duty to the purchase of the lady, to the affected astonishment of the mandarin, of whom he understood her to be either the wife or the daughter. Another gentleman, in returning one day from the town to the river side, was accosted by an elderly woman, who made signs to him to follow her into her cottage, where she presented him with her daughter, very nearly in that state in which she came out of nature's hands; and the eyes of the old lady sparkled with joy at the sight of a Spanish dollar.' I couldn't help but wonder what desperate straits the old woman found herself and her daughter in to have produced this little drama. Barrow found that 'the women had but slender pretensions to beauty; yet the want of personal charms was in some degree compensated by lively and cheerful temper. The dress of the women was by no means fascinating, a loose blue or brown frock reaching down to the middle of the thigh and a pair of black napkin trousers made very wide.'

'For a festive occasion, a lady puts on three or four frocks at once, of different colours and lengths; the shortest being uppermost. Their long black hair is sometimes twisted into a knot and fixed on the crown of the head and sometimes hangs loose in flowing tresses down the back, reaching frequently to the very ground.

'Short hair is not only considered as a mark of vulgarity, but an indication of degeneracy.' Everyone went barefoot with the exception of a few officials, 'they wearing a kind of sandals or loose slippers.' Men wore handkerchiefs tied round the head like turbans; others wore hats or caps to protect their faces from the sun. They used 'umbrellas of strong china paper or the leaves of *borassus* or fan palms, or fans might be made of feathers.'

The buildings that Barrow saw were very humble, even the temples. Hardly surprising when the town had been burnt only a few years previously by the Tay Son. In their mud and bamboo cottages, 'nothing met the eye that could impress the mind of a stranger with high notions of the happy condition of this people.

154

'That Hoi An had suffered considerably from the recent revolution was evident from the ruins of larger and better buildings than any which now appeared, and from the inequalities of surface indicating a former existence of walls and forts . . . from the remains also of gardens and plantations of fruit trees and flowering shrubs, that were not run into wildernesses, but no traces appeared to indicate former opulence, or convey the impression of fallen magnificence.'

Being a man of the sea, Barrow remarked that the Cochin Chinese excelled in naval architecture, for which 'they are not a little indebted to the size and quality of the timber employed for that purpose. The row-gallies for pleasure are remarkably fine vessels . . . from fifty to ninety feet (16-30 m) in length, sometimes composed of five single planks, each extending from one extremity to the other, the edges mortised, kept tight by wooden pegs and bound firm by twisted fibres of bamboo, without either ribs or any kind of timbers. At the stem and stern, they are raised to a considerable height, and are curiously carved into monstrous figures of dragons and serpents ornamented with gilding and painting. A number of poles and spears bearing flags and streamers, pikes ornamented with tufts of cows' tails painted red, lanterns and umbrellas, and other insignia denoting the rank of the passenger, are erected at each end of the boat.

'The company always sit in the fore part of the boat . . . it being considered a breach of good manners for the rowers to turn their backs on the passengers, they stand with their faces towards the bow of the boat, pushing the oars from them instead of pulling towards them, as is usually done in the Western world.'

The vessels employed in the coastal trade, the fishing craft and those used to collect swallows' nests, like Chinese sampans, he explained, were covered with 'sheds of matting' under which a whole family resided; others resembled the common *proas* of the Malays, both in their hulls and rigging.

'Their foreign traders are built on the same plan as the Chinese junks . . . as they have subsisted some thousands of years unaltered, they are at least entitled to a little respect from the antiquity of the invention . . . Security rather than speed was the object of the owner . . . and as the merchant was both owner and navigator, a limited tonnage was sufficient for his own merchandise; the vessel was therefore divided in order to obviate his inconvenience, into distinct compartments, so that one ship might separately accommodate many merchants. The bulk-heads by which these divisions were formed consisted of planks of two inches thick, so well caulked and secured as to be completely water-tight.'

And then he remarks on the same sturdiness of design that Marco Polo described five hundred years earlier.

'A ship, thus fortified with cross bulk-heads, may strike on a rock and yet sustain no serious injury; a leak springing in one division of the hold will not be attended with any damage to the articles placed in another; and by the ship being thus so well bound together, she is firm and strong enough to sustain a more than ordinary shock. It is well known to seamen, that when a large ship strikes the ground, the first indication of her falling in pieces is when the edges of the decks begin to part from the sides; but this separation can never happen when the sides and the deck are firmly bound together by cross bulk-heads . . . In fact, this old Chinese invention is now on trial in the British Navy, as a new experiment.'

Barrow found that the people of Cochin China followed a form of Buddhism, often placing small wooden boxes or wicker baskets, hanging or fixed among the branches of trees as tiny shrines, and that they offered the first fruits of the earth to their deities. He also found that the government made an annual contribution to support the monasteries and that the Buddhist priests were considered to be the best physicians.

Contrary to China, he noted, where they hardly passed a town or village in which the British were not offended at the sight of a *cangue* (pillory) or heard the cries of someone being beaten with a bamboo stick, in contrast in Cochin China, 'not a single punishment of any description occurred to our notice. At all events, the spirit of the people of Turon did not appear to suffer any depression from a too severe exercise of the hand of power.'

LOST CITADEL

A friend in London, looking up the town where I was going, emailed me a map of the area, probably taken from an old Ordnance Survey map. 'Looks like some interesting ruins nearby,' he said. At the time, I thought of Myson, but when I printed out the map, there was a neat square, definitely *not* Myson. When later I read that the Nguyen lords had built a garrison ten leagues from Hoi An, a citadel to guard the harbour against foreigners and to house the officers who collected harbour fees, of course, I was determined to find it.

At the motorbike repair shop next door, I ask if they know a *xe om* I can hire. To my delight, the wife of the owner, Anh, takes up the challenge. She studies the map and reckons it's about six miles (10 km) We agree a price and set off at half past eight on a Sunday morning, the sun already blazing. One week into April, the half-ripened heads of the rice are just beginning to droop and here and there a woman is out in her paddy, checking how soon the rice will be ready to harvest.

Sunday in central Vietnam feels much like any other day. Only banks and government offices are closed. The roads are full of bicycles, motorbikes and lorries; even the schools are open.

Anh is a careful driver, pausing before pulling out round bicycles ridden two abreast by chatting matrons. She hoots as we pass schools where children wobble unpredictably on their bikes. When we reach the little town of Dien Ban, according to the map, the road to right and left of the T-junction travels along what should be the perimeter of the walls of the Nguyen citadel. We stop and Anh asks.

A pavement conference ensues with differing opinions raised, amidst many doubtful glances and the need to retain face – by knowing. According to the map, the nearest walls should lie right in front of us, or behind the shops facing us, the shops, of course, built cheek-by-jowl, so no possibility of actually seeing a wall if there is one. A narrow road directly in front of us runs straight through what well might have been the entrance into the citadel. We follow it, looking for anything remotely resembling a ruined wall.

No walls. Houses line the narrow road, but not so close together that we don't catch glimpses of rice paddies behind. This should have been the interior of the garrison built by the Nguyen lords in Hue during the period when Japanese Street and Chinese Street were flourishing. We stop at a school to inquire. The children in the playground giggle and shout hello, retreat shyly, then lead us to their teachers, who have no knowledge of a citadel, nor walls, although the school is built right in the middle of where it maybe once stood. The teachers at the school suggest we ask another teacher in a house opposite. She gets out her glasses, looks at the map and suggests that we go back to the main road and turn right towards a pagoda – the direction suggested by the men on the pavement – although even considering my lack of comprehension, it seemed clear that they had no notion of any walls. Quite how the pagoda figures in the scenario remains uncertain, perhaps just a road direction. We retrace our way, then turn.

Anh drives very slowly along the main road where the houses cling to one another, permitting only the odd glance down a narrow side road. No wall. We reach what I first take to be a pagoda and stop. Over a humpback bridge – over what just might possibly have been a moat – I climb the steps of not a pagoda, but what turns out to be a war memorial listing the names of the fallen beneath the gold star on the red field of the Vietnamese national flag. The raised platform of the monument provides a view out over rice fields for some distance, which could easily have been – or not – the parade ground of a garrison. Only the bridge across a span of water four meters wide beneath the memorial might suggest the possibility of a former moat. Defeated, I suggest to Anh that we go home.

Instead, she suggests that we go on to the pagoda.

We continue along the same road and I notice on the right – the same side as the war memorial – that along here, houses have been built on stilts, over the remains of a moat? Turning off to the left – the wrong direction for the citadel if the map is correct, but towards Hoi An – we head into the countryside. Phuoc Lan pagoda, off a track to the right, is totally lacking in distinction, or one could say, even great beauty. We are met by two old ladies, no monks, a snarling dog and a toddler who dances over the tile floor of the upper worship hall where a gold painted Buddha presides, flanked by a *bodhissatva* carrying a vase to provide refreshing water, much to be appreciated in a hot climate. Another *bodhissatva* wears a crown, the pagoda's most curious feature being a pink, electric lotus tree, mercifully not lit.

158

Suddenly, Anh drops to her knees, raising her hands three times in an attitude of prayer.

Returning along this back road towards Hoi An, a different way from which we had come, Anh keeps pausing to check with passersby that we are headed in the right direction and I suddenly realize that there are no road signs in Vietnam; people have to ask the way as they go. Can it possibly be that Anh has never been six miles (10 km) outside of Hoi An? Perhaps not, as people work seven days a week. Anh pauses at each pagoda where dragons, phoenix and wing-flapping geese glitter along their roof ridges, all flashily new, pagoda building reflecting the prosperity of the area. Disappointed at not finding the walls of the garrison, I am not interested in modern country pagodas. It is only afterwards, guiltily, that it occurs to me that perhaps our excursion might have been a longed-for pilgrimage to various pagodas for Anh. At the time, I only wondered if any of them had been built of the stones from the old Nguyen citadel.

MYSTERIOUS CONCUBINE

Heading towards Cua Dai beach, Pho turns right, then crosses the bridge over the Do river. From here, Pho starts to ask old people for the way to Cam Thanh village – Pho being the only man I have ever known, willing to stop and ask for directions. It isn't far, a turn right, then another right and maybe half a mile between a ripening patchwork of paddies.

At the edge of Cam Thanh, villagers are tidying up a graveyard. Tra Quan temple lies opposite on the right, behind an old and decaying concrete screen, a rampant tiger threatening the road, a crane on the backside of the screen. The wooden doors of the temple are tightly locked.

An old, bow-legged woman in a brown flecked pyjama suit under a conical straw hat approaches, coming from the cemetery, smiles and offers to lead us to the man who holds the key. We walk along a concrete road through the village, which looks relatively prosperous, stuccoed houses amongst banana trees, vegetable gardens and corn patches. Reaching the bank of the Dinh river, the road abruptly turns right, the riverbank densely edged by water palms, reminiscent of the Mekong delta. Amongst these tightly packed palms was a Viet Cong hideout during the war years, the woman tells Pho, probably during both wars, the French Indo-China War, then later in what the Vietnamese call the American War.

About the same distance again and finally, the woman turns into a house where a sinewy man wearing a slouch hat, his tanned face grooved with deep laughter lines, squats, repairing a palm-plaited gate, surrounded by baby chicks in front of his large, single storey house. Head-high corn encroaches on his front garden. Lang Tra Quan temple, he says, was built by the government 'for the top mandarin of Tan Dam hamlet in feudal times.' He then tells us a tale of how Mieu Ong Tien temple, opposite Lang Tra Quan temple, happened to be built. It seems that a long time ago, it was a Mr Tien from this village, who discovered that swallows nests were edible.

'He became trapped in a cave in Cu Lau Cham (island) by flood waters. He had nothing to eat – so he had to eat the swallows' nests. Many people drowned in the floods, but he was saved by the

160

swallows. The people from this village started to gather swallows nests and Mr Tien built the temple to give thanks to the swallows for saving his life.

'A few people from this village still collect swallows nests, but they work for the government. Since independence, collecting nests is not open and free as it once was. It is strictly controlled by the government and the gatherers earn a salary.'

Last autumn, he tells us, the typhoons brought floods to the village, water up to the roofs and the villagers had to move elsewhere until the flood waters subsided. The village is, after all, on a low-lying island in a river delta.

As well as the two temples, my real purpose in coming to Cam Thanh village is to search for the tombs of 'the royal concubine of King Quang Trung and the Tay Son commanders,' as one guidebook puts it. The mysterious lady's name was Quy and she was from the local Tran family. I am wondering if she is the same wife, who penned the poignant, now famous poem on the death of her husband, the Tay Son king, Quang Trung. Her husband died at the age of forty in 1792, she left a grieving widow at only twenty.

Wind pours its cold into the room
Orchids wither on the veranda
Smoke covers the crypt of the deceased,
The shadow of the royal coach is gone.
Alone, I weep over my fate.
Heaven, why did you shatter our union?
How to tell my misery, my pain
Deep as the ocean, boundless as the sky,
I look to the East, sails glide in all directions,
I see only immensity of sky and water.
I look to the West,
Mountains and trees spread as far as the eye can see.
To the South, wild geese wander,
To the North, mist covers forests with a white shroud.
Though I search, the more this separation weighs upon me,
Will my affliction awaken echoes in that far beyond?
I see the moon through sorrow, its brilliance tarnished,
A fine dust veils its silvered glow.
I am ashamed to look at myself in the mirror,
My love shattered, alone, I wander on the deserted shore.

161

The flowers I look at return my grief.
Camellias cry tears of dew.
Watching the flitting bird, my heart is torn,
A turtle-dove flies solitary, seeking its companion.
Each landscape wears its own desolation,
Where are the joys of former days?
One moment only and the world collapsed,
So life goes, to whom can I complain,
Love and fidelity, as immense as heaven and earth,
My grief grows as my days endure.
To whom may I confide my torment and pain?
Let sun and moon bear witness!
                                        (tr Huu Ngoc)

On the way back, we stop to ask two old men, busy pruning a potted jasmine bush in front of Ho Tu Duong, the chapel of the Ho clan, if they know whether it was Quy who wrote the poem.

One of them greets me in French, introducing himself as Monsieur Ho Huong and to my surprise, writes his address as: 37 Rue du Marshal, à Faifo – Faifo being the seventeenth century name for Hoi An! Monsieur Huong volunteers that he is seventy-nine years old and asks my age. The Vietnamese often ask your age and find it difficult to understand that Western women are sometimes reluctant to divulge it. I always say 'a hundred', which usually results in a pause before they realise I am hedging. He doesn't know if Quy was the lady who wrote the poem.

Entrance to the Tra Quan temple is guarded by two small, almost comical looking, pink and blue temple lions, encrusted with bits of broken china. Obviously, the temple has been recently restored. Tra Quan translates as the Five Elements, but Pho suggests that it is only a name and has nothing to do with the five elements: fire, water, earth, lightning, metal. Once inside, there are five painted altars, predominately yellow and brown, depicting clouds, flowers, dragons, birds, deer, turtles, cranes and bamboo.

To get to the tomb of the royal concubine, the old lady points to a narrow dirt dyke between rice paddies. So, me hanging onto Pho, we bounce off along the dyke on his motorbike.

At first, we think the tomb of Quy is one of the two set behind a screen, each bearing a marble slab, the inscriptions in *chu nom*, the old Chinese script adopted by the Vietnamese to express

162

their hitherto unwritten language. Then Pho finds the tomb of Quy – he reads a bit of Chinese – a few meters away, its monument a semi-circle, the tumulus or raised grave mound, indeed, shaped like a mango stone as the guide book had said.

Another very old grave in one corner of the low-walled enclosure is so overgrown that we cannot get near enough to see the inscription. One of the Tran commanders, perhaps? The two graves side by side, also have mango-shaped tumuli and appear to be of the same vintage. Were the three Tran commanders brothers, cousins, a father and sons? Had Quy travelled with the invading army, along with her relatives? The size of her tumulus suggests that she was quite small, although it is the tradition in Vietnam to dig up the bones and rebury them after a year, so the size of her tumulus may be no indication of her size. If only all gravestones told the stories of the deceased – some do.

The man who kept the keys to the temple had suggested to Pho that someone at the local government office might know the story of the tombs. We present ourselves at an office with an open door. I show the man at the desk a photocopy of my letter of introduction from the Hanoi publisher – in Vietnamese. Official introductions are necessary in Vietnam – 'Otherwise, we don't know who you are.' The official asks why I don't have the letter with the red seal. I bring out the original letter with the red seal and hand it to him, hanging onto it and he laughs, understanding why. The Vietnamese have a habit of whisking any letter or paper out of your hands and you never see it again. He allows me to retain the original letter and takes the photocopy to another office, then comes back and writes a note with a biro on the photocopy and asks a young man in his office to conduct us to the leader of the Tran clan, who he thinks will be able to answer my questions. In parting, he grasps my hand in both of his and wishes us well in our search. So, a cordial welcome, after all.

We follow the young man's motorbike through the village and a few turns later, stop at a house – no one at home. We follow the young man on to another house, where we are told that, in fact, the person we are seeking is at the graves at this moment – where we started from. We retrace our way, take the dirt path again along the dyke, getting off to edge our way round a cart blocking the dyke. At the cemetery, several villagers are tidying up the graveyard.

Pho shows the letter and the scribbled note to one and he shouts to a thin man some way off having only one good eye, wearing a checked shirt, trousers, sandals and a red baseball cap – head of the Tran clan. Pho explains why we have come. The man introduces himself as Tran Cong Tinh and announces proudly that he is the sixth generation of the Tran after the lady I am seeking.

The two graves, side by side, that I had imagined might be brothers, were 'the graves of the lady's grandmother and grandfather, Tran Cong Thuc. The overgrown grave was that of her uncle, Tran Cong Thanh, commander-in-chief of the Tay Son Navy. Where her father is buried is unknown.

'When her husband, King Quang Trung died', the man explains, 'the lady fled to this area because this was her home, but instead of coming to Cam Thanh, she and her two ladies in waiting hid in the village of Cam Kim, now Kim Bong, the boat building village, nearby across the river.

'But they were discovered by the Nguyen mandarin, she was arrested and executed – they cut off her head – and floated her body on the river. Her head they took to Hue. Her body floated to the coconut palms' – the very water palms we had passed on our walk through the village. In early days, adulterous women and even 'adulterous widows' were set afloat on a boat with no oars as punishment to perish in the sun or waves.

'Someone found the body and they buried her here.'

Knowing the Vietnamese custom of burying for a year, then digging up the bones for a final burial, I ask if the mango-shaped mound holds only her bones.

'This was her first burial,' he replies dolefully.

Under the freshly victorious Nguyen Anh, newly established as King Gia Long, the first king of the Nguyen dynasty, perhaps no one dared to perform the second burial rite.

(Note: The poet was Princess Ngoc Han, daughter of the deposed king, Le Hien Tong, who the Tay Son king, Quang Trung, married on defeating her father in Thang Long.)

GOLDEN SWALLOWS

In Vietnam, age pulls rank. When I learned that the village of Cam Thanh, where the Lady Tran Quy is buried, had been the original swallow-gathering village, naturally I wanted to return to meet a nest gatherer. This was not to happen. A new friend, Le Thi Thu Thuy, who would act as translator, arranges to take me back to Cam Thanh to meet a swallows' nest gatherer, only this time, his father pulls rank.

Ho Thanh Nhut, sixty-seven, is a retired policeman. He has never gathered a swallow's nest in his life, but his son, Ho Trang, thirty-six, gathers nests. A trifle miffed that I am not to meet an actual nest gatherer, when he hands me a list of twenty-one of his ancestors, who have gathered nests going back to 1804 – the time of Nguyen Anh, King Gia Long – I have to be satisfied. Doubtless, he knows a thing or two about nest gathering.

'My father followed that career, but I didn't, I became a policeman. My father and grandfather gathered nests. I feel a shiver when he tells me, 'When I was young, there was the American War, so I had to take part in the Vietnamese Army to fight against the Americans, here in this area' – perhaps hiding amongst the water palms I had walked past in Cam Thanh village.

'The swallow gatherers go by boats and the bamboo (scaffolding) is attached to the cave walls. There are two seasons, one in March and one in August. They make frames for the two seasons each year, take the old ones down and replace them with new frames. The frames can be from six to eight meters (18-24 ft) high from the highest to the lowest points.'

How long are the gathering seasons?

'Three to five days per season. It takes time to make the frames, about two days and after that, they steady the frames, then climb to get the nests, one day per cave and four or five days for the caves in Cu Lau Cham.' Between seasons, his son acts as a guard to keep the caves safe.

'Yes, he lives here,' despite the swallows' nests being in the caves of Cham Island(s). Depending on the labour of the teams, they divide their time to keep the caves safe. When he is in Hoi An, he cleans the swallows' nests.'

165

How many people work collecting nests?
'Forty to fifty.'
And how many clean and prepare the nests for shipping?
'Forty to fifty men, the same men who gather, clean the nests. Women only work in administration.'
And how much do they sell for? When he replies, my head spins – swallows' nests are the caviar of South East Asia!
'One kilo costs forty to sixty-five million *dong* – US$2,105 to $3,421. And is the team allowed to keep any nests, are they allowed to eat them or to sell them?
'No, the team cannot eat them, just a piece to taste. They don't taste like anything else, a little salty.' No, he himself has never eaten one, but the nests are very good for old and sick people, he says. When his father was collecting nests during the French colonial time, the Chinese rented the caves from the French and his father was an employee of the Chinese.
Was your father well paid for such a dangerous job?
'Not well paid, but enough to bring up the children and look after his family.'
Is it well paid now?
'It is well paid, nest gathering is a profession, very dangerous, so they get a salary and an extra fee for danger and poison – danger when you climb to the nests and the odour, the smell in the caves – and because he has to go to a remote area, the government pays extra fees.' He then tells me that one of his ancestors was the man who first discovered that swallows nests were edible. The discoverer, he says, was Ho Van Hoa – under King Gia Long. He then hands me the list of Nguyen kings and the names of his ancestors who served under each king as administrators over the gathering of swallows nests. Then comes the story.
'There are no historical documents, but from generation to generation, the story has been passed on of the couple, my ancestor and his wife, who went to the sea fishing. At the time, the wind came up and he could not get back to land – in those days they were rowing. His boat was pushed towards Cu Lau Cham where they took refuge in a cave and as he was very hungry and thirsty, he ate a small piece of a nest and felt better.
'He took a piece for his wife and he took more back to the mainland to give people to taste. From that time on, he began to gather nests, but he didn't know what it was, so he submitted it as

food – and Gia Long gave him the honour of general management of the nests.' This man, Ho Van Hoa, first appointed by King Gia Long to look after the nests, was the seventh generation of Ho Thanh Nhut's family; his own generation is the nineteenth – so that was twelve generations back.

Traditionally, Vietnamese sons follow the trade of their fathers, but not him. Nor have all of his offspring. He has five sons, no daughters. Only one gathers nests, the second son. Of the other sons, two are policemen and one is a carpenter in HCMC, one a cyclo driver. He tells me proudly that he has five grandsons and three granddaughters, ranging from one month old to ten years old.

'The Ong Tien temple', he says, 'is dedicated to the people who gather swallows' nests. It's proper name is Mieu To Nghe Yen – Temple for the Worship of Ancestors Who Discovered Swallows Nests.' He explains that Ho, his ancestor, asked Mr Tien to look after the temple, so people here call it his temple, 'but it is not for worshipping Mr Tien, but for honouring the people who gather swallows' nests. There is another one on Cu Lao Cham where they worship Mr Ho and others who gather nests.'

As a policeman, Ho Thanh Nhut earned much more than his son, the nest gatherer – 'but I had many years of experience. Ho Thanh Nhut is now retired, but his monthly salary was seven million *dong* ($368). He receives extra pension now because he is disabled and a war hero. His son, the nest gatherer, earns 2.5 million *dong* ($131). Under French colonial rule, the people of Cam Thanh (Thanh Chau) lost their right to the sea swallows' nests; the gatherers became mere wage earners. After 1975, the government claimed the resource and the Hoi An sea swallow nest collection brigade came into being; again the gatherers became wage earners.

The swallows are a particular subspecies of sea swifts *(collocaliafuciphaga germaini outstalet),* a bit like a sparrow, having a grey breast, a brownish black body, a long thin beak, short legs and sharp claws. In English they are called salangane, in French *hirondele de mer,* in Vietnamese *chim yen.*

The birds secrete saliva to form their nests, attached to high cliffs and grottoes in caves. The hen swallow lays two eggs once a year, which are incubated and fed by both the hen and cock. A year later, the young swallows reach maturity and build their own nests.

Cham Islands with their dry cliffs and airy caves, waves lapping against the rocks, provide high humidity and plenty of insects for food, a perfect incubator for the young swallows. The number of nests gathered is strictly limited to enable the birds to reproduce and increase their numbers.

These days concrete barriers protect the entrance to the caves from high waves, cracks in the cave walls are filled with cement to prevent leaking water from harming the birds and their nests, and artificial cave walls of brick have been built to provide more space for the birds to build their nests.

Motorboats have replaced the old rowboats, torches have replaced lanterns and the gathering seasons have been reduced from three to two per year to protect the swallows. The nests are said to have high nutritional value – thirty-five to fifty per cent protein – and to cure various illnesses: tuberculosis, asthma and inflammation of the arms or legs.

Later I read with astonishment that the sale of swallows' nests in Hoi An is worth billions of *dong* per year. In 1990 (no more recent figures available), swallows nests were Hoi An's number one export, representing 20 per cent of the town's total income. The annual harvest is reported to be around 1.4 tonnes, selling at US$4,000 per kilo retail. A nice little earner for the government, then.

PART IV

WITHIN MEMORY

BEGINNING OF THE END

The French priest, Adran, despite his illustrious titles – the Bishop of Cochin China and Ambassador Extraordinary and Plenipotentiary to the Court of Cochin China – continued to call himself simply the Apostolic Vicar of Cochin China. He died in 1799, not living to see his protégé, Nguyen Anh, retake Phu Xuan (Hue) in 1801, nor to crown himself King Gia Long of all Vietnam in 1802.

Having lost his own father at fifteen, Nguyen Anh had loved Adran like a father and when he died, bestowed upon him an epithet usually reserved for Confucius, Illustrious Master. Nguyen Anh never forgot that he owed everything to Adran: his succour and support during the desperate years in Pulo Wai (Phu Quoc) and above all, Adran's having raised the funds to mount the naval force that brought him to power – for which North Vietnam, having lost power, has never forgiven the South, nor for allowing the French that all-important toehold in Vietnam.

After Adran's body had been interred by his brother missionaries according to the rites of the Roman Catholic Church, much to the consternation of the French priests, Nguyen Anh insisted that Adran's body be disinterred and buried again – this time according to Buddhist funeral ceremonies. Not a few in Nguyen Anh's entourage must have sighed in relief at the priest's death, as he had been entrusted with the education of the heir apparent – a foreigner, who neither respected the traditional laws nor professed the faith of their ancestors.

Entrusting the education of his heir to a foreigner, however, was not altogether lacking in foresight. From his experience, Nguyen Anh realized that the traditional weaponry of South East Asia was finished. Modern weaponry and tactics relegated traditional warfare to feudal history. If his heirs were to retain power, they needed Western techniques and armaments.

When Nguyen Anh himself died in 1820, his fourth son, who came to reign as Minh Mang, had been taught modern warfare by the

169

French, who had helped his father to gain power and he was highly respected as a general. The little prince who had accompanied Adran to the French Court, having grown up, had died just before his father conquered Hue.

In Hoi An, even as early as the latter part of the eighteenth century, the volume of trade had begun to fall off with the cessation of the silver and copper trade with Japan and as spices began to be shipped from Africa and South America, resulting in loss of the monopoly of the Moluccas over the spice trade. The swashbuckling days of the European trading companies were winding down and with them began the slow decline of Hoi An as an international port. Meanwhile in Hoi An, the sands were shifting, literally. Historically, the most popular entry for ships bound for Hoi An had been from the north, Cua Han. Towards the end of the eighteenth century, this northern route from Danang along the Co Co river, quite a large river, started to silt up, threatening to close this approach to Hoi An.

When the Co Co river threatened to close altogether, Minh Mang had a canal dug in 1819 to replace part of the river. When the canal proved to be too narrow and too shallow, it was widened and deepened in 1826. Yet each monsoon brought more silt, clogging the canal. It was dredged again and again to keep the vital connecting waterway open. An old Vietnamese text, *Dai Nam Nhai Thung Chi,* after describing how the Co Co river once ran past Thanh Chau village (the old name for the village of the royal concubine's tomb and the swallows' nest gatherers), states brusquely: 'That river has dried up now. Boats can no longer sail along it.'

Traces of the dried up, dead riverbed suggest that the De Vong river, which now flows into the sea near Cua Dai in the south and the Cau Lien river near the Han river in the north, were the upper and lower parts of the dead Co Co river. Now lying in between is a series of valleys called Con Hoi, the old river bed having yielded up pieces of broken masts and anchors and place names evocative of its maritime past: Isle of Boats at Cam Chau, where vessels en route to Hoi An once anchored; Ferry River at Cam Thanh.

Worse, it was precisely at this time that deposits along the coast and the Thu Bon estuary itself began to build up significantly. The lakes were no longer deep or large enough for boats and barges to moor. The channels through the Cua Dai estuary changed frequently, the river bed filling with sandy shoals, creating serious threats to boatmen. It was the beginning of the end for Hoi An as a port. As bigger ships, particularly steamships, started to arrive from the West, Danang with its deep water bay, drew more and more business away from Hoi An.

The log of a Portuguese ship states bluntly: 'Big ships that could not travel along the Hoi An river had to unload at Danang.'

Finally in 1835, Minh Mang decreed that all Western merchant ships coming to Vietnam must berth at Danang and puzzlingly, that Chinese merchants would have to use their own vessels if they wanted to do business in other ports – Hoi An.

While Hoi An was fighting the silt in the Co Co and Thu Bon rivers, French influence was spreading in Vietnam. From early on, France had been jealous of Britain's lucrative trade with China. Following the Opium Wars of 1842, the British had obtained Favoured Nation trading rights with China in the treaty of 1857. The thinking of the French must have gone something like this. By establishing a foothold in South East Asia, by controlling the deltas of the Mekong river in the South and the Red river in the North, whose sources arose in China, French merchants would be able to penetrate along these two rivers, deep into the heart of China to trade.

However, in an early expedition up the Mekong led by Francis Garnier and Daudart de Lagnee, the shallow rapids of southern Laos known as the Four Thousand Islands, proved to be an insurmountable obstacle to shipping.

Not to be deterred, the French built a short railway alongside the rapids and a railway bridge over the river a bit further upstream. It was with utter amazement a few years ago that I stumbled upon a rusty old French engine on an isolated length of track, stranded in a village in southern Laos, the remains of this wildly optimistic, tropical misadventure. How they got the heavy engine there – they must have disassembled and reassembled it. The Mekong in the South having proved un-navigable for heavy shipping, France decided to focus on Tonkin in the North of Vietnam, to gain access to China up the Red river from Hanoi.

To thread our way through the labyrinthine chronology of France's creeping advancement into Indo-China, although the Nguyen came to power through French military support, the fourth Nguyen king, Tu Duc (reign 1848-1883), had become hostile to Western influence, particularly to Catholicism, which he considered a foreign threat to Confucianism. Although Louis XVI had reneged on the military support promised in the Treaty of Versailles, the French with the approval of Nguyen Anh, had established a trading presence in Danang and Hoi An.

Using Tu Duc's later persecution of French priests as a pretext, the French attacked Vietnamese ships in Turon (Danang) harbour in 1858, leaving Tu Duc little choice but to agree to a full-blown, official French trade concession in the port of Turon. The French were now on the military offensive. A year later in July of 1859, they took Saigon and a treaty of 1864 recognised French control over three cities and provinces in the South: Saigon, My Tho and Bien Hoa. In spite of dogged Vietnamese resistance, the French occupied three more cities and provinces in the Mekong Delta in 1867: Vinh Long, Ha Tien and Chau Doc. Now, despite continuing resistance, they nominally controlled the entire Mekong delta.

In November of 1873, a small expeditionary force of fewer than two hundred men led by Francis Garnier – the same Garnier who had made the expedition up the Mekong – captured Hanoi's citadel, no longer the seat of power, but ardently defended by Hanoians nonetheless. If a small expeditionary force could take Hanoi's citadel, Tu Duc realized that he had little chance against a full French army.

On 15 March 1874, he therefore agreed to a treaty, preserving the independence of Annam (Central Vietnam including Hue, Danang and Hoi An), but opening the Red river in the North to international trade. The treaty granted a land concession for a French Navy Cantonment along the Red river in Hanoi. The French had obtained their goals, control of both rivers, the Red river (Song Hong) in the North and the Mekong river in the South – not that either gave them a gateway to China.

Following the death of Tu Duc in 1883, the French forced Tu Duc's brief successor, Hiep Hoa, to sign the first Convention of Protectorate. It was ratified 6 June 1884 by the Treaty of Patenôtre (named after the French negotiator), which relinquished sovereignty over all three regions of Vietnam: Cochin in the South, Annam in Central, and Tonkin in the North. From this moment on, Vietnam was under French colonial rule; Vietnamese emperors in Hue, despite resistance, were reduced to puppets and their mandarin forced to follow French orders. The Indo-Chinese Union proclaimed by the French in 1887, which included Cochin, Annam, Tonkin and Cambodia – Laos was added in 1894 – may have ended the legal

172

existence of independent Vietnam, but active Vietnamese resistance continued in various parts of the country right up to World War II and then, of course, afterwards in the French Indo-Chinese War.

Over the years, the creeping sands had taken their toll. Records for 1887 – the same year that the Indo-Chinese Union was proclaimed – state that 623 vessels called at Danang: 54 French, 2 British, 65 German, 8 Danish, the remainder Chinese and Vietnamese – a total of 65,840 tons. There were 719 departures with a total tonnage of 75,676. Some of this business still was conducted through Hoi An.

Statistics for that same year expressed in French francs, however, reveal the underlying truth. Hoi An remained a vital *entrepot,* the collection point to which produce was brought from up and down the coast and from the hinterland, but it had lost its prominence as a port. Even as late as 1905, to ease the lack of a connecting water route, the French colonial authorities built a railway between Danang and Hoi An. When the railway was washed away by a storm in 1916, it was never rebuilt.

With increasingly larger vessels requiring a deep harbour, maritime trade came to revolve around Danang. Hoi An was left up a shallow river, a provincial backwater with a treacherous, tidal harbour entrance, its merchants clinging to their role as middle men and forwarding agents for up-country and down-country producers and farmers, who had supplied their families for generations. Hoi An's days as an international port had come to an end.

THREE WARS

'The biggest and ugliest building in Hoi An' – is one resident's opinion of the new Revolutionary Museum (and now also the History Museum) at the corner of Nguyen Hue and Tran Phu Streets. Monumental staircases lead to a modern block, its heavy design bordering on social-realism, totally out of scale with the rest of the town. How much more fitting if the mementos of the early stirrings of the local Communist party and the grass-roots resistance during the French Indo-Chinese War and the Vietnam War had been placed in an old historic house, the kind of house in which these stirrings and movements first began.

Offices occupy the upper ground floor; the museum occupies two rooms above, one devoted to the French Indo-Chinese War, the other to the Vietnam War. Photographs of long-dead cadres, their secret meeting places, parades and certain artefacts add up to a rather forlorn collection: the Duc An house where the Vietnam Revolutionary Youth organization was established in 1927 and the Van Sanh Bookshop where they were based from 1926-30; the photograph of a lone pine on a sand dune, one of the places where Hoi An town and Quang Nam province Communist Party used to meet (1930); a blurry photograph of Hoi An people in white uniforms, marching with guns 'taking the government in 1945' – at the end of the Second World War.

When the Japanese invaded Vietnam during World War II, requisitioning so much rice that two million Vietnamese died of starvation, Hoi An suffered along with the rest of the country. During the occupation, the Japanese incarcerated the French. Following the Japanese surrender on 19 August 1945, Ho Chi Minh's Revolutionary Committee rushed to the balcony of the French built opera house in Hanoi, unfurled their banners and announced the establishment of the independent Socialist Republic of Vietnam.

Two months later on 2 September 1945, Ho Chi Minh read out his historic, freshly penned Declaration of Independence at Ba Dinh Square in Hanoi. Ironically, he had borrowed heavily from America's Declaration of Independence. The newly appointed Minister of Internal Affairs, Vo Nguyen Giap – later the victorious general of the Vietnam War – took his turn as speaker, discussing the domestic situation and the new government's policies. The royal seal and the sword, imperial symbols of the Nguyen dynasty, were shown to the people. Only days before, standing high in the red lacquered Five Phoenix Pavilion of Ngo Mon (gate) at Hue's Citadel, the last Nguyen king, Bao Dai, had abdicated, saying he 'would far rather be a common man than ruler of an enslaved nation.' The ceremony in Ba Dinh Square was a bit premature, as it turned out. The French had other ideas – the French simply returned to business as usual in their Indo-Chinese colony. Armed Viet Minh resistance against them began in earnest and the French Indo-China War dragged on for nine years until the French surrender at Dien Bien Phu in 1954.

Hoi An's Revolutionary Museum displays a few bamboo spears – 'set up at Con 198 Kiem dune to resist landing of the French in 1953 by the people of Cam Thanh village' – once again the village of the swallows' nest gatherers where the royal concubine lies entombed. I remembered the farmer pointing out the hideout in the water palms along the river's edge. A display case contains 'one of the rifles presented by Ho Chi Minh to the people of Hoi An to honour their 'best achievement' in resistance against the French (1950).'

Sentiments ran high during the struggle against the French. I was told by one man in Hoi An that his grandfather had been murdered by his sister-in-law. I immediately imagined a crime of passion until he went on to tell the story.

His grandfather had been working as a translator for the French in Hanoi while his son worked for the Viet Minh in Hoi An. When his grandfather come home to visit his village between Hoi An and Danang, his sister-in-law denounced him. He had arrived home late in the afternoon and at midnight, there were knocks on the door. He was tied up and his throat slit by the Viet Minh, who saw him as a traitor 'because he was trying to earn a living to support his family.' For many reasons, the family was unable to retrieve his body from the village at the time, so he was buried there. It was years later before his son could move his bones away from the village and bury him in Hoi An.

Following Dien Bien Phu, in 1959 the North's determination to 'liberate' the South began in earnest. Historically, going back to the days of the Nguyen lords, Vietnam had been divided since 1627, Central Vietnam a part of the South. Families were spit between those who had fought with the Communists, who with nationalistic fervour had driven out the French, and those – Catholics, Buddhists and many others – who feared the Communists in the North.

After several years of providing American military advisers to the army of the South, over three thousand American marines landed on Nam O Beach in 1965 and set up a huge base at Danang. The Viet Cong responded by installing gun emplacements and a military hospital in the caves of nearby Marble Mountains.

The Americans positioned their evacuation hospital on nearby Nam O beach on the Danang peninsula. What was to become known as China Beach, just south of Danang, now dotted with luxurious resorts, served as the rest and recreation area for the American military in the Danang area. There were even rooms to rent where the men could take their girlfriends. By and large, American troops were discouraged from going into Danang, but at times, permits were allowed. It became the town where the American military went for a night out to bars, restaurants and nightclubs. A doctor, then posted to the Danang military evacuation hospital, recalls one night, driving back to the base – and having a flat tyre.

'We were very scared and ran on the flat tyre. It was rumoured that the Viet Cong – or just locals – would put nailed boards in the road, so we would have to stop and get out and they could rob the gas can, or tyres, or us. Sometimes a person would pretend to be hit and lie in the middle of the road to get us to stop at night. The rule was, don't stop. This was all after the Tet offensive (in Hue) of 1968. Before that, the military could go about more freely. Hoi An and Marble Mountain were definitely off limits. The Marine air base at the foot of Marble Mountain would get rocketed regularly from the cave at the top. I didn't even know about Hoi An then.'

During the Vietnam War, with the agreement of both sides, Hoi An remained almost completely undamaged. Yet it did not escape skirmishes. One elderly resident told me that seven people were killed in his garden. Motioning to an altar in his courtyard, 'We set up an altar for them.'

Hoi An's Revolutionary Museum displays some touchingly personal mementos from this period: A shovel used by Tran Binh to dig tunnels to protect comrades (1963-65); a long, cracked wooden boat used by Le Van Duc to ferry soldiers and cadres (1965-1972) – the boat in which he died; jars used for leaving secret messages; a soldier's water bottle, pith helmet and 'handguns used to kill the enemy (1967).'

Several months after the Tet offensive in Hue, Ho Chi Minh died on what has become Vietnam's national holiday, 2 September 1968. Seven days later on 9 September 1968, a solemn memorial service in his honour was held, once again in Ba Dinh Square in Hanoi. By 1973, all US military personnel had left Vietnam and US prisoners of war had been released. The war between the North and the South continued, only now – without the Americans. In January 1975, the North mounted a massive ground offensive across the seventeenth parallel, which panicked the South Vietnamese army.

Soldiers from the South fled south, melting into the population, leaving Hue, Danang, Hoi An, Quy Nhon and Nha Trang unprotected from the northern advance. When Hue fell to the North, all chaos broke loose. People were fleeing and soldiers from the South were looting. Two truckloads of Communist guerrillas drove into Danang and without firing a shot, declared the city liberated.

On 30 April 1975, a North Vietnamese tank smashed through the gates of Saigon's Presidential Palace, since renamed the Reunification Palace. The war was over. Vietnam had been reunited.

Since 1975, Vietnam has rebuilt itself, at first slowly with Russian aid, then after the break-up of the Soviet Union, little by little opening its doors to international investment. Direct foreign investment in Vietnam reached a peak of $64 billion (£43 bn) in 2008, up from only $20 billion (£13 bn) in 2007, now having fallen back during the world financial crisis. The country began to open its doors to tourism in 1990.

(Note: The Hoi An History Museum has moved to the same floor as the rooms dedicated to the French Indo-Chinese War and theVietnam War.)

A LOCAL SUCCESS STORY

From the Revolutionary Museum, I stroll round the corner into Nguyen Hue Street to Miss Ly's restaurant for an early lunch of fresh spring rolls, iced Vietnamese tea and frozen yoghurt. Ideal for a hot day. Miss Ly's restaurant is in an appealing old house, dark wood panelling, pot plants hanging from the eaves. A table in each of the windows faces the street on each side of the central doorway, entered through low wooden gates. The restaurant is a study of elegant simplicity: dark wooden, curved, high-back chairs, white cushions, white tablecloths, the over-cloths a black square placed diagonally under glass – less laundry when technique-less foreigners battling chopsticks have mishaps.

I watch as a man squats on the pavement in front of the restaurant, assembling electric fans, destined for the restaurant. The current fans blow straight down from the beams above, whipping diners' hair and cooling the food. So, an upgrading of fans, which he installs one by one along the walls.

An amputee sits opposite under a tree, leaning on his crutch, selling sweet potato crisps in plastic bags from a cart. Another amputee with a peg leg stumps by and they exchange greetings. A man pushes his motorbike, piled high with a mountain of baskets, then hops aboard and splutters off noisily. This is the no-motorbikes area; he is only allowed to push the bike through the area, motor-less.

Half a dozen young girls stroll past en route home to lunch from high school, wearing white *ao dais* and jackets in thirty-degree heat to protect their arms from the sun, floppy-brimmed hats and masks to cover their faces from the dust and pollution. The boys in neat black trousers and white shirts, scuff their sandals, swaggering a bit to attract attention as teenage boys will. A woman pushes her cart, loaded with plastic tables and chairs, cooking pots and bowls, en route to wherever she will set up her pavement cafe. A granny in a conical straw hat brings her bicycle to an abrupt halt, stoops to pick up a flattened cardboard box from the new fans, then sets off again on her bicycle. The morning rubbish lorries that play a plaintive flute tune every morning over a loudspeaker to announce their arrival, will have one less box to collect. Perhaps she can sell it, or has a use for it.

As I am early for lunch, Miss Ly sits down. I am her first customer of the day, significant in Vietnamese and Chinese tradition, because the first customer foretells how the rest of the day will go. Miss Ly is a slim, wiry woman of indeterminate age, who opened the restaurant with her mother in 1993. She lost her father when she was only four. 'I was just a little girl, we started out small, a few plastic chairs and a couple of tables, serving *cao lau,*' a specialty of Hoi An. Miss Ly and her mother had started out like the woman who just passed by, her cart piled high with plastic stools and tables, pots and dishes. 'Our family has lived in this same house for sixty or seventy years. We rent it from the government. It's so small here, I now live with my brother, but my mum still lives here.'

In what would have been the shop or the sitting room, she can now seat a maximum of thirty-six and is expecting a group of twenty people this evening.

Tentatively, I ask if she is married.

'I was married, but not anymore. He was Belgian and a very good man, but sometimes things happen; people are not always good together,' she replies philosophically.

Does she have a boyfriend, I ask timidly? The Vietnamese are very open people, but one does feel intrusive.

'Yes, I have a boyfriend and we plan to live together. He calls me every day from California.'

Is he a *Viet kieu* (an overseas Vietnamese)?

'No, he is an American-American, he teaches art, he is a very good guy. He is going to move to Hoi An. He has to give up everything to move here, rather than me moving there.'

And what will he do here?

'He has to find something to do to make him feel proud of himself. I don't want his family to worry.'

I ask if she has children.

'No, nor does he.'

I wonder aloud if he is about to retire? So often older Western men fall under the spell of a younger Vietnamese woman.

'No, he's forty, like me. His mother might want him to have children. He has a sister, an older sister, so she is unlikely to have children. I don't want to have children, I am so busy.'

Clearly, she has given a lot of thought to his decision to move to Vietnam and it is easy to see her own ties: the restaurant which she and her mother have built up together over the years, which her mother is now too old to run on her own – and her devotion to her mother. Traditionally, the Vietnamese always look after their elderly relatives, it being unthinkable that they should be shoved out of the family home.

Miss Ly and her artist have bought a property together on the way to the beach.

'In the countryside. It is really nice, in a big rice field. It's very quiet there. Westerners like it, but my mother thinks it is too quiet. In a few days he has one week off for school holidays and he will come and take one more week. In July, he will be here for good.'

Some days later, during his brief spring school holidays, I meet Nathan, a pleasant, open-faced man, who is very much looking forward to life in Hoi An and above all else, to sharing his life with Miss Ly. He understands and accepts her strong ties, her rootedness to Hoi An, to the restaurant and above all else, to her mother.

'She helps so many people,' he says when she is out of earshot. It is her uncle who sells sweet potato crisps from the cart across the street. He lost his leg in the Vietnam War – fighting for the South, like her father.'

GOOD MORNING HOI AN!

Mr Phung, a friend of my landlady, is a grasshopper-thin man with intense, intelligent eyes. From my description he instantly recognizes the woman with the glass-cutting cry as the vendor of coconut juice, *nuoc dua*. Sold in plastic bags with a straw, it is very refreshing to shopkeepers on a hot day. To my delight, he suggests a tour of Hoi An's pavement breakfast stalls. At 6.45 a.m. we set off on his motorbike. Rush hour in Hoi An starts about six, if not earlier. People open their shops at eight o'clock and many are meant to be at their desks by 7.30. Consequently, the pavement cafes open around six. We no more than cross the junction. Street stalls on low tables and tiny plastic stools crowd both sides of a narrow lane.

'We used to eat breakfast at home. I always ate breakfast at home when I was young, but now, because it takes so long to prepare, we go out,' explains Mr Phung. 'Breakfast for an adult, perhaps two dishes, costs ten thousand *dong* ($0.53) and one bowl for a child costs five thousand *dong*' ($0.26).

The women breakfast cooks sit on tiny stools surrounded by large bowls, pans and plastic bags holding various ingredients and huge metal pots with lids, simmering gently over portable gas burners. In the past, it would have been flower pot charcoal burners. This is fresh food, freshly cooked before your eyes, doubtless the legacy of a time not so long ago when no one had refrigerators. Only pork or a meat *paté* will have been cooked at home the night before and most cooks start their preparations – there is a lot of grinding and sauce-making – at three or four in the morning.

The first stall is selling the Hoi An specialty, *cao lau,* the dish that Miss Ly and her mother started out selling in just such a pavement cafe: thick steamed noodles and fresh greens, topped with thin slices of pork and chopped peanuts.

'*Cao* means high, *lau* means storey,' Mr Phung explains. 'When we eat *cao lau,* it's very special. In the past, we never ate it on the ground floor, we had to go to the top storey. This name *cao lau* comes from a very long time ago. In the seventeenth century when we made *cao lau,*, we had to spend a lot of time making it.' Mr Phung then tells me a bit about how to make the basic ingredient of *cao lau* the noodles, and how they differ from other noodles.

'First, we had to choose good, soft rice. We put the rice in a huge bowl – a basin – with water, because when we made it, we made it for many people. Into the water we put some ash – from Cham Island, from the wood there. The water had to come from the Ba Le well in Hoi An; the fresh vegetables had to come from Tra Que village and the pork from the other side of Kim Bong village. It took a long time in the past to gather all these ingredients.

'There is still an old woman who makes it in the traditional way. She is known as Ba Be and they are thinking of using her name as a trademark, a brand name. Now everyone makes *cao lau,* but not using the ingredients from the original, traditional sources.'

Next in the line-up is a woman selling *banh goi.*

'*Banh* means cake, *goi* means wrapped,' in this case a rice powder cake, wrapped in a banana leaf with prawns and pork inside.

Banh beo is made of soft, sticky rice, ground to a powder and it is served in bowls topped by a red paste made of ground peppers and prawn with pork on top. It can be sweet or savoury topped with chilli sauce and ground peanuts. Children, of course, prefer the sweet, made with sugar and green pea powder.'

The cooks and their customers are much bemused by our visit and obligingly lift their lids to show us the assortment of ingredients that go into their particular specialties.

'*Bun'*, Mr Phung explains, 'are noodles made from rice powder and go into a soup with beef or pork – in a soup because some people like to chew a lot. Beef is tough. You can eat it here or it is sold in plastic bags to go, along with fresh mint and chilli. It is very popular with older people.'

Across the lane is a *bun man* stall.

'*Bun* means noodles, *bun man* is rice noodles in fish sauce. There are two kinds of fish sauce, *nuoc mam,* brown or red,' I learn for the first time. In the first process of making *nuoc mam,* he explains, the anchovies are placed in the bottom of a jug where they ferment to a powder; the thick brown sauce that results is called *mam cai.* In the second process, the brown sauce drips through a cloth filter – this strained liquid becomes *mam trong.*

'Some people can't use *mam cai* because they have high blood pressure.'

At the *bun man* stall, into a bowl go pork and young star fruit chopped finely, chilli, softened onions, chopped peanuts and of course, *nuoc mam.*

182

'It has a very strong smell.'

Not half. I remember encountering *nuoc mam* for the first time, years ago in Cambodia, approaching a village that specialized in making it. You could smell the fermenting fish from miles away as we approached. Having said that, it is the all-purpose, slightly salty base of seasoning in Vietnam and in much of South East Asia, a bit of sugar, lime, or chillies added for variety. And very good it is, too, particularly as a salad dressing, and extremely nutritious.

The last woman in the lane is sitting behind a huge galvanized pan of tiny black fish – anchovies – the same fish that go into the fish sauce, *nuoc man*.

'She is selling *chao gao do* – or *chao ao nau*. *Chao* means soup, *gao* means rice, *nau* means brown and *do* means red – but we never say *chao gao nau.*'

So it's brown rice soup with red *nuoc mam*. The vendor very carefully picks up each anchovy with her chopsticks, one by one, and puts them into a plastic bag, then adds the juice – for the takeaways. Spiced cucumber and a few ground peanuts accompany it.

'It is very good for sick people, very nutritious.'

From here we take Mr Phuong's motorbike into Nguyen Truong To Street where a little beyond the Revolutionary Museum, Mr Phuong pulls over to the curb, saying that we are lucky, this old Chinese man isn't here every day, sometimes only once a week and that he is the last, the very last vendor to sell his concoction: black sesame seeds ground to a powder, a bit of flour and sugar added to make a thick black sauce or soup called *si ma*.

Mr Phuong explains that when the Chinese came to Hoi An in the seventeenth century, they brought their cuisine with them and many of Hoi An's specialties have derived from these early southern Chinese cooks.

'He has been selling his sesame soup on the pavements of Hoi An for seventy years.'

My mind scrolls back through the history that this old man has lived through! His name is Ngo Thieu and he says that he is ninety-five years old and was born in 1912 – which by my reckoning would make him ninety-eight. The soup must be good for longevity.

'It is not only a food, but medicine, good for the stomach. You take it hot. He starts his preparations at 3 a.m.'

The large pot of black soup steams over a charcoal fire in a metal container.

He is a gruff old man, not particularly friendly. Poor man, for far too long he has become a curiosity for tourists. He asks for a tip and Mr Phung explains that usually, people tip him for taking photographs. With only a notebook, I look problematical. Mr Phung suggests ten thousand dong, which doesn't bring a smile.

Further up Nguyen Truong To Street, we come upon another string of pavement cafes.

'*Chao xuong* is another kind of rice soup, this time using stewed pork bones. Or it can be rice soup with beef paste, chopped onion stalks, mint and quails' eggs. You ask for the beef paste and quail egg, extra. It is not only for old people, but it is easy to digest.'

Babies snuggle on their mothers' laps, being fed *chao*.

Moving along, Mr Phung defines *cha* as 'pork salad in a banana leaf,' but the pork salad, once unwrapped, to me looks more like a sausage-shaped pork *paté*.

Cha, I had thought, was tea. It's all in where the Vietnamese place those infernal little accents that indicate which of the five tones – or six in the North.

'*Cha* with a different accent, means father and *tra*, pronounced exactly the same to the Western ear as *cha*, does indeed, mean tea. Another vendor here is selling *chao gao do*, sticky red rice soup, served with a baguette, 'very nutritious.'

At last I see something recognisable – a huge pan of bean sprouts – which go into the *cao lau*, Miss Ly's mother's specialty. Here, the cook places the thick brown rice noodles in a bowl over which go a selection of bean sprouts and fresh green salad leaves, among them mint and purple onions in vinegar, on top of which go a slice of pork, chilli and brown juice from cooking the pork. Sometimes soya sauce.

'The woman starts her preparations at 4 a.m. She makes some things in the morning, some the night before. She cooks the pork and the sauce the night before.'

Bun mam are rice cakes shaped like the halves of apricots, sweet and savoury, served in a bowl, a kind of noodles with fish sauce and pork salad on top, again the sausage-shaped pork *paté* unwrapped from a banana leaf.

Khoai lang are unadorned, baked sweet potatoes, sold by an old lady, sitting behind her tray of stacked sweet potatoes and ordinary baked potatoes. At the next stall, Mr Phung orders a bag of *banh it*.

'*It* means very, very small, tiny. They are wrapped in banana leaves. We take them as a present to show warm feelings towards a friend. They are made of powdered rice and green pea powder and are eaten as desert.'

Perhaps the strangest and possibly the most elaborate dish to prepare of the entire lot is *banh cuon*. A huge round plastic bowl is heaped with what look like thin sheets of semi-transparent, soft rice paper, tiny flecks of carrots and mushrooms embedded in it.

Shredded green papaya goes into the bottom of a serving bowl. Then the vendor gently lifts a sheet of the rice paper with her chopsticks. Sometimes it sticks and tears. In any case, as she lifts each one, she cuts the rice paper into bite-sized widths with scissors – easier for chopsticks. On top go the pork salad, the sausage-shaped pork *paté* from a banana leaf, sometimes beef, more greens, onions and chilli sauce.

At the next stall, Mr Phung announces, '*My Quang* are rice noodles' – so many kinds of noodles. 'We are in Quang Nam, so *mi Quang* are the special noodles from here,' rather like Italy, where every district has its own style and shape of pasta. *Mi Quang* are served with vegetables, pork and prawns.

'What is your plan for the day?' Mr Phung asks.

I have no plan for the day, so to my delight he suggests that we go for breakfast at his favourite cafe, the only difference from the pavement cafes being that it has a tin roof over the top. He orders *mi Quang*, the Quang noodles topped with fresh greens and a savoury sauce, then *banh beo*, a small, shallow saucer, the bottom of which holds a kind of jellied noodle, shaped to the bowl, topped by one red prawn and pork paste, happily, eaten with a spoon. Neither are chilli hot, both delicious.

'The base of *banh beo* is made from *mi* rice powder. We have rice, so much rice, and rice can be boring, so we have to think of many different ways of eating it.'

My head jumbled with noodles, my heart sinks when Mr Phung says brightly, 'But that is only breakfast. We must do lunch and supper as well.'

Another day Mr Phung invites me to meet the *cao lau* noodle lady. From an unpaved lane in Truong Le hamlet of Cam Chou village, we turn into a stuccoed house behind neat rows of pomegranate bonzai trees in the courtyard.

185

Noodles piled on large straw trays lie cooling and drying on the terrace. Off to one side in an open shed, four people are busily working. Their family name is Ta. Mr Phung introduces me to Dinh, his wife Trai (who has taken her mother-in-law's name) and two employees. In Vietnam, children often adopt a parent's or a parent-in-law's given name, rather like a nickname – out of respect.

The Ta family has been making *cao lau* noodles, unique to Hoi An, for at least three generations and the old lady, Dinh's mother, still sells *cao lau* noodles in Hoi An market.

Making *cao lau* noodles is a hot and labour intensive business. A wood fire burns in a dark shed next door to where three women are cutting noodles, beside Dinh, who rolls out the dough.

The first step is leaving the rice to soak for two or three hours to soften in water to which ash has been added. Three huge basins stand outside full of milky looking liquid. The softened rice is then put through a grinder to make powder – rice flour. The rice flour is then steamed under a lid over a wood fire for about an hour. Dinh then places the rice flour and water in a large motorized mixer to make the dough. Afterwards, Dinh takes a wodge of dough from the mixer and rolls it into a neat rectangle, roughly ten by twenty inches (25 x 51 cms) long.

The women take the rolled out dough, brush it with peanut oil and cut the noodles. Two employees squat with curved, two-handled knives, rocking the knives back and forth from side to side, cutting astonishingly uniform noodles by hand, a quarter of an inch (1 cm) wide, noodle by noodle. Dinh's wife, Trai, runs the dough through a mechanical noodle-cutting machine. Noodles cut by hand are more expensive. The noodles then are placed in neat handfuls, spread over straw trays on banana leaves, covered with more banana leaves and steamed again for an hour after they have been cut.

From the noodle factory, we set off for the market and eventually find Trai, an old lady of seventy-seven with a wizened face, salt and pepper hair, her front teeth blackened from chewing betal, standing behind trays of noodles with three of her female relatives. The family works at noodle making from 1 a.m. to 11 a.m. every day, their only day off being *Tet,* New Year's Day. The family does not get rich from noodle making, but makes a modest to comfortable living – everyone in Hoi An has to have *cao lau* noodles and the Ta family supplies them.

A BUDDHA OR TWO

When I first rang the young Italian archaeologist, Federico Barocco, I found him at the other end of his mobile, more than a hundred miles (200 km) south of Hoi An on a dig and not expected back for some days. 'Go round and meet my wife Thanh,' he suggested. 'She has just opened a restaurant called Bazaar at 36 Tran Phu Street.'

Pale violet morning glories shower their blossoms from the eaves over the open terrace where deep purple silk lanterns hang above two tables, ideal for market and people watching. The old house yawns back and back to a large garden on several levels, the rustic furniture reflecting a deep affection for old things and a love of *objets trouvées*. Fishing baskets and birdcages hang as lamps, tastefully transformed by a flow of silk. The wooden drums used to press dried sardines into the highly nutritious fish sauce, *nuoc mam*, find themselves as low tables in the bar.

Thanh is Vietnamese, but a chic, Paris-born *Viet kieu*, who met her husband on a boat to Cham Island while on a family holiday to visit her unknown homeland. He was already working in Vietnam as an arachaeologist. Bright eyed, tawny skinned, her lovely black hair swept back casually in a ponytail and her slim frame lend her a natural elegance, her kindness and generosity of spirit only exceeded by her quick perception and intelligence. Despite her tender years, in Paris she organized international conferences in countries bordering the Mediterranean. 'I have a book that might be useful to you,' she said on first meeting and when I told her that I was eager to meet and talk to old Hoi An families, immediately she introduced me to her neighbour across the street. It was also Thanh who found me a translator, Pho, the uncle of a friend, and the charming restaurant remained a cool oasis throughout my stay in Hoi An, whenever I found myself near the market.

'Do you know *lemoncello?*' Thanh asked. As Federico's mother had taught her to make *lemoncello,* an innocuous tasting, unexpectedly lethal Italian liqueur, she had been experimenting with *mangochello* – with excellent results.

Thanh also introduced me to her locally born partner, Nguyen Viet Linh, who also owns a carving factory. Linh has one of those merry faces that tells you instantly that he has a keen sense of humour and mischief. At thirty-seven, already smile lines crinkle the corners of his quick, darting eyes, and as most Vietnamese marry young, he must be one of the most eligible bachelors in Hoi An. It is Linh, who had translated my letter of introduction into Vietnamese.

Since Federico's Italian parents happen to be visiting Vietnam for the first time, Linh asks if I would like to join Federico's father in a visit to his carving factory.

'Of course.' Federico's father hops gamely onto the back of Linh's motorbike. A *xe om* is hired for me and we zoom off. *Xe om* translates as motorbike huggy, because the passenger riding pinion hangs on for dear life to the motorbike driver.

The tightly packed houses of Hoi An end abruptly, giving way to lush, iridescent green paddies. Crops of vegetables thrust their way lustily through the rich alluvial soil of the river banks and the river bed, left high above the watermark in the dry season. So fast do vegetables grow in this hot, moist climate that several crops of vegetables can be harvested from the river bed between January and October, the start of the rainy season. This being a river estuary, temporary fields in river beds appear and disappear with the monsoons. On crossing the bridge at Nam Phuoc, the motorbikes turn off the main road into paved village lanes, past neat stuccoed houses behind concrete or sometimes courtyards of packed earth where a haystack clings to a central pole, always behind some kind of fence or wall, flowering plant pots and fruit trees, occasionally a bougainvillea covered gateway.

Vietnam's standard of living has improved dramatically in the past thirteen years. Blinking into memory, in country lanes I recall only occasional stuccoed houses, most village houses built of wood, sometimes straw, the walls of plaited matting with thatched roofs, sometimes boasting one dangling electric light bulb, or one up on the financial ladder, a high florescent bar lighting the room. These days there are modern light fittings, even down-lighters in false ceilings and always, motorbikes parked out front. Now, only the very poor, the young and the very old peddle bicycles and some of them have motorbikes. Everyone seems glued to a mobile phone.

Our two motorbikes splutter to a halt at the entrance to a large open shed, eighteen miles (29 km) from Hoi An in a village called Dien Hong Go Noi.

The shed is what Linh calls the carving factory, the company fancifully named Au Lac, one of the ancient names for Vietnam. His partner in the carving business is Tran Thu, 'my best friend since we were little boys.' Inside, the heady scent of freshly cut timber fills the air; sawdust, shavings and wood chips litter the floor. The workers squat on stools, eating watermelon, 'their afternoon break.' Half a dozen overpowering statues of the goddess, Quan Am The Am, stand in a group, facing one another in a *tête-à-tête* of deities, no two alike. Sometimes a goddess stands with a child in her arms, sometimes with a toddler at her feet, sometimes childless.

In the story of the Vietnamese Quan Am Thi Kinh, a reincarnation of the Chinese Kwan Yin, holding a baby has nothing to do with the birth of Buddha. According to the story, the last trial of a good monk before reaching nirvana is to endure one life – living as a woman. She married, but one night when she attempted to trim a whisker from her husband's chin while he was sleeping, he awoke and thinking she was about to slit his throat, beat her and banished her from the house.

The poor wife took refuge in a pagoda disguised as a male monk and was besieged by the unwanted attentions of the village belle, Thi Mau. Despite the monk's rejections, when Thi Mau fell pregnant through another liaison, out of spite she pointed to the monk, who obviously did nothing to support her/his innocence by offering to adopt the baby. When the monk(ess) finally died, it was discovered that he was a she, and much was made of the wrong that had been done to her. Not surprisingly, having endured this greatest of afflictions and mortifications – life as a woman – the monk(ess) attained nirvana and has since been known as the Vietnamese Quan Am Thi Kinh. That is why she often appears, holding an infant.

In another incarnation, she is the goddess of a thousand arms and a thousand eyes, the all-seeing goddess of mercy. Naturally, she is a very popular and much in demand.

A roly-poly wooden Buddha, the Buddha of the future, sits hunched over his tummy, laughing at a secret joke that might have been cracked by a crony, only I don't recall ever seeing a really fat Vietnamese man.

The watermelon break over, the sculptors take up their tools and the cacophony of hammers tapping metal rings round the shed. A factory, this is certainly not, more an *atelier* of artisans working under a master sculptor. Three young men tap away at the base of a huge

189

Quan Yin. Another taps at a reclining Christ, who will soon be joined to his cross. Beside the sculptor lies a twelve-inch-long wooden crucifixion, which he is using as a guide to create the life-sized statue. It has been commissioned not by a church, but by a private individual who will donate it to a church. Amongst the Quan Yins, waiting to be sanded and oiled, stands a large crowned figure.

'A monk, commissioned by a pagoda in Thailand. Commissions come in not only from Vietnam, also from Thailand and America, and other countries,' says Linh.

Nearby, the life-sized figure of a young boy holds out 'a fire ring,' the loose wooden ring in his hand having been carved from the same piece of wood as the boy, the folds of his tunic falling as though blown softly by the wind.

Linh's partner, Tran Thu, joins us. The master sculptor, he manages the factory. Life-sized statues of the goddess, Quan Yin The Am, are their most popular product. They carve some twenty-odd Quan Yins a year, which sell for up to three thousand US dollars (£2,000). Tran Thu learnt the art of carving in Hue where he lived and worked with a family of sculptors. Linh and Thu opened the factory six years ago.

'The factory takes on young people and teaches them to carve. It takes one and a half years before they can produce anything and three years to be fully-trained.' Au Lac has ten to twelve boys in training – and one girl. They start at eighteen. Normally, women finish the work, sanding and polishing.

'The workers earn from one million eight hundred to four-and-a-half million Vietnamese *dong* ($100-250) per month. That may not sound like much, but it is quite good for here.'

Along one wall, the name of each worker is painted above a space on an open shelf 'where they store their tools,' a set of thirty or so tools of different sizes. There are flint stones for sharpening.

Surprisingly, the factory employs several handicapped people, surprisingly because one would think that physical strength is required to be a sculptor. Linh explains that they have one worker who cannot speak, one who is deaf and an amputee and that often, the handicapped are the best workers 'because they are more focused.'

The factory has also employed a reformed alcoholic and an ex-prisoner, both of whom through learning to carve have found their way back into normal and fulfilling lives. In the beginning, the factory produced carvings of flowers, portraits of famous artists and well-known people, but as time passed the business gravitated towards religious statues. They also make furniture, but only to order. As go-ahead young entrepreneurs, Linh and Tran Tru market their business on the internet, have presented their work at exhibitions in Hanoi and Ho Chi Minh City and will take it to an exhibition next month in Danang. We come to an enormous perforated wall panel on the floor, the size of a large door, two young men tapping on it. It will take them two months to finish. 'We use ironwood, redwood, red mahogany and Vietnamese cherry wood. Some of the wood comes from this area and some from Laos – red mahogany. But it is not as good as red mahogany from Vietnam.' They season their wood for at least six months.

At several low work tables, intricately perforated panels are emerging. Birds, attached only by one wing, attempt to flutter free from the panel; chrysanthemum petals peal open and cherry blossoms cling to almost freestanding twigs. So delicate is the minimal attachment to the panels! Sharp bamboo leaves lift and curl away from the filigree. The astonishing craftsmanship reminds me of England's seventeenth century master carver, Grinling Gibbons. However, he joined pieces of wood together; here the work is carved from one piece of wood.

The filigree panels begin with a design drawn in ink on paper, glued to the wood panel. Little by little, the design is patiently tapped out, while alongside lies a full copy of the design to refer to during carving. A curious wooden arc looks rather like part of a crossbow, but no, it will hold a solid wooden guitar on which the portrait of a famous Vietnamese musician from Hue, Trinh Cong Son, has been carved. 'He is well known throughout Vietnam.' The guitar, balanced in its arc will be shown in the exhibition in Danang next month. In a back corner, a turtle is rearing his arrogant wooden head from a hunk of redwood. 'He will go to the shop in Hoi An.'

The carving factory is very much a village enterprise. Linh's partner, Thu, lives next door to the factory, Linh's mother lives across the street, his sister's house is next door, his brother's house and bicycle shop next door on the other side. Linh himself lives in Hoi An. We cross the street to meet Linh's mother, who invites us to sit in beautiful, dark wooden armchairs, opposite a wooden settee, separated by a tea table. A curtain of wooden beads, tied together, reveals the family altar. In the adjoining room hangs a hammock. Four dogs, overjoyed to see Linh back home, romp about the room and in and out of the open doors to the terrace. Linh's mother, Tam, serves hot Vietnamese tea in glasses.

I ask about the framed certificate hanging on the wall. Linh explains that his family received the certificate as an award for being 'a good family,' as five children from the family had gone to university. One of five sisters and three brothers, Linh went to university in Dalat and studied to become a journalist. Three of his sisters went to university and became teachers; his brother, who studied engineering, runs the bicycle shop next door.

As we are climbing back on the motorbikes, a saw bites into a seven-foot-long virgin log – another Quan Yin perhaps. Tap, tap, tap, then suddenly the ear-splitting screech of a chainsaw hacks its way into what will become the body of the turtle.

Another day, I visit Linh's shop in Hoi An at 152 Tran Phu Street. It is early morning and the shop assistant, Nhung (a flower), has time to show me around. A huge, bald-headed Buddha carries a walking stick with a dragon's head, a gourd of wine and a huge Chinese cherry. He has been carved from dark red ironwood, a local hardwood. Rosewood is not so dark, Nhung explains. All of the statues remain unstained, natural wood. Opposite the old Buddha stands a fierce, famous Chinese warrior, Quan Yu, wearing a crown and carrying a long pike. Two plastic objects alongside look entirely out of place amongst the wood. 'Awards my company won in 2003 and 2004,' Nhung explains.

High on the walls hang exquisitely carved panels of windblown bamboo, flying birds, chrysanthemums and peach blossoms: the four seasons. If only wood weren't so heavy.

Upstairs, an old man from the highlands with a pipe and numerous strings of beads slung round his neck, stares balefully from a huge panel. Other panels portray the Lord's Supper; a stylistically modern head of Christ wearing a crown of thorns; a sword-wielding Buddha, – 'Van Thu Su Li, he always rides a lion' – and two nude figures, male and female beneath a banana tree from which hangs a heavy bud – 'No, not Adam and Eve, Phyllis and Demophoon, Ovid's separated lovers.'

Nhung leads me to a window where there is an archetypal Hoi An roof-scape: double and triple-hipped roofs, their tiles weathered and mellowed with age.

192

'Ring her between four and five – when she's not praying,' advises my friend Robyn Morley, an extraordinary Australian woman, who has lived in Hoi An for ten years and single-handedly founded Children's Hope in Action. Her charity helps children with desperate disabilities, health or educational problems. When I ask her about the disabled men selling the *Vietnam News,* who wheel around in carts, operated by push-pulling a lever back and forth, she says, 'They are the lucky ones. You should see the rest.'

Her 'praying friend' is a Buddhist nun. 'Call her Co Lai,' she says thoughtfully, saving me the anguish of not knowing how to address a Buddhist nun. Behind a long, low wall, a tangled garden and an ageing ochre villa stands a newish two-storey house, entered from a narrow lane.

A young woman leaving on a motorbike beckons me to a stairway leading to an upper, terraced walkway where I discard my shoes and enter an open doorway. A pile of pennants streaming iridescent red, yellow, blue and green ribbons lie stacked on a polished table, which I recognize, having seen them hanging in pagodas. As it is February, Hoi An's winter, Co Lai greets me wearing a fleece over the grey tunic and trousers of a Vietnamese nun's habit. A close fitting, grey woolly hat frames her lean, smooth-skinned, wrinkle-less face with soft, dark eyes. She looks maybe forty – much younger than she is.

The pennants are swept off the table and a tea tray is brought in. There are five leading families in Hoi An, Co Lai explains, her own, the Pham, being one of them. Her father had a wine business and his shop was in the position now occupied by a silk shop. Her parents built what is now the ageing villa in front of her house in 1933. Her mother also had a business, shipping seasonal farm produce from the countryside around Hoi An to Hanoi.

'In April it was green beans, different months by region. They brought it into Hoi An and she kept everything in the two-storey house until she would go to Hanoi by boat. In Hanoi she would buy imported things to bring back to sell. Always, after almost every trip, she would build a house. Altogether she had sixteen children. There was no birth control in those days. My parents were the first (Vietnamese) people to buy a car, a French Tracion. We had a driver, we also had horses. Every weekend we would go to the beach on the horses. Everything about the house was French, the style of the villa, the fridge, the toilets.'

Where now a terrace of small charity shops line the lane beside the house, stood a gaol, first a French prison, later used by the new Communist Government, she tells me. During World War II, Co Lai's family fled from Hoi An. For this reason, she was 'born in 1945 in a small village far from the river.' Her father died from an illness when she was only a year old. Her father had a lot of farmland before the Communists came to power in 1945, after which he gave it to the tenants. Her family were also important contributors to Chua Phap Bao, the pagoda's name now changed to Chua Tinh Hoi, 'the main temple for the city of Hoi An.'

The family returned to Hoi An in 1954, following the defeat of the French at Dien Bien Phu. 'My three older brothers had to join the army; they went to Hanoi when they were only sixteen, seventeen and eighteen. They volunteered, they felt they had to. The call to join was very strong, all the young people were caught up in "fight against the French and keep your country."'

With nationalization of private property by the new Communist Government, how had they managed to retain their family property in Hoi An? I wondered aloud.

'A Vietnamese governor took the house while we were away, but then my older brother came back to take care of the house. My older brother had been in the Communist Army. The government agreed to rent it as a tax office. My second brother died in the war, a martyr, so they could not take my parents' property.'

Co Lai is one of nine children, she thinks – her mother had a first marriage with six children. 'Then she married my father and he had two children. She had sixteen babies delivered,' which suggests a high level of mortality. 'After 1975, my brothers and sisters came back and half of us went to America, to California mostly.'

Co Lai married young, was married for many years and has three children living in America. 'When my husband died eight years ago, I decided to be a nun.' She went to stay in a pagoda in California.

'But after three months, I asked the master to let me come back to Vietnam to spend half the year and half the year in California. I don't want to belong to any one temple because if I belong to one

194

temple, I would have to stay in the temple and I want to stay in my own house.' She prays and meditates three times a day, early in the morning, in the afternoon and in the evening and sometimes goes to the pagoda to join a group to pray.

During the Vietnam War, a rocket hit the roof of her mother's house in Hoi An. 'It burned for three days. No one would come to help my mother put it out.' In her own house, two large blue and white china vases dominate the room. Intricately carved chairs inlaid with mother-of-pearl and a small, elegant table stands along one wall; shelves along another wall hold statues of Quan The Am, the goddess of mercy and a white china statue of the reclining Buddha.

And what are the responsibilities, duties and activities of a Buddhist nun?

Co Lai helps in the preparations for celebrations for Phap Bao pagoda – hence the pennants – helps in the Life Start and leprosy charities here in Hoi An, as well as helping the old and homeless.

And can any Buddhist woman become a Buddhist nun?

'To be a nun you must have a strong conviction and an understanding of Buddha. And be a vegetarian. In your mind you must want to be a strong helper to the Buddha. When you give away this body, you want to be in the land of Buddha and not come back to this world.' What if a woman is married? 'Yes, even if a woman is married, she can leave her family, if her husband and family agree. As a nun you belong to one master (a Buddhist monk). He has power and can teach you the right way to go.'

Co Lai's husband was in the army of the South (her brothers fighting for the North). He served as an interpreter for the American Marines. At the end of the American War, he escaped by boat. Luckily, he was picked up by a German boat and taken to Germany. In what must have been a terrifying journey, Co Lai and her three young children – at the time they were ten, nine and five – followed in a boat a year later, landing in Malaysia where they were placed in a refugee camp for two and a half years.

'But I didn't want to go to Germany – too cold and too hard to learn that language. That is why we had to wait two and a half years – to go to America.' While she and the children were in the refugee camp, she kept in contact with her husband – by letter.

After the refugee camp in Malaysia, they were held for a further six months in a camp near Manila. Finally they were allowed to go to California, to Alhambra between Los Angeles and Santa

Anna, where they lived for twenty years, she working as a primary school teacher. Her children now live in Ohio. Since 2001, she has spent six months of the year in Hoi An (November to April) and six months in California near her master.

Two large altars fill her private chapel in the adjoining room. The altar in front, a beautifully inlaid cabinet, holds offerings of bananas, two glasses of tea, brass candlesticks, a ceremonial wooden knocker for prayers, a Buddhist text 'like a Bible' and a triptych portraying a master monk in the centre, a woman on each side, beneath a white statue of Quan The Am and a larger statue of Buddha, his head encircled by an illuminated mandorla.

The second, intricately carved gilt and vermillion altar behind is dedicated to Buddha and her ancestors. Here photographs of both her grandfathers, her father and mother, the brother killed in the war and several other members of her family, face her during daily prayers. She gets out her prayer mat and cushion to show me where she kneels. 'And this is my bedroom,' she points through a window to a wooden bed with a mat in one corner, a mattress on the floor in another corner and a small cabinet – indeed, a nun's cell.

'And there are the flowers,' she waves to the garden below, eyes sparkling as she leads me along the covered walkway. Round the corner, an open bower explodes in a shower of orchids – yellow, white, violet, deep purple. 'The white one is five years old', she tells me, 'and blossoms so profusely, it is like a bush – it had twenty-eight blooms.' Water gurgles in a fish tank in one corner; a larger fish pond opposite holds larger fish.

A jolly, white china Buddha perches jovially atop one wall. 'Dilao, Buddha of the future. The others are Phat Thi Chi, Buddha of the past and Phat Adida, Buddha of the present.' Petunias tremble from a hanging basket and bougainvillaea gushes over a wall, a perfect respite from the bustling commercial life of Hoi An.

Back inside, Co Lai gets out a photo album, an album showing mostly the elderly that she and various charities have helped: aged people so thin and fragile that I wonder that they can even walk, peering out of thatched huts, sometimes missing an arm or with a dent in the forehead from an exploding mine, a person with seemingly no body below the waist, smiling up from a mat bed.

She tells me of one poor woman who had a cancer of the eye as large as a hen's egg and points to three children who were left orphans when their father murdered their mother, then killed himself.

196

Vietnam's war wounds are beginning to heal, but poverty in the countryside still runs very deep.

The following day, I stroll past Co Lai's pagoda in Hai Ba Trung Street, (Chua Tinh Hoi), and am met by what sounds like romantic ballads over a tannoy system. An enormous china statue of Quan The Am and a round tummied Buddha of the future regard the proceedings from one side of the courtyard where temporary altars have been set up beneath a marquee. One monk stands out in his dark brown robe, engaged in conversation, opposite a long table where several nuns in grey sit above signs in Vietnamese and English, saying Donations. In the hall alongside the temple, rows and rows of nuns sit in their pale grey habits, young nuns, old nuns. It is the annual ceremony for the 'induction' of new nuns.

A BANK AND A BRIDGE

The modest entrance is through a narrow garden to one side of a bank. Opening the slatted, wooden door, Huynh Thi Chi Nga is a fine boned woman with a high forehead, a slim face and stylish, frameless glasses, her black hair swept high in a bun. She is wearing a single strand pearl necklace and earrings, a neatly tailored, black fitted jacket over a black top and black corduroy trousers, very understated, very elegant.

'Leave your shoes on,' she commands Pho and me. She is wearing flip-flops. She leads us through a large white tiled kitchen with dark, varnished wood cupboards – surely a French built kitchen – and into the salon, a long, narrow room with art deco floor tiles, white walls, dark varnished wood ceiling and woodwork, its tall, arched doors and windows opening onto a covered, tiled veranda at the back of the house – straight out of *Indochine*.

'Please sit down,' she beckons to a carved, cherry wood settee. A huge floral painted screen occupies one wall, black lacquer paintings another.

'The house is a hundred years old. It was my grandfather's, designed by a French architect. The furniture is from my grandparents, some from my parents.'

Co Lai had named her family, the Nghe Thanh, as one of the five families of Hoi An.

'My grandparents sold tea and dried betal nuts for export. My father had a famous photography studio in Danang. It was called Huynh Phat Loi. The studio ended with my father.'

Pho adds an aside in English, 'Her grandparents were very rich, they had many houses in Hoi An and in Danang as well.'

Chi Nga's precise mannerisms strike me as peculiarly French, yet she is too young to have been educated under the French. I am even more perplexed when she tells me that she was a midwife until she retired eight years ago. Then it comes out. When she was young, she did a *stage* – a period of study in Lausanne (Switzerland) 'before liberation.' Then in 1996 and 1997 she went again to France, this time to study French. When I tell her that I live in France, the conversation switches to French and poor Pho suddenly feels redundant.

198

She has one sister and one brother. Her younger sister teaches English and French here in Hoi An, her brother is a reporter for a Vietnamese newspaper in California. So once again, a family split, perhaps by politics, perhaps by ambition.

'As a young child until I was seven, I lived here, then went to school in Danang and only came back to Hoi An for holidays. I graduated in 1966' – just as the Vietnam War was accelerating. The marines landed and set up a base in Danang in 1965.

'During the years while I was working as a midwife at the hospital in Danang where my cousin was a doctor and director of the hospital, I lived in Danang. Since retiring, I have lived in my grandparents' house in Hoi An. My grandfather's name was Dinh Van Tung. Chi Nga has one daughter, who is studying in Ho Chi Minh City. Other relatives live in America, in Houston, Washington, DC and Los Angeles.

'You're going to love upstairs,' she says, her eyes shining.

At the foot of a flight of steep, varnished stairs, we all leave our shoes. Upstairs, we pass through a small room holding little more than a traditional wooden Vietnamese bed and mat. The dark, varnished floorboards feel cool and curved to the feet; old wood swells in the humidity.

The long, narrow main room above the sitting room, open to the rafters and roof tiles, is entirely devoted to family altars, the family chapel. Between parallel sentences hanging from columns, the central altar is presided over by Quan Am. Among the shorter joss sticks is one very long incense stick, burning. Also standing in the bowl is the curled ember of an already burnt incense stick.

Chi Nga explains. 'When the incense curls, it is a sign that it is a good family, a good sign from the ancestors and thanks to their kindness, when we dream anything, it will come true.'

The altar to the right is dedicated to Chi Nga's ancestors. Electric candles glow and pink plastic lilies warm the photographs: her grandparents in the centre, her parents on the right, and on the left, her 'other mother,' presumably, a stepmother. Her aunt on the left is wearing blue; an uncle on the right and an older sister make up the assemblage, surrounding a couple of enormous biscuit tins on the altar – in case they feel peckish in the night. The altar on the left is devoted solely to her husband. Artificial tulips and orchids surround his photograph, which rests against a bottle of champagne – perhaps her husband was partial to a glass of bubbly.

'My husband, Professor Nguyen Phuong Vo, was an architect. He was head of the Department of Architecture at the University of Danang.' She pauses before going on.

'There was a competition for the design of the Song Ham bridge in Danang. He won the competition.' Another pause. I remember the bridge, the graceful, gleaming suspension bridge, seen in the distance from the bus when I went to visit the Champa Museum in Danang.

'But because of the strain, he died of high blood pressure in 2001.' Facing her husband's altar is a modern settee with white silk cushions – white is the colour of mourning in Vietnam. Perhaps this is where she sits to commune with her dead husband; it is the only furniture apart from the altars in the entire room. I ask about the large red lacquer tableau bearing gilt Chinese ideograms, hanging high on the wall at the far end of the room.

'It's a long story. A long time ago, a cousin from Hanoi came here and my mother had a small room where he stayed. He borrowed the documents of the house and made a false document. He had a plot to occupy this house . . .' she trails off, eliminating much of no doubt an entangled story.

'The lacquer panel was a present from a friend in thanks to the ancestors that he (the cousin) did not succeed in getting the house. It was a congratulatory panel, given by my close friend in the winter of 2003.' So on top of grieving for her dead husband, she had to fight to keep the roof over her head.

Back downstairs, through the double, arched doors at the back of the house, her sister and three friends sit playing cards on the narrow veranda beside a paved, walled garden.

'Four-colour cards, played by old men and women,' Pho explains. A craggy rock garden rises from the fish pond, where large orange carp and tiny black fish come to nibble at the surface, the pond softened by papyrus, lotus pads and floating, delicate water plants. Flowering pot plants add to the effect of tranquillity.

Chi Nga brings out a photo album, not a family album – a photo album of her dog, performing various antics. How very French! The perky little dog wearing a dress with a skirt; the dog reading a comic book; the dog cutting her whiskers with giant scissors; the dog with her forepaw on a mouse, looking intently at a laptop screen; the dog with her head on a pillow and a photo of the dog's very own bed, like any good Vietnamese bed, the mat made of straw.

As soon as the photo album is closed, we are introduced. The door to a room I had not suspected is opened and Lucky bounces out, wearing the dress with the skirt, tail wagging a million a minute. As we are leaving, I ask if the bank in front is her bank.

'Oh no, the bank rents my house,' she replies, and I suddenly realize that the large villa has been divided lengthwise, the bank occupying the front half, Chi Nga residing in the rear – to earn an income.

Just beyond the Japanese Bridge, through a small shop selling embroidered cushion covers and bags, Pho and I are led inside to where we find an old woman, who rises from a portable hammock, her grey hair pinned back with a single hairpin.

Tran Thi Ngo is wearing tiny, round, steel-framed glasses and a two-piece pyjama suit of dark brown and cream print fabric, similar to that worn by the old peasant woman in Cam Thanh village, who led us to the man with the temple key. Because it is a grey day and to the Vietnamese, chilly at twenty-four degrees (67 F), she has tucked a dark leopard print scarf into the collar of her short tunic. Her only jewellery is a thin jade bracelet.

She invites us to sit at an ebony table in elaborately carved chairs with marble insets in the chair backs, like those in the Hainan Community Assembly Hall. When suddenly, she pulls her hair back and clips it in a hair clasp, an instant transformation takes place from a tired old woman to a smooth, dignified face of character.

I remark on the beauty of the old chairs and she says, 'Sometimes the chairs are borrowed for ceremonies. Then they are covered with embroidered cloth.'

The floor is cement. The balusters of the staircase have been rough-sawn into intricate shapes, not turned as in many old houses. Tran Thi Ngo goes to fetch tea.

Framed paintings of the four seasons hang on one dark-stained wooden wall; wild horses leap in another. A huge blue and white vase occupies the place of honour on a hexagonal stand with spindle railings.Tran Thi Ngo returns and serves hot tea in glasses in the traditional Vietnamese manner.

Two blue and white vases stand on either side of the door leading to the rooms at the back of the house. When I remark on the huge vases, she says, 'My father had a precious, old Chinese vase. During the American War, someone bought it in the sixties to offer to Ngo Dinh Diem, the president of South Vietnam. They replaced it, but the replacements are new. People have offered to buy the hexagonal stand, but I decided not to sell.'

'In 1945 during the French time and again in the American time, many people had to flee Hoi An because they were afraid. Many people had to sell items in the house in order to live.'

How old is the house?

'1785' – a few years after the Tay Son Rebellion.

How many generations have lived here?

Tran Thi Ngo counts on her fingers, presumably through the grandfathers. 'Eight generations. Only my father was rich. Where is the house of Cuu Cang? Everybody knew.'

Co Lai had written down Cuu Cang, her father's name as one of Hoi An's five families. Her father and Huynh Thi Chi Nha's grandfather were cousins. In the old days before the wars, both families were prominent landowners in Hoi An.

'Many families in Hoi An were rich because of betal nut, tea and scented wood, which they brought from the mountain areas. I have always lived in this house,' she tells us. She is keeper of the family's ancestral chapel. Her parents have both died, her father in 1961, just before the Vietnam War; her mother lived until 1985. She had five brothers and sisters, but because she is the eldest, she has taken responsibility for the house. She lives here with one sister. One sister runs the Faifoo restaurant in Tran Phu Street, another sister owns Des Amies restaurant in Bach Dang Street and one sister now lives in Phan Chu Trinh Street.

'We have always lived in Hoi An, we didn't come from anywhere else, we are pure Vietnamese – not Chinese.

'My grandparents were very poor, their business was selling dried betal nuts, scented wood and dried tea which they took to Hanoi and some other places in Vietnam to sell. In small boats, no engines.'

Since before independence in 1975, her brothers and sisters were all teachers. Chi Nha was a primary school teacher. Later, some ran small businesses, one stopped to have a baby and one reached retirement. Chi Nha stopped teaching in 1983 because of ill health.

'My business became selling, just cigarettes and water' – individual cigarettes and bottles of water to passersby, sitting on the pavement in front of her house. There is still an old woman further along the street selling bottles of water. The embroidery shop at the front of the house belongs to her sister-in-law; the family runs an inn: two rooms to rent downstairs. The two sisters live upstairs. Tran Thi Ngo never married. 'It is no longer rare for people not to get married.'

Her unlined face belies her sixty-eight years. She laughs when I remark on her fine skin. 'Because when I was young, I ate lots of swallows' nests. My father was very rich then. They now cost $6,000-$7000 per kilo. In the past, they were cheap.'

She and her sister live very modestly on the rent from the rooms, two hundred thousand *dong* ($10) a night. She doesn't advertise. News of the rooms travels by word of mouth; also it is in a guidebook published in Hanoi. And of course, there is the sign hanging out front. She brings out a guest book in which numerous guests from many countries have penned their appreciation of the hospitality they have enjoyed and the pleasure of staying overnight in an authentic old house.

The back of the house, past the two small interior bedrooms – the inn – leads to a courtyard where an open kitchen runs along one side, toilets along the other, a melon vine growing over the roof next door. A gate at the back opens to a narrow, paved courtyard where clothes are drying, another gate to the street beside the river. Music blares from across the river.

Upstairs, nothing has been changed since the upper story served as a warehouse. In the room at the back, river end of the house, two beds, hers and her sister's, stand side by side under mosquito nets. Two rather tired, red silk lanterns hang on the covered veranda across the back of the house, looking out over the river. She points to the wooden columns, riddled with termites.

At the front of the house, an open lattice trap door still has the pulley hanging above it, for lifting merchandise or furniture upstairs. More chairs like those downstairs have been stacked in neat, dusty rows along one wall. Wooden shuttered windows open to Nguyen Thi Minh Khai Street, a few steps from the Japanese Bridge.

Looking out of the shuttered windows, Thi Ngo explains that her family once owned the two old houses opposite, Phung Hung house and the bookshop; her father had two wives and the property was divided when he died.

'After Independence Day, the government seized the property of the rich – my father's as well. The bookshop was seized and now the government owns the bookshop.'

How did you manage to keep the house?

'Because the whole family was living here. But my wooden columns are being ruined by termites and I cannot afford to have them replaced.'

It is only as we are leaving that I notice the family altar, tucked to one side of the sitting area. The altar itself, the elaborate lacquer and gilt frame around it and the artfully carved, hanging pennants, now decaying, echo of past grandeur.

'My father is in the middle.' An austere looking face under a black headband stares out from his high-necked black tunic. She points to 'two mothers,' one on each side of her father's photo and one brother. 'My mother was my father's second wife. He had four – not at the same time.' Brass candlesticks stand on each side of a brass incense burner and slightly behind, a bottle of Remy Martin cognac – for her father.

Once again outside, two gilt characters proclaim the proud clan name, high above the front door, just behind the sign: Nha Tro Guest House.

SILK AND CERAMICS

It was my friend Thanh from the Bazaar restaurant who introduced me to her neighbour opposite, Bich Lan. At first glance the clothes shop at 23 Tran Phu Street looks like a hundred other tailor shops in Hoi An, silk lanterns dangling from the eaves, pots of yellow chrysanthemums beside the door beneath red and gold door eyes, two open bays to welcome passers-by, bolts of cloth stacked on shelves along the walls, trendy mannequins and vertical parallel sentence panels with gilt characters attached to the columns.

However, unlike other clothes shops, in dead centre of this shop stands a glass case. On top of it, several colourfully painted porcelain opium pipes lie beside a dozen or so fist-sized, round-bellied opium pots.

'The smoker inhales through a metal straw,' says Bich Lan casually, one of those oriental beauties of indeterminate age, no longer quite young, not yet old, a woman in her prime. Tiny Japanese figures march around a jug with an elaborate metal lid.

'Not originals, all copies,' she says off-handedly. Very appealing for all that. From the cabinet beneath the opium pipes, Bich Lan draws out a cellophane bag holding small brown cones of incense. She has 'an incense factory in the mountains' where the incense cones are shaped by hand from sandalwood.

The name of the shop, B'Lan, is a simplified abbreviation of her name, 'easier for foreigners.' Her husband's family name is Tran and the old house is her husband's family's ancestral home, going back eight generations to 1822, when the family finally migrated from Canton to Hoi An.

'The grandparents' – she means the ancestors – 'first came to Hoi An to do business as seafaring traders. The first time they stopped here just for water, travelling in a sailboat. Then step by step – many ships came to Hoi An in those days – they began to stop to do business. At first while they were in Hoi An, they stayed in the Five Chinese Communities Assembly Hall. They would come for six months to Vietnam, then go back to Canton. They brought fabrics from China and in Vietnam they would buy cinnamon, cotton, rice and salt. Then when the grandparents decided that it was a good place to stay, they bought the land and had a small house built. This is the family house. We have a tableau upstairs, telling when they came. Three generations from China came here and married Vietnamese women.' Bich Lan's father-in-law is now dead.

'My aunt and uncle are in America. Before 1975, they lived here and were working for the Americans – my father-in-law was working for the Viet Cong – all living in the same house. Afterwards, they went to America to live.'

Again and again I hear stories of Vietnamese families in Central Vietnam having been politically divided by what the Vietnamese call the American War. And the women were equally active in the war effort.

It is now Bich Lan and her husband who occupy the house. Formerly a professor of history at the University of Quy Nhon in Binh Dinh Province some distance south, her husband now has a house in Danang where he works, possibly unable to concentrate at home, working over the busy shop.

'He is a writer. He writes for films, love stories. He works there but comes back every night.'

In 1990, Bich Lan opened the shop. Between 1988 and 1997, she worked for Hoi An Tourist Information where she met her husband. He was her boss and is twelve years her senior. Later Pho, who knows her well, tells me that she had qualified as a chemical engineer and her work for the Tourism Office was helping to preserve the historic houses.

'When Vietnam opened the door in the nineties, many foreigners started to come to Vietnam, so I opened the clothing shop. Mine was one of the first souvenir shops to open in Hoi An – the fourteenth to open.'

Bich Lan has three children, a daughter of nineteen studying economics at university in Saigon, a daughter of seventeen in high school and a son of twelve. Up worryingly steep stairs – they might have been taken from a ship – to the second floor where glass case after glass case holds a collection of ceramics: faint blue and white, red and white painted vases and plates, tiny blue and white pots, a few celadon plates, rows of varying sized earthen pots, cabinet after cabinet, shelf after shelf. This is Bich Lan's own personal collection, ranging from prehistoric Sa Huynh through Cham and Viet ceramics. When she worked in the Tourist Office, part of her job was to research their age when pieces were brought in.

'This gave me the opportunity to buy for my collection. The fishermen would bring them to us; they have all come from shipwrecks.'

The tiny round pots with a hole in one side, she explains, were for lime ash to be used in chewing betal nut. Opening a glass display case, she takes out a small terracotta pot.

'An oil lamp, you put the oil here and the fire. From China, seventeenth century, but made in Vietnam.'

From another shelf, she takes out tiny blue and white pots, 'for lipstick,' she says with a smile. In the display case opposite, she points to low, round, slightly flattened, blue and white pots with lids. 'For powder, fourteenth to sixteenth century, from shipwrecks.'

I gasp at a graceful curved vase with an elongated neck, decorated with a flying bird. 'For wine. They are decorated with flying birds and the four sacred animals – the phoenix, the dragon, the turtle and the lion – also poems. All of these have come from shipwrecks. The blue and white ones are called *men lam.* The yellow, green and red are called *tam thai.'*

She reaches for a large beige, glazed jug with six small protuberances around the curved top – handles? 'These were for a general's family in feudal times, not for ordinary people.'

Her most treasured object is a seventh century Cham bronze kept under glass to protect it from Hoi An's humid climate, a figure of Siva sitting on a Nandina bull, the bronze coated with green verdigris. That it was dredged up from a shipwreck sets off my imagination. A Cham ship fleeing attack, carrying royal treasures? A Javanese, Khmer or Viet aggressor sunk in battle or shipwrecked as it was pursued with its loot?

'I have a friend from the Louvre who says that anytime I want to sell the seventh century bronze, that money is no object, just let him know.'

The bronze is not for sale; nor are any of the ceramics. Beside the bronze, also under glass, is an old wooden panel, maybe eight by twenty inches (20 x 51 cm) long. On the left side, a carved Buddha waves several arms, the rest of the panel incised with Chinese characters, 'a Buddhist text.'

By far the oldest pieces are the Sa Huynh pots. One has stayed so long under the sea that shells have become embedded in its rusticated surface. I wince when she points to a round, fat pot, saying, 'thought to have been a coffin for a baby.'

The furnishings of the house, also are traditional. Mythical beasts and dragons grasp a standing cheval mirror. Two deeply carved, heavy wooden beds glint with mother-of-pearl. The peachy, inlaid mother-of-pearl of the display cabinets confirms their antiquity. Newly inlaid mother-of-pearl gleams white, I was told years ago when I first visited Hoi An.

The house, like most merchant houses, is divided into two parts, or more precisely, there are two houses with an atrium, formerly a courtyard opening through to the second floor, now roofed over. Several enormous, faintly tinted stone crystals, line the retaining wall of a rectangular fish pond along one side of the courtyard.

Upstairs in the front portion of the house, a dark stained, wooden veranda overlooks Tran Phu Street, the Chinese style railings of the central span, a curved, broken arch. Here in the front of the house, more glass cases and shelves hold what must be several hundred pieces of china and pottery. Two old swords rest in their gilt wooden sheaths, handed down through generations. They came with the family from China. Antique ebony chairs stand at a high, round, marble topped tea table. For meals, carved benches with spindle backs and Chinese characters stand rigidly alongside a highly polished rectangular table.

Always an integral part of family life, the ancestral altar dominates the room. A white china Quan Am gazes down over a bronze incense burner, guarded by a snarling temple lion. A pair of cranes balance on the backs of turtles – turtles with monster heads. Photographs of the grandparents rank just below Quan Am. Three gilt characters engraved in the red lacquer panel above the family altar translate as: 'Tran, the family name; small pagoda in the house; the third indicates the place where the family celebrates the death anniversaries of their ancestors.'

Wandering through this lovely old house and pondering its treasures, I only wish that the pots and vases could whisper their stories of pirates and traders, of storms and shipwrecks, of battles and looting, of the lives and funeral ceremonies of the early Sa Huynh settlers – and what happened to them. How I long to talk to the people who crafted these beautiful, enigmatic objects, and to their original owners, to discover how these rough, earthen pots and delicately painted vases came to find their way here so many centuries, in some cases more than two thousand years later.

I came here to live and look after the house six years ago.'

She is a pretty woman, her face full of lively animation. The house she has come to look after is one of Hoi An's finest, Tan Ky, certainly its most famous historic house and the first house ever to open its doors to the public in 1983.

The lady's name is Huynh Thi Tan Xuan – Xuan means spring. She is the daughter-in-law. Vietnamese women do not change their names when they marry; the family name of her in-laws is Le. She married at twenty-seven, twenty-nine years ago.

'The house is two hundred years old; seven generations have lived in it. The family originally came from Fukien province in China. They fled a revolution, the fall of the Ming dynasty.'

Asked if there were any particularly memorable ancestors, Xuan points to the photograph of her great-grandmother-in-law on the wall above her, a thin, balding old lady with sunken cheeks, her hair pulled back austerely in a bun, holding a Buddhist rosary.

'The photo was taken when she was very old. My mother-in-law told me about her.'

Her mother-in-law, Phan Thi Dao, would have been the woman I met when I first visited the house thirteen years ago. I have an image of her still, sitting with great dignity at her desk, wearing black. In those days she greeted each visitor individually, serving tiny cups of Vietnamese tea. Having asked which country I came from, she had turned to the page in her visitors' book where an earlier British journalist had written a few lines. She is now eighty-three and living in Danang. If she only left the house six years ago, she would have kept open house to visitors every day of the year for twenty-one years until she was seventy-seven.

'My great-grandmother-in-law's name was Thai Thi Lan,' says Xuan, referring to the photograph. "She knew how to work and how to enjoy her life and she looked after her family very well. She had just one son.' His photograph faces that of his mother from the wall opposite, the young man in the photograph wearing a brocade silk, Chinese-style tunic, white trousers and a headband called a *than dong*. His name was Le Huynh – Xuan's husband's grandfather.

210

'He was a teacher of English and French. He was fluent in Chinese, English and French.'

Xuan's husband is also a teacher – of English – teaching in the University of Danang. Her husband has two sisters, one who lives just outside Hoi An, the other down the coast in Tam Ky. Xuan and her husband, Le Dzung, have two sons, both engineers working in telecommunications in Danang.

'Both the sixth and seventh generations of the family have graduated from university,' Xuan says proudly.

The dark stained beams of this beautiful old house, built of local hardwoods – jack fruit, ironwood and peck-wood – are works of fine craftsmanship, exquisitely carved and inlaid with mother-of pearl. Slabs of stone and traditional brick tiles pave the ground floors. With thick tile roofs and wooden walls, the old houses stay warm in winter and cool in summer. Spindle railings allow air to pass between the rooms. A pulley formerly lifted goods, now furniture, through a well in the ceiling from the ground floor upstairs to escape the floods.

A curved, crab shell ceiling shelters the narrow sitting room just behind the front room. Carved carp, en route to becoming dragons, the symbol of how hard-working people could better themselves in the old days by passing the mandarin examinations, serve as finials to the roof beams. Xuan points to a beam bearing carved crossed sabres 'representing power', wrapped in a carved ribbon, 'denoting flexibility.'

Xuan points to three horizontal beams at both ends of the room, each successively higher beam diminishing in length. 'These are Japanese-style *chong ruong* beams, representing the earth, humanity and the heavens. The five vertical carved columns between the beams and the roof represent the five elements: metal, wood, water, fire and earth.' Oddly, because it would have been built some years after the Japanese departed from Hoi An in 1636, the house contains both Chinese and Japanese architectural features.

Through the generations, the family has changed the house very little, discretely adding electricity. There is a well in the courtyard and what was the fish tank, now serves as a planter. The oldest furniture is not in the sitting room where we sit sipping tea – beautiful furniture inlaid with glittering mother-of-pearl – but in the back house, a round ebony table and chairs with marble insets in the chair backs, standing opposite a built-in bed compartment, the bed surrounded by high, turned spindle balustrade railings.

On the wall beside the bed are the high-water marks from the floods of previous years. The mark from the typhoon of September 2009 is higher than I can reach – at least seven feet (more than two meters) above floor level – and the floor of the house is perhaps eighteen inches above the ground level of the courtyard. When floods come, the water stays for one to five days and families move their furniture and themselves upstairs. Glass cases hold blue and white china, 'Chinese and Japanese.'

And the furniture?

'All of the furniture was made in Hoi An' – the ebony and marble chairs, the inlaid mother-of-pearl settee and tea table.

Having heard that her husband is a professor of English, I am most anxious to meet him.

A few days later, Le Dzung, a slim man wearing steel framed glasses, is back from Danang and welcomes me into his family home, sitting at the desk where his mother once sat. He tells me that the house was built towards the end of the eighteenth century.

'My great-grandmother came to Hoi An with her little son – she came on her own – her husband had been killed, most probably in the revolution against the Ming. Her son was only seven or eight years old at the time.' I shudder to think of the long voyage in a sailing junk, alone with a young child.

'When she came to Vietnam, she had almost no relatives, so she lived with some very distant relatives named Truong. Then after a while they lived independently. She bought a house and her son grew up and started his own business. Then he almost lost everything, I don't know why.

'After many years, his daughter-in-law – the old lady whose photo hangs on the wall – 'took over as head of the family and started up the business again and this time, she could pay off all the debts of her father-in-law. In her time, many of the old houses in Hoi An belonged to her. She owned over twenty old houses in Nguyen Thi Hoc and Tran Phu Streets and a lot of land.

Le Dzung doesn't know why her father-in-law's business failed. 'My great-grandmother continued her father-in-law's business, but she was much more successful than he – dealing in agricultural products: pepper, cinnamon, timber, spices and rice. My great-grandmother sent boats up the river to the mountainous area. She bought the products there, then brought them back here and exported to other countries.'

212

Le Dzung never knew her. 'She died before I was born. When my mother first married, she lived with her for two years before she died – after the French Indo-Chinese War, when she came back.

Back?

'From a village in the countryside about forty kilometers (24 mi) away from Hoi An, where they lived during the French War.'

Le Dzung was born in 1953, a year before Dien Bien Phu. The family continued to live in the house in Hoi An throughout the Vietnam War.

'Fortunately, Hoi An was not a strategic site, the war was mostly round about, not in Hoi An. At the time, I had a lot of American friends at the university in Saigon.'

Le Dzung attended university during the Vietnam War. He should have graduated in 1975 – 'but we had the big upheaval, we all had to stay on a year more to complete the political training course, so I graduated in 1976.

'One day I came back to see my parents – the first time since 1975, and my parents were looking very happy. Of course, I was happy to see my parents, but I asked, "Why are you looking so happy?" And my father said, because he had just given all the houses and land to the government and they had accepted his proposal. I asked why he was so happy and he said, "Maybe something very bad would have happened if the government had not accepted my proposal." So that's why he looked so very happy!'

Le Dzung's father died only two years ago in 2008.

'My father was a French language teacher, he also taught English, so he could speak both French and English very well. He was also a teacher of Vietnamese literature; he was very interested in Vietnamese literature.'

On leaving university, Le Dzung taught at a high school in Quang Nam province about twenty-odd miles (32 km) from Hoi An.

'It was a very poor area – and it is still very poor. I taught there for two years, then was transferred to a junior college of foreign languages in Danang. Then I was sent to Australia, two times, to study there to get my Master's Degree.

'It was very, very difficult to get a scholarship', he pauses to emphasize how very nearly impossible it had been, 'especially if you did not have a good political record like my family.' By this, he does not mean that there was anything particularly unsavoury about his family, merely that they had been wealthy property owners.

213

'I was fortunate enough to get a scholarship, first for Canberra, then for Sydney. But before you could go out of the country, you were surrounded by many policemen.'

Policemen? Why?

'Because they didn't think you would come back. So my local police department in Danang gave me a big party – because before, some of my friends had gone and would never return.'

It sounded rather peculiar psychology. Was the thinking that if so much were made of his departure, then he would feel too guilty not to return? I do a bit of mental calculation – but you were already married, leaving your wife behind?

'Yes, I was already married and the father of two young sons. But my friends, despite being married, had left behind families and never returned.'

It took two years to finish the Master's Degree. He explains that he had to spend the first year in Canberra doing a course for foreign students. 'They didn't accept degrees from foreign universities,' then another year in Sydney doing the Master's Degree, which he completed in 1996.

Le Dzung is the author of several books. 'Most of my books are on linguistics. I am teaching linguistics.

'The name of the house, Tan Ky, came from the second generation. The little boy who had fled China with his mother called his business Tan Ky, which means "wish for progress, or prosperity." It was here, his business, his shop in the front,' where the windows that opened onto Nguyen Tai Hoc Street now remain boarded and closed. 'The courtyard was built when I was young, seven or eight – it is not old – and the well. The Vietnamese don't permit people to build a well within a house because they think it *damages* longevity,' he says with a twinkle.

I ask why, if the house was built a century after the Japanese community departed in 1636 and after the town of Hoi An had been burnt during the Tay Son Rebellion in 1773 – why Japanese-style rafters? 'When the Japanese left, they left their Japanese style houses. The local people liked the Japanese style houses and imitated the style.' As he is teaching linguistics, I ask Le Dzung about the Hoi An dialect. 'It is quite different from other regions – perhaps I should do more research before giving an answer,' he replies with a chuckle. It seems that Le Dzung teaches and writes about English linguistics, not Vietnamese linguistics.

214

Then he explains a bit about the Chinese immigrants to Hoi An. 'In the past, of the people who came here from China, families when they settled, many married local people, so they couldn't speak Chinese from the second generation. Many others kept their traditions and married Chinese women, so they could communicate both in Chinese and Vietnamese. Although in Saigon, some Chinese live there all their lives and cannot speak any Vietnamese.'

Then he tells me about how the old historic houses of Hoi An happened to be opened to the public.

'Tan Ky was the first house to open to the public. It was the idea of a complete stranger, a foreigner, a Pole, Kazimierz Kwaitkowski. Tan Ky was one of the first old houses that he visited, he met my father several times and they talked about many things. He became one of my father's close friend. The world didn't know anything about Hoi An until after Kwaitkowski came. He told the Vietnamese authorities about his project – to open the historic houses and get Hoi An listed as a World Heritage Site – and suggested that this house be part of the project.'

The oldest furniture in the house, the ebony table and chairs with the marble insets 'were bought during the second generation – whether bought or given as a present, I'm not sure.' The old built-in bed compartment, the bed surrounded by turned-spindle balustrade railings? 'My great-grandmother's bed.'

On close examination I find that the inlaid, mother-of pearl, Chinese characters of the parallel sentences, hanging from the columns at the front of the house, have been achieved by the artful entwining of numerous tiny birds. What exquisite craftsmanship!

No doubt, with their love of Vietnamese literature, it was Le Dzung's father or his grandfather, who placed these inlaid mother-of-pearl, parallel sentences on the columns at the entrance to the sitting room. Two lines to a column, the poem translates:

A row of firs only a hundred metres long,
Receives rains from thousands of miles away.
A bright moon only ten centimetres wide
Lights a whole floor full of books.

LEGACY

An unexpected benefit of Hoi An having lost its prosperity as a port is its rich, largely untouched treasure of historic architecture, the finest concentration of old wooden merchant houses in Vietnam, possibly in South East Asia.

Of the 1,254 buildings in Hoi An identified as Historic Heritage, 929 houses are privately owned, 205 state owned, 120 collectively owned, such as Chinese assembly halls, pagodas and community halls. Hoi An's lovely old buildings have been studied, surveyed, and carefully classified into four categories. Meticulous colour-coded maps, identifying every single building, hang rather incongruously in Hoi An's Trade Ceramics Museum.

The historic core, the Old Town, has been declared a protected area. Repairs and alterations to its precious historic buildings are strictly controlled. This central core consists of only five east-west streets: Phan Chu Trinh, Tran Phu, Nguyen Thi Minh Khai and two 'new' streets, Nguyen Thai Hoc and Bach Dang Streets, added in 1840 and 1878 as the river silted up and the riverbank extended further south.

North-south streets include those from Hoang Dieu in the east to part of Hai Ba Trung Street in the west. Only the first few houses in Nguyen Thi Minh Khai Street, among them Tran Thi Nha's and her father's two houses opposite, have been designated Class 1.

The cheek-by-jowl houses that created these narrow streets and lanes, preserve the original street patterns of this old Asian port, its architecture influenced by a mixture and progression of Chinese, Japanese, Vietnamese and French inhabitants, who have left their legacy in wood, bricks and tiles.

Between 1997 and 2007, 168 government-owned and 1,125 privately owned historic buildings were restored. Owners are required to obtain permission from the Hoi An People's Committee and the Hoi An Centre for Monuments Management and Preservation before work can begin. Some financial assistance for restoration is available; how much depends upon the classification of the building according to its historic merits and its position. For a Special Category building located on a main road, the government subsidizes sixty per cent of the total restoration cost, the remainder borne by the home owner.

For a Special Category house in a side street, the government pays up to seventy-five per cent, houses in smaller streets receiving larger subsidies because buildings on main roads are deemed to have more opportunity to earn revenue as businesses or shops.

Hoi An's oldest shophouses date from the late eighteenth century, the most recent from the French colonial period. Although the older houses are very much of a period style, the differences are not subtle amongst the five main types of houses:

one-storey with a separately roofed veranda,
two-storey having eaves over both the ground and first floor,
two-storey with wooden balconies and railings,
two-storey brick with a veranda on the ground floor and a balcony on the first,
two-storey French-style houses with veranda and balcony, dating from the early twentieth century.

The French-style houses are mostly found at the eastern end of Nguyen Thai Hoc Street, but dotted here and there along Tran Phu Street and elsewhere.

The floor plans of the pre-colonial merchant houses are remarkably similar, almost to the point of uniformity. Long, narrow shophouses run back from the street, originally to the river's edge. At the front is the shop. Behind is a narrow, decorative room, often the family's sitting room. Each of these rooms has a hipped, tiled roof, slanting down to the street. Sometimes a crab shell roof curves over either the narrow sitting room or an upstairs balcony.

An open courtyard paved in brick or stone slabs separates the shop from the back building, bringing fresh air and light and the cooling sound of trickling water from the fish pond on one side into the house. Often there are pot plants and a bird cage. Along the opposite side of the courtyard, the 'bridge building' provides shelter between the front and back sections of the house, in fact, two houses. The building at the rear contains bedrooms on one or both sides of a central hallway with a back yard beyond, an outdoor kitchen to one side, toilets and a shower room opposite. Occasionally, I have encountered a hen or rooster in a backyard in the centre of Hoi An – Hoi An remains a village!

Apart from preserving its historic buildings, Hoi An has been at pains to improve the town, both for its inhabitants and for visitors.

Streets are being paved, new sewers laid, a palm-lined promenade installed on the river bank across the river in An Hoi, a new wooden footbridge built to break the bottleneck of the Japanese Bridge and a new bridge for vehicles erected farther west linking Hoi An and An Hoi island. New houses have leapt up along new streets across the river in An Hoi and newly paved roads to the west, both in Hoi An and in An Hoi, leave land for more new houses to be built.

Motorbike and vehicle traffic is strictly controlled in the Old Town, leaving the streets blissfully free of motor vehicles for visitors to stroll during business hours – and classical music over loud speakers lulls Europeans into feeling at home. Festive, red silk lanterns hang along the eaves of the houses, have been strung across streets and across the bridges. Tucked up in the trees, they act as street lamps.

Every full moon, the entire town turns out to float paper boats on the river, each bearing a candle and a wish. It is an enchanting sight, the river lit by a flotilla of tiny paper boats. Come nightfall, every night in an open triangle beside An Hoi bridge, locals gather for an animated 'bingo' game in which the leader sings out the 'calls', providing lively entertainment for residents and visitors alike.

On my last day in Hoi An, just before eight o'clock in the morning, I sit at Treats cafe over a Vietnamese coffee, watching the opening of the shops on Tran Phu Street. Wooden shutters come down, display cases are dragged out into position, bicycles are pushed through the shops to be parked somewhere behind. Steps are swept, followed by buckets of water thrown over the pavement to lay the dust.

A man pedals his bicycle past, pulling a cart carrying his wife and merchandise to market. A woman laden with baskets of fruit, dangling from her bamboo carrying pole, pads by rhythmically, her baskets of fruit swinging gaily: green oranges, shocking pink dragon fruit, tangerines, grapes, pamplemousse, golden mangoes, ragged rose rambutans, custard apples. A salad woman, her greens piled high in her baskets, pads past. Spiky, pale yellowy-green durians pass on the back of a motorbike. Motorbikes loaded with toddlers tucked in front of their grandpas, behind their fathers or between their fathers and mothers, growl past – before the witching hour when the street closes to motorbike traffic. A boy stops his bicycle, selling the English language newspaper, *Vietnam News*. A few minutes later, another boy stops, also selling *Vietnam News*.

Shopkeepers light joss sticks, placing them either in cracks in the pavement near the doors of their shops, in holders or on altars inside their shops. Old ladies wearing cool, baggy, long-sleeved pyjamas and straw hats scuff along in plastic slippers – why do they so often have too-short slippers, their heels hanging off the back? A passing vendor shouts her wares – she could be calling buffaloes. Two young schoolgirls pedal past, red ties over crisp white blouses and dark blue skirts.

Coffee finished, I stroll to the corner of Tran Phu and Le Loi Streets where a woman squats on a plastic stool behind a basket of sticks – scented agar wood to burn in the morning offering bowls. Chopin tinkles from loudspeakers over Tran Phu Street. Tiny pavement cafes are being tidied up after the breakfast trade.

At the corner of Le Loi and Tran Hung Dao Streets, old ladies sit in a genial row on the pavement behind their baskets of clay whistles: 'You buy?' Another seems to be permanently stationed at the Hoi An end of An Hoi Bridge, warbling her whistles, when she's not chewing betal nut. Sometimes, she gets her mouth so full of betal that the whistles won't warble.

A cheerful woman sits at the corner of Hai Ba Trung and Tran Hung Dao under a parasol selling pineapples, the peel trimmed in neat spirals, each eye meticulously removed. In the distance I hear the plaintiff flute melody that heralds the arrival of the rubbish lorry, accompanied by blue uniformed female collectors wearing gloves, caps and masks.

When I first started strolling along Nguyen Thi Minh Khai Street on the far side of the Japanese Bridge, the shopkeepers would call out: 'You have a look my shop?' . . . 'You buy something?' . . . 'Madame, please come in my shop!' With the odd exception of a jewellery shop or an art gallery, it is always the women who do the selling, the hectoring and the cajoling. After the first month, they stopped trying to get me into their shops but continued to call out, 'Hello, how are you today?'

Favouring the friendly shopkeepers in Nguyen Thi Minh Khai Street – my neighbours – I make last-minute gift purchases: a pair of silk slippers with cane mat insoles, a beautifully embroidered silk jewellery case for travelling, a silk tie, a rosewood toothpick holder with inlaid buffalo horn.

There is a power cut, no electricity until who knows when in all but the Old Town. Ironically, in an old town that floods, there has

219

been too little rain this year; the reservoir up in the mountains is low and they are conserving energy.

For my last night out in Hoi An, I take myself to one of my favourite restaurants over the bridge in An Hoi, where they place tables on the pavement opposite Hoi An. Red and white lanterns glow along the eaves of the Old Town across the river. Sipping a fresh beer, I watch as the boats draw into the darkling river for the shelter of the quay. Rain has been forecast, which means storms at sea. The air hangs balmy after a hot day. Palms silhouette their drowsy outlines against the azure sky. Children lark in the grassy strip of the promenade. Mothers follow their toddlers, a bowl and spoon in hand. Neighbours sit on stone benches gossiping. A lone diner feels a part of the friendly community.

Suddenly, a large black people-carrier – which in Vietnam means they are rich – draws up to the curb and a family disembarks: a very elderly couple and a middle-aged couple. They are met and greeted by the waitresses from the restaurant, the elders each with a cane, solicitously helped to a table and tenderly looked after by the waitresses as though they were their own parents.

I sit ruminating on the things I cherish most in Hoi An: the wandering vendors of fruit, coconut milk, tea; the old women selling clay whistles; the smiling woman who sells pineapples – the people of Hoi An, the Vietnamese for that matter – who live so publicly, their shophouses open from early morning to well after dark, taking their meals on tiny plastic stools on the pavement in front of their houses, the old women sitting after dark on their front steps, smiling and nodding as you pass – and not bothering to invite you into their shops, just being friendly and neighbourly; the *xe om* drivers who assure you that they are 'good driver, go slow.'

I shall never forget the Rolls Royce of *xe oms,* his super-bike having the cushioned passenger seat raised so high that I simply could not lift my leg high enough to get on – he had to get off so that I could climb aboard and slide backwards!

And the flowers: roofs dripping lavender morning glories and the trailing vines the Vietnamese call yellow bells; the astonishing orchids and the flowering tree with watermelon pink and white petals in the same blossom – and the cheery, chirping of birds in bamboo cages dangling from the eaves.

I think of the delicious Hoi An food that I will miss: the refreshing green papaya and green mango salads, flavoured with lime juice and *nuoc mam* on a hot day; the fresh spring rolls dipped in *nuoc mam;* an entire fish smothered in garlic, lemon grass and vegetables, grilled in a banana leaf; crayfish in tamarind sauce, when I get sticky to the elbows, peeling the shells – the Vietnamese eat them shells and all; the fresh beer, a cooling mug of mild iced Vietnamese tea, the jackfruit and pineapple shakes; the luscious mangoes and rambutans; the mango-flavoured yoghurt; and not least, at which my oenophile friends will wince, a glass of red Dalat wine with ice – the best thing to do with Dalat wine in a hot climate.

Their meal completed, the middle-aged man turns to me – a lone diner in Hoi An, in Vietnam for that matter, is to be pitied. No friends, no family? They are his parents, he says by way of introduction with a wave of an arm. His father is ninety-one, his mother eighty-seven, he says proudly. He has looked after them well. I look at the fragile old man, his hair thin, back slightly bent, born in 1918 and I think of the changes he has witnessed in Hoi An during those ninety-one years: Hoi An as the home of a small French colony, the winding down of Hoi An as a port. He has survived three wars and witnessed the South being reunified with the North. He has seen Hoi An sink to an impoverished, sleepy backwater and rise again to become a prosperous, major site on the international tourist circuit.

The town may no longer be the important port it was for two thousand years – or even much of a port at all, but Hoi An is still a bustling town of traders, a city of hustlers and entrepreneurs and it will probably always remain so, for as long as the Thu Bon river rushes past. Only the customers have changed – from traders from afar, to tourists from near and far.

These days an old banana seller has turned photographic model. So many visitors asked to take her photograph and gave her money that she no longer wanders around weighed down by bananas. She simply sits with her bananas, waiting for the tourists. So yes, Hoi An is changing, but then, it always has, to suit the trade.

HISTORIC APPENDIX

300 BC-200 AD	Sa Huynh people settle in river valleys along the coast of Central Vietnam
179 BC	Chinese invade northern Vietnam and set up three territories
111 BC	Han Chinese take over these three southern trading territories
200-100 BC	Arrival of Chams in Central Vietnam
3rd C	Earliest Cham inscription, the Vo Canh, near Nha Trang
192 AD	Rebellion and founding of the breakaway kingdom, Linyi
4th-13th C	Myson towers and temples built and rebuilt by Chams
380-413	Supposed reign of first Cham king, Bhadravarman
446	Chinese Song army loots Linyi, carrying away much gold
Early 6th C	Hon Cuc, earliest Austronesian language inscription, near Myson
7th C	Brick temples begin to appear at Myson
605	Sui Chinese invade Linyi, burning Cham Buddhist texts and looting golden tablets
749	Linyi disappears from Chinese records, replaced by Huanwang

756	Chinese annuls report the death of the last king of Lam Ap
850	Two Arab journals mention Champa in their itineraries
875	King Indravarman II establishes a new capital, Indrapura
938	The Viets gain independence from the Chinese and set up their capital at Hoa Lu, south of Hanoi
982	Viets sack Indrapura, killing King Phe Mi Thue, carrying off Cham dancers and musicians
1000	The Chams abandon Indrapura for Vijaya (Qui Nhon), Cham Buddhism shifts back to Saivism
1010	Le Thai To moves the Dai Viet capital from Hoa Lu to Thang Long (Hanoi)
1044	Viets sack Vijaya, killing the Cham king, capturing elephants and the Cham queen, who throws herself into the sea
1068	King of Vijaya, Rudravarman III (Che Cu) attacks Dai Viet, the Chams are defeated, the Viets burn Vijaya (Qui Nhon)
1069	Vijaya again sacked by Viets, Rudravarman III taken prisoner and forced to cede three northern territories for his freedom.
1080	Khmer attack Vijaya and other Cham cities, Chams repel the invaders

1145	Khmer King Suryavarman II occupies Vijaya and destroys the temples of Myson
1150-60	Cham King of Panduranga (Phan Rang), Jaya Harivarman IV, defeats the Khmer, restores Po Nagar in Nha Trang and builds Group G temples at Myson
1167	Cham King Jaya Indravarman IV secures peace with Dai Viet, invades Cambodia, sacks the capital and kills the Khmer king
1181	New Khmer king, Jayavarman VII, drives the Chams out of Cambodia
1190	Cham King Jaya Indravarman IV launches another attack against the Khmer
1203	Khmer King Jayavarman VII takes Vijaya, which becomes a province of Angkor
1220	Champa regains independence, but goes into gradual decline
1257, 1284 1288	Kublai Khan invades Dai Viet (North Vietnam) and Champa
1271	Marco Polo departs from Venice with his father and uncle
1285	Marco Polo visits Champa
1288	Mongols defeated at the Battle of Bach Dang
1292	Marco Polo visits Champa on his return voyage to Venice
1307	Cham King Jaya Simhavarman III (Che Man), cedes two districts to Dai Viet in exchange for a Viet princess

1371	China halts maritime trade, beginning a Closed Door Policy that lasts nearly 200 years
1372	The last strong Cham king, Che Bong Nga, the Red King, attacks Thang Long (Hanoi) from the sea
1388	Che Bong Nga defeated by Viet General Ho Quy Ly, founder of the Ho Dynasty
Early 15th C	Malacca founded by the Thais
1431	The Thais defeat the Khmer and sack Angkor, ending Khmer power
1446	Viets invade Champa and Vijaya falls
1447	The Chams drive the Viets out of Vijaya
1450	Bui Thi Hy fashions the vase, now in Istanbul's Topkapi Saraji Museum
1453	The Turks take Constantinople and restrict trade in the eastern Mediterranean, pressing European maritime powers to reach Asia via a yet undiscovered sea route
1471	Viets destroy Vijaya, sending first wave of Cham immigrants fleeing to Cambodia and Malacca
1487	Portuguese Bartholomew Diaz rounds the southern tip of Africa, opening the route from the Atlantic to the Indian Ocean
1493	The Pope draws a north-south line through the Atlantic: west of the line goes to Spain; east to Portugal

225

1498	Portuguese Vasco de Gama reaches India by sea, breaking the monopoly of Arab and Venetian traders and setting off a frenzy of competition between European merchants for the Moluccas spice trade
1535	Antonio De Faris anchors in Danang and visits Faifo (Hoi An), Portuguese ships begin to visit Faifo regularly
1558	Nguyen Huang, first of the Nguyen lords, moves South and establishes his capital at Phu Xuan (Hue)
Around 1560	Japanese begin to trade in Hoi An, later building merchant houses in Japanese Street
1567	China ends her Closed Door Policy to maritime trade
1592-1636	Era of Japanese Red Seal *shuinsen* ships visiting Hoi An
1602	Dutch East India Company (VOC) founded
1613	Richard Cocks of the English East India Company in Japan, dispatches emissaries to Hoi An to investigate trade prospects
1614	Jesuits expelled from Japan, move to Hoi An, introducing Christianity and Catholicism to Vietnam
1631	Christoforo Borri publishes *An Account of the New Mission of Jesuit Fathers in the Kingdom of Dang Trong* in Rome
1636	Japan slams the door to trade in a Closed Door Policy, ordering the Japanese home

1636-1685	The Dutch East India Company (VOC) sets up a trading factory in Hoi An, taking over the Japanese *shuinsen* trade
1644	Fall of the Ming Dynasty sends waves of immigrants fleeing south to Hoi An, who establish Minh Huang village
1644-1581	Chinese Qing dynasty closes China to trade against pirate, Koxinga
1651	French priest, Alexandre de Rhodes, publishes his *quoc nhu* dictionary and catechism
1653	Viets defeat the Cham kingdom of Kauthara (Nha Trang), leaving only Panduranga (Phan Rang) as a remnant of Champa
1678-80	Chaya Shinrokuro Masachika draws his Sea Map – Trade with the State of Jiaozhi, describing 17th century Faifo (Hoi An)
1683	China ends its Closed Door Policy towards Japan
1697	Viets defeat Cham principality of Panduranga (Phan Rang)
1712	Lord Nguyen Phuc Chu makes the Treaty of Five Articles with Cham lord, Po Saktiray Da Patih, in force until 1832
1773-1788	Tay Son Rebellion
1773	Hoi An, as the port of the Nguyen lords, is burnt in the Tay Son Rebellion
1786	As a result of the Tay Son Rebellion, Cham Lord Chei Krei Brei and his court flee to Cambodia

1787	Treaty of Versailles, signed in Paris by King Louis XVI, promising military support to Nguyen Anh in exchange for Hoi An and French trade concessions
1788	Nguyen Hue, eldest of Tay Son brothers, crowns himself King Quang Trung over Central and North Vietnam
1792-93	John Barrow travels with Lord Macartney to China, stopping in Hoi An, later publishing *A Voyage to Cochinchina in the Years 1792 and 1793*
19th C.	As Hoi An's Thu Bon river silts up, Danang gains preference. Hoi An's role as an international port declines
1801	Nguyen Anh attacks the Tay Son retainers and takes Hue
1802	Nguyen Anh takes Hanoi, unites the country, crowns himself King Gia Long and establishes his capital at Phu Xuan (Hue)
1804	Representatives of the British East India Company again try to negotiate trading rights with King Gia Long, later with King Ming Mang in 1821 and 1822
1819	Minh Mang digs the Vinh Dien Canal to keep the Co Co river passage open between Danang and Hoi An
1832	Minh Mang defeats and annexes the remaining Cham territories, Panduranga (Phan Rang), placing them under Viet 'protection'
1835	Minh Mang decrees that all Western ships must berth at Danang

1847	After the French attack a Vietnamese warship, the English ask to build a fort at Danang to form a British-Vietnamese alliance against the French, the British approach fails
1858	The French attack Danang, Tu Duc forced to grant a trade concession to the French in Danang, beginning a century-long French-Vietnamese struggle for power
1859	The French seize Saigon
1864	Treaty recognizing French control over three provinces in the Mekong Delta including Saigon, My Tho and Bien Hoa
1867	The French occupy three further provinces in the Mekong Delta, including Vinh Long, Ha Tien and Chau Doc
1873	A small force under Francis Garnier captures Hanoi's Citadel
1874	Tu Duc signs a treaty with the French, granting a Navy Cantonment on the Red river in Hanoi
1884	The Treaty of Patenôtre relinquishes sovereignty over Cochin, Annan and Tonkin: Vietnam falls under French Colonial rule
1885	Father Bruyere leads a French military attachment to Myson
1887	Indo-Chinese Union including Cochin, Annam, Tonkin and Cambodia, announced by the French, Laos added in 1894

1903	Henri Parmentier and Charles Carpeaux begin their survey of Cham ruins, Parmentier producing his *Inventoire sommaire des monuments Cham de l'Annam*
1905	The French build a railway connecting Danang and Hoi An
1940-45	World War II, Japanese occupation of Vietnam
1945-54	French Indo-Chinese War, ending at Dien Bien Phu
1965-75	Vietnam War. Americans establish a base at Danang; American troops withdraw from Vietnam in 1973
1975	Reunification of Vietnam
1980-86	The Polish-Vietnamese Committee for Conservation of Cham Architectural Heritage does archaeological work at Myson
1985	Hoi An declared a Historical Site by the Vietnamese government
1999	Hoi An and Myson designated World Heritage Sites by UNESCO
2000	The Hoi An Town Preservation Cooperation project receives a UNESCO Excellent Project Award
2003	The Italian team of archaeologists and architects from Lerici Foundation of Milan Polytechnic start work at Myson

BIBLIOGRAPHY

Abott, Carroll, *In the Far East: A Narrative of Exploration and Adventure in Cochin-China, Cambodia, Laos and Siam,* Thomas Nelson and Sons, London, 1879

Barrow, John, *A Voyage Made to Cochinchina in 1792-93,* (engravings by Medland, original drawings by Messrs Alexander and Daniell), printed for T. Cadell and W. Davies in The Strand, London, 1806

Clavell, James, *Shogun,* Random House, New York, 1975

Dieu Khac, *Champa Sculpture,* VNA Publishing House, Hanoi, 2004

Farrington, Anthony and Massarella, Derek, *William Adams and Early English Enterprise in Japan,* London School of Economics, London, 2000

Glover, Ian, *Early Trade Between India and South-East Asia,* Univ. of Hull, (occasional papers No. 16), Hull, 1989

Glover, I. C. and Yamagato, M., *The Origin of Cham Civilisation – Indigenous Chinese and Indian Influences in Central Vietnam as Revealed by Excavations at Tra Kieu, Vietnam, 1990-1993,* Hong Kong University

Glover, Ian and Bellwood, Peter, *Southeast Asia from Prehistory to History,* Routledge Curzon, Abingdon, England, 2004

Glover, I. C., Nguyen Kim Dung and Prior, R., *The 2000-2001 Excavation Seasons at the Ancient Cham City of Tra Kieu and Go Cam, Quang Nam Province, Central Vietnam,* paper presented at a Conference to celebrate 100 Years of Archaeology in Vietnam, Hanoi, 2001

Guillon, Emmanuel, *Cham Art, Treasures from Da Nang Museum, Vietnam,* Thames & Hudson, London, 2001

Hammer, Ellen, *The Struggle for Indochina 1940-1955,* Stanford University Press, Redwood City, California, 1966

Hardy, Andrew; Cucarzi, Mauro and Zolese, Patrizia, eds. *Champa and the Archaeology of My Son (Vietnam),* NUS Press, (National University of Singapore), 2009

Higham, Charles, *The Bronze Age of Southeast Asia,* Cambridge Univ. Press, 1996

Higham, Charles, *Early Cultures of Mainland Southeast Asia,* River Books, Bangkok, 2002

Hoi An Center for Monuments Management and Preservation and Showa Women's University, Institute of International Culture, *Heritage Homeowner's Preservation Manual,* UNESCO Bangkok and Hanoi, 2008.

Hoi An Center for Monuments Management and Preservation, *Hoi An, Some Typical Relics and Scenic Spots of Hoi An,* Hoi An, 2007

Hoi An Center for Monuments Management and Preservation, *Impact, Cultural Tourism and Heritage Management in the World Heritage Site of the Ancient Town of Hoi An,* UNESCO Bangkok, 2008

Lam Thi My Dzung, *Sa Huynh Regional and Inter-Regional Interactions in the Thu Bon Valley, Quang Nam Province, Central Vietnam* IPP Bulletin 29, Hanoi National University, Hanoi, 2009

Lee Xuan Diem and Vu Kim Loc, *Artefacts of Champa,* National Culture Publishing House, Ho Chi Minh City, 1996

Lerner, John, *Marco Polo and the Discovery of the World,* Yale University Press, New Haven and London, 1999

Moule, A. C. and Pelliot, Paul (trans.), *(Marco Polo's) The Description of the World,* George Routledge & Sons Limited, Abingdon, England, 1938

Nguyen Lam Thi My Dzung, *Sa Huynh Culture in Hoi An,* in Klohke, M. and Bruyn, P. (editors), *Southeast Asian Archaeology,* Hull Univ. Centre for Southeast Asian Studies, Hull, 1996

Nguyen Van Xuan, *Hoi An,* Danang Publishing House, Danang, 2008

(Numerous international academic contributors), *Ancient Town of Hoi An,* The Gioi Publishers, Hanoi, 2006

O'Reilly, Dougald J. W., *Early Civilisations of Southeast Asia,* Alta Mira Press, Lanham, Maryland, 2006

Rawson, Philip, *The Art of Southeast Asia,* Thames and Hudson, London, 1967

Tucker, Spencer, *An Encyclopedia of the Vietnam War: A Political, Social and Military History,* Oxford University Press, Oxford, 1999

Wood, Frances, *Did Marco Polo Go to China?* Secker & Warburg, London, 1995

Yule, Col. Sir Henry (trans.), *Book of Ser Marco Polo,* John Murray, 1903. Also, *The Travels of Marco Polo: the complete Yule-Cordier edition,* (London 1903, 1920, New York 1993)

No w/chairs
Border security, police, 2 lade
GF meal - ✓
Minsk, top caspian sea, Bukhara,
Islamabad — 10 Lrs